ROYAL HISTORICAL SOCIETY

STUDIES IN HISTORY

New Series

CONQUEST AND LAND IN IRELAND
THE TRANSPLANTATION TO CONNACHT, 1649–1680

PAST & PRESENT
a journal of historical studies

CONQUEST AND LAND IN IRELAND
THE TRANSPLANTATION TO CONNACHT, 1649–1680

John Cunningham

THE ROYAL HISTORICAL SOCIETY

THE BOYDELL PRESS

First published 2011

A Royal Historical Society publication
Published by The Boydell Press
an imprint of Boydell & Brewer Ltd
PO Box 9, Woodbridge, Suffolk IP12 3DF, UK
and of Boydell & Brewer Inc.
668 Mt Hope Avenue, Rochester, NY 14620, USA
website: www.boydellandbrewer.com

ISBN 978–0–86193–315–0

ISSN 0269–2244

A CIP catalogue record for this book is available
from the British Library

The publisher has no responsibility for the continued existence or accuracy of
URLs for external or third-party internet websites referred to in this book, and
does not guarantee that any content on such websites is, or will remain,
accurate or appropriate.

Papers used by Boydell & Brewer Ltd are natural, recyclable products
made from wood grown in sustainable forests.

Printed and bound in the United States of America

Contents

List of Maps

Acknowledgements

I wish to acknowledge the financial support received in 2005–6 from the College of Arts, Social Sciences and Celtic Studies at National University of Ireland, Galway, and the receipt of a postgraduate scholarship from the Irish Research Council for the Humanities and the Social Sciences in the period 2006–9. The Moore Institute for Research in the Humanities and Social Studies provided the necessary infrastructural support and intellectual environment for my work.

Professor Nicholas Canny has provided direction and inspiration since the latter stages of my undergraduate study; I owe him considerable thanks. His expertise and generous guidance have done much to shape what follows. I also wish to record my gratitude to Dr Ciarán Ó Murchadha for advice on early drafts and on the completed thesis. Dr Toby Barnard has provided significant assistance, for which I am grateful.

Professor John Morrill, my advisory editor for the Royal Historical Society's *Studies in History*, deserves thanks for his enthusiastic support in preparing this work for publication, as does the executive editor Christine Linehan. I would also like to acknowledge the input of the anonymous reader whose report drew my attention to several points of importance. The earlier comments offered by Professor Jane Ohlmeyer, Dr John Gibney and Dr Jason McHugh have proven very helpful too.

Part of the content of chapter 3 has been published in 'Oliver Cromwell and the "Cromwellian" settlement of Ireland', *HJ* liii (2010), 919–37. I am grateful to the editors for permission to reproduce this material here.

Many other people have helped in a variety of ways. I wish to acknowledge in particular the personnel of the various libraries where research was conducted, staff and colleagues at the Moore Institute and the Department of History, NUI Galway, and good friends both there and elsewhere. I am grateful to my parents, Peter and Frances, and my family for their unfailing support in this and in all endeavours for as long as I can remember. Finally, my thanks to Ashling; her patience and love have helped to make this work, as so much else, worth the while.

John Cunningham
April 2011

Abbreviations

CJ	*Journal of the House of Commons*
CSPD	*Calendar of state papers, domestic series*
CSPI	*Calendar of state papers relating to Ireland*
DIB	*Dictionary of Irish Biography*
EHR	*English Historical Review*
HJ	*Historical Journal*
IHS	*Irish Historical Studies*
IUC	*Ireland under the Commonwealth*, ed. Robert Dunlop, Manchester 1913
ODNB	*Oxford Dictionary of National Biography*
P&P	*Past & Present*
TSP	*A collection of the state papers of John Thurloe*, ed. Thomas Birch, London 1742

BL	British Library, London
Bodl. Lib.	Bodleian Library, Oxford
HMC	Historical Manuscripts Commission
IRC	Irish Record Commission
KIL	King's Inns Library, Dublin
NAI	National Archives of Ireland, Dublin
NLI	National Library of Ireland, Dublin
NLW	National Library of Wales, Aberystwyth
NUI	National University of Ireland
'Ormond list'	'List of the transplanted Irish, 1655–9', HMC, *Ormonde manuscripts*, ii. 114–76
RIA	Royal Irish Academy, Dublin
SP	State papers
TCD	Trinity College, Dublin
TNA	The National Archives, Kew

Introduction

The history of Ireland in the 1650s is synonymous with Oliver Cromwell and with his supposed pronouncement on the fate of the Catholic population: 'Go to hell or to Connacht'. This slogan is shorthand for the policy of transplantation, the forced relocation of people. The transplantation to Connacht was a central aspect of the land settlement implemented in the aftermath of the Cromwellian conquest. It was designed primarily to clear the ground for a Protestant colonisation of the other three Irish provinces. The present work constitutes a reassessment of the history of the transplantation, examining its background, its implementation and its outcomes between 1649 and 1680.

The 'Cromwellian' slogan offers a useful point of entry into the complex of interpretations which have been constructed around the transplantation across the centuries. It in fact originated in 1790s Ulster in the same vicinity as the Orange Order, and it was seemingly first linked explicitly to Cromwell by a French writer only in the 1830s.[1] Thereafter, the 'Cromwellian' became a nationalist byword for perceived shortcomings in Britain's rule of Ireland past and present. As late as 1965 the Irish minister for lands explained that his preferred policies were necessary 'to undo the work of Cromwell'.[2] Even today, individuals or groups deemed to be obstructing the 'progress' of the country run the risk of being labelled as Cromwellians. In a televised speech in 2009, a government minister aimed fierce criticism at financial institutions by claiming that 'there is no parallel for the damage they have done to this country, except perhaps Cromwell'.[3] Others would soon level the same accusation back at the government, as it negotiated the so-called 'Oliver Cromwell package' with Brussels and the International Monetary Fund.[4] These are just some of many examples which suggest that the Cromwellian episode of the 1650s remains integral to Irish identities, even while the old problems with which it was connected – land, religion and British rule – have either been resolved or are seemingly becoming less contentious.

Many other layers of meaning can also be discerned. Some of those ordered to transplant interpreted their fate in terms drawn from the book of Exodus, with the Irish Catholics filling the role of the Israelites going down to slavery in

---

1   *The speeches of the right honourable Henry Grattan, in the Irish, and in the imperial parliament*, ed. Henry Grattan, Dublin 1822, iii. 220; Gustave de Beaumont, *L'Irlande: sociale, politique et religeuse*, Paris 1839, i. 62.
2   Terence Dooley, *The land for the people: the land question in independent Ireland*, Dublin 2004, 181.
3   <http://www.irishtimes.com/newspaper/breaking/2009/0228/breaking43.htm> accessed 15 Apr. 2009.
4   <http://euobserver.com/9/31302> accessed 1 Dec. 2010. The phrase has been attributed to Irish officials in Brussels.

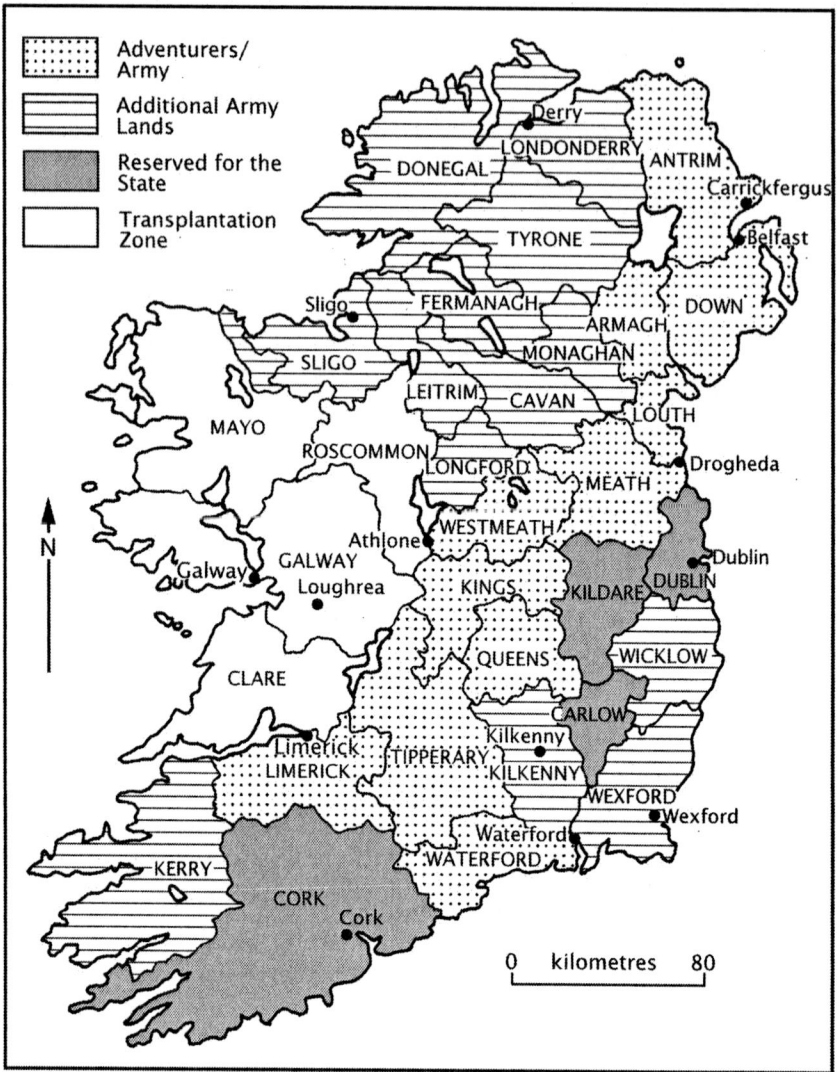

Map 1. The Irish land settlement of the 1650s

Egypt.[5] From the perspective of the exiled Jesuit Peter Talbot matters were even worse: 'all the world seeth how the whole Irish nation is murthered by the transplantation into Conaght and by transporting them into the plantations of America'.[6] Just over a century ago the transplantation could be compared to 'an enormous scheme of eviction' or to 'the dealings of the United States govern-

[5] An *duanaire, 1600–1900: poems of the dispossessed*, ed. Thomas Kinsella and Seán Ó Tuama, Mountrath 1981, 104–9.
[6] Peter Talbot, *The polititians cathechisme, for his instruction in divine faith and morall honesty*, Antwerp 1658, 158.

2

ment with the Red Indians'.[7] In 1915 the socialist leader James Connolly represented the episode as a key moment in the establishment of landlord and capitalist domination of the working class, while W. B. Yeats later identified the triumph of 'Cromwell's murderous crew' with the eclipse of a more traditionalist Irish society.[8] In 1985 Margaret Thatcher referred to the Cromwellian precedent in arguing that the relocation of Northern Irish Catholics to the south would soon bring an end to the conflict there.[9] More recently, a leading English historian has described the transplantation as 'possibly the greatest act of ethnic cleansing in European history'.[10] This multiplicity of readings, from Exodus to ethnic cleansing, highlights perceived connections between the transplantation and some of the enduring problems of the human experience: religious and racial hatred; captivity; dislocation; and the struggle for the possession of land.

The enduring level of awareness that exists concerning the transplantation, and Cromwellian Ireland more generally, has ensured that the events of the 1650s carry a symbolism matched in Irish history perhaps only by the Battle of the Boyne or the Great Famine. It is therefore remarkable that the subject has not recently received any sustained attention from historians of early modern Ireland. None the less, the past decade has witnessed the appearance of several important specialist studies focused on other aspects of Ireland in the 1650s. Micheál Ó Siochrú's God's executioner is the latest work to examine the violent and destructive period of conquest with which the decade opened, while Aidan Clarke's Prelude to restoration in Ireland carefully explored its less familiar end.[11] W. J. Smyth's work in the field of historical geography, although spanning a much broader period, has also introduced a range of fresh and valuable insights.[12] In addition, Crawford Gribben's God's Irishmen: theological debates in Cromwellian Ireland has built upon the solid foundations laid by Toby Barnard in the 1970s.[13] In 1973 the latter author noted that 'At the most basic level there is still a need to establish exactly what happened, especially in the years of peace after 1652.'[14] His Cromwellian Ireland sought to fulfil this need across a range of topics, while generally avoiding the 'rebarbative subjects' of massacre and transplantation.[15] The

7   Emily Lawless and Mrs Arthur Bronson, The story of Ireland, New York 1896, 267; Justin McCarthy, Ireland and her story, New York 1903, 86–7.
8   James Connolly, The re-conquest of Ireland, rev. edn, Dublin 1983, 9–14; William Butler Yeats, The collected poems of W. B. Yeats, Toronto 1956, 302–3.
9   <http://www.independent.ie/national–news/news–digest–508869.html> accessed 1 Dec. 2010.
10   John Morrill, 'Introduction', in Peter Kenyon and Jane Ohlmeyer (eds), The civil wars: a military history of England, Scotland and Ireland, 1638–1660, Oxford 1998, p. xx.
11   Micheál Ó Siochrú, God's executioner: Oliver Cromwell and the conquest of Ireland, London 2008; Aidan Clarke, Prelude to restoration in Ireland: the end of the Commonwealth, 1659–1660, Cambridge 1999.
12   William Smyth, Map-making, landscapes and memory: a geography of colonial and early modern Ireland, c. 1530–1750, Cork 2006.
13   Crawford Gribben, God's Irishmen: theological debates in Cromwellian Ireland, Oxford 2007.
14   Toby Barnard, 'Planters and Policies in Cromwellian Ireland', P&P lxi (1973), 31–69 at p. 31.
15   Ibid. and Cromwellian Ireland: English government and reform in Ireland, 1649–1660, Oxford 2000.

'post-revisionist' revival of interest in Irish massacres has inevitably seen attention devoted to the mid-seventeenth century.[16] On the other hand, apart from
frequent analyses of the series of pamphlets published by Vincent Gookin and
Colonel Richard Lawrence in 1655–6, scholarly study of the transplantation to
Connacht has not hitherto experienced any similar revival.[17]

Alongside the recent studies concerned with aspects of Cromwellian Ireland,
further scholarship has served to situate that decade in multiple wider historical
contexts. Most notably, research on three-kingdom history and the Atlantic
world has helped to locate 1650s Ireland firmly within those particular transna-
tional perspectives. For example, fruitful comparisons have been made between
Ireland and Scotland by scholars such as David Stevenson, David Menarry and
Patrick Little.[18] Little has also examined aspects of the complex constitutional
relationship which existed between England and Ireland.[19] Patricia Coughlan
and Alison Games have analysed transatlantic connections, with the latter
tracing the minor but fascinating role played by New Englanders in Cromwellian
Ireland.[20] The 1650s have also been situated in the wider chronological framework of Irish history. For example, Nicholas Canny has depicted the events of the
1650s as in many ways the completion of the Spenserian agenda of the 1590s,
while other works have linked Cromwellian Ireland firmly to the subsequent
period of Protestant ascendancy.[21] In addition, the wider Irish world inhabited by
exiles on the continent in this period has been receiving welcome scholarly
attention.[22] These rich and various scholarly contributions focused on and
beyond Cromwellian Ireland provide an appropriate context for a fresh examination of the transplantation to Connacht.

A further vital framework is supplied by the historiography of the transplantation in the *longue durée*, a span of 350 years during which scholarly interest ebbed
and flowed while manuscripts decayed and burned. For a century after the event,
the main controversy between Catholic and Protestant historians was focused on

---

[16] David Edwards, Padraig Lenihan and Clodagh Tait (eds), *Age of atrocity: violence and
political conflict in early modern Ireland*, Dublin 2007.
[17] For a discussion of the literature on Gookin and Lawrence see John Cunningham, 'The
Gookin-Lawrence pamphlet debate in Cromwellian Ireland', in Ciara Breathnach, Liam
Chambers and Anthony McElligott (eds), *Power in history: from the medieval to the
post-modern world* (Historical Studies xxvii, 2011), 63–80.
[18] David Stevenson, 'Cromwell, Scotland and Ireland', in John Morrill (ed.), *Oliver Cromwell and the English revolution*, London 1990, 149–80; David Menarry, 'The Irish and Scottish landed elites from regicide to restoration', unpubl. PhD diss. Aberdeen 2001; Patrick
Little, *Lord Broghill and the Cromwellian union with Ireland and Scotland*, Oxford 2004.
[19] Patrick Little, 'The first unionists? Irish Protestant attitudes to union with England,
1653–9', *IHS* xxxii (2000), 44–58.
[20] Patricia Coughlan, 'Counter-currents in colonial discourse: the political thought of
Vincent and Daniel Gookin', in Jane Ohlmeyer (ed.), *Political thought in seventeenth-century
Ireland*, Cambridge 2000, 56–82; Alison Games, *The web of empire: English cosmopolitans in
an age of expansion, 1560–1660*, Oxford 2008, ch. viii.
[21] Nicholas Canny, *Making Ireland British, 1580–1650*, Oxford 2001, 551–78; Toby
Barnard, *A new anatomy of Ireland: the Irish Protestants, 1649–1770*, New Haven–London
2003.
[22] Mary Ann Lyons and Thomas O'Connor (eds), *Irish communities in early modern Europe*,
Dublin 2006.

the 1641 rebellion and the alleged massacres associated with it. In 1689 Sir Richard Cox's *Hibernia Anglicana* essentially glossed over much of what had occurred in the 1650s: 'The Interval between the end of the War, and *Cromwell*'s Death, affords but little matter for an Historian.'[23] The eventual publication of the earl of Clarendon's *Life* in 1759 offered a brief appraisal which was broadly sympathetic to the transplanted Catholics: 'They required all the Irish to retire by such a day, under the penalty of death ... many did die every day of famine.'[24] Over the following decades, the transplantation emerged as a minor element in several works whose chief contributions were to the ongoing and bitter debate relating to 1641. These included the *History of the rebellion* published by the English clergyman Ferdinando Warner in 1767 and Thomas Leland's *History of Ireland*, published in 1773.[25] Warner explained that the transplantation was implemented to enable the English 'to plant without disturbance, or danger of being corrupted, by intermixing with the natives in marriage or otherwise', a sentiment echoed by Leland.[26] The Irish Catholic response to these writings came from John Curry in 1775. Curry reproduced verbatim Clarendon's depiction of the transplantation before taking Leland to task: 'grievous and shocking as it appears in this authentic description of it, it has been represented by a late historian, rather as a piece of necessary, and useful policy at that time, than as an act of severity, and injustice to the Irish'.[27]

There the controversy rested until the publication of John Prendergast's *Cromwellian settlement of Ireland* in 1865. This work altered fundamentally the historiography of the subject.[28] Prendergast was the first historian to make extensive use of the Commonwealth records, a substantial archive of official documentation from the 1650s preserved in dusty obscurity in Dublin Castle. A century earlier Warner had dismissed this collection as 'a few meagre dry annals'.[29] The new availability of the Commonwealth records and other sources allowed Prendergast to construct a narrative of Catholic suffering in the 1650s designed to parallel and to overshadow established accounts of Protestant hardships in the early 1640s.[30] At the same time, the credibility of the chief primary source for those latter accounts, the 1641 depositions, was increasingly beleaguered by sceptical writers, particularly Irish nationalists. Taking place against a background of growing political and agrarian tensions, these developments helped to foster what Barnard has referred to as 'the heroic age of Irish historiography' between the 1860s and 1922.[31]

---

23 Richard Cox, *Hibernia anglicana, or the history of Ireland, from the conquest thereof by the English, to this present time*, London 1689–90, ii, sig. Aaaaa.
24 Edward Hyde, earl of Clarendon, *The life of Edward, earl of Clarendon*, Oxford 1759, ii. 116–17.
25 Ferdinando Warner, *The history of the rebellion and civil war in Ireland*, London 1767; Thomas Leland, *The history of Ireland from the invasion of Henry II*, Dublin 1773.
26 Warner, *The history of the rebellion*, 546–7; Leland, *The history of Ireland*, iii. 396–7.
27 John Curry, *An historical and critical review of the civil wars in Ireland*, Dublin 1775, 276–7.
28 John Prendergast, *The Cromwellian settlement of Ireland*, 2nd edn, London 1870.
29 Warner, *History of the rebellion*, 546.
30 Prendergast, *Cromwellian settlement*, passim.
31 Toby Barnard, '1641: a bibliographical essay', in Brian MacCuarta (ed.), *Ulster 1641: aspects of the rising*, rev. edn, Belfast 1997, 173–86.

During this 'heroic age', the controversy surrounding the 1641 rebellion was renewed as the 'massacrists', J. A. Froude and Mary Hickson, joined battle with the 'anti-massacrists', J. T. Gilbert, Robert Dunlop and Prendergast.[32] The latter's ground-breaking study of the 1650s ensured that the transplantation now bulked much larger in the public consciousness and in histories of mid seventeenth-century Ireland than had previously been the case. Furthermore, initial attempts to undermine Prendergast's emotive account of the transplantation proved rather ineffective. Against the mass of primary materials so masterfully harnessed by Prendergast, Froude could offer only a reiteration of the arguments of Warner and Leland concerning the danger of degeneration, and a misrepresentation of Clarendon's views. His additional claim that the transplantation 'was conceived and carried out in no ill-will to those who were removed' contradicted entirely Prendergast's portrayal of the scheme. The latter, quick to take offence, was unlikely to subscribe to Froude's explanation of their differing opinions: 'He writes as an Irish patriot – I as an Englishman.'[33]

As Prendergast's narrative continued to shape outraged Irish Catholic and nationalist perceptions of the 1650s up to the end of the nineteenth century, two Englishmen, Robert Dunlop and Samuel Gardiner, came to suspect that his scholarship was somewhat biased. The former, after extensive research in the Commonwealth records and first-hand exposure to the problems bedevilling Ireland in the 1880s, largely changed his mind.[34] On the other hand, Gardiner, in an article on the transplantation published in 1899, argued that government policy had been substantially moderated after 1655 as Oliver Cromwell came to accept the arguments against universal transplantation published by the Munster Protestant Vincent Gookin.[35] However, Gardiner's scholarly intervention did little to dampen enthusiasm for Prendergast's more chilling version of events among Irish and Irish-American audiences up to 1922. His *Cromwellian settlement* entered its third edition in that year.

The destruction of the Commonwealth records in an explosion at the Four Courts in Dublin, also in 1922, had profound consequences for the historiography of Cromwellian Ireland. Half a century was to pass before Karl Bottigheimer and Robert Simington produced substantial new quantitative studies of the land settlement. The latter's non-contentious statistical work on the transplantation served largely to reinforce Gardiner's finding that the scheme had been aimed only at landowners.[36] However, while Barnard was subsequently able to draw upon a broad range of scattered materials in his study of Cromwellian policy, the make-up of the sources for transplantation exploited by historians has not evolved much further since 1970. The latest trend has been to synthesise the discordant conclusions reached by previous historians who used

---

[32] Walter Love, 'Civil war in Ireland: appearances in three centuries of historical writing', *Emory University Quarterly* xxii (1966), 57–62.
[33] James Anthony Froude, *The English in Ireland in the eighteenth century*, London 1872–4, i. 134–6.
[34] Charles Firth, 'Robert Dunlop', *History* xv (1931), 320–4 at p. 320.
[35] Samuel Gardiner, 'The transplantation to Connaught', *EHR* xiv (1899), 700–34.
[36] Karl Bottigheimer, *English money and Irish land: the 'adventurers' in the Cromwellian settlement of Ireland*, Oxford 1971; Robert Simington, *The transplantation to Connaught, 1654–1658*, Dublin 1970.

very different sources. In particular, Simington's warnings regarding the legacy of 'ingenuous and erroneous calculation' bequeathed by some earlier scholars have not been heeded. Although he roundly denounced the work of nineteenth-century historians such as W. H. Hardinge, their respective and contradictory findings have recently been presented side by side as wholly complementary.[37]

The historiography of the transplantation reflects not only the concerns of the worlds in which successive historians lived and moved, but also the evolution of the extant source base. Unfortunately, the most recent efforts to traverse old research in search of new findings could be seen to suggest that there exists little scope for further research. Given the importance of the subject in question, such an outcome would be altogether unsatisfactory, particularly as the extant source base is sufficient to sustain and to reward renewed scholarly efforts.

This study draws upon a wide range of these surviving quantitative and qualitative sources. The evidence preserved in contemporary printed pamphlets and official declarations, published for the most part in London or Dublin, are a central element. In addition, various state papers, Irish, Domestic, Thurloe and Clarendon, each shed light on important aspects. Although the destruction of the Commonwealth records has been frequently lamented, a substantial amount of data extracted from that collection before 1922 has in fact survived. Apart from the two-volume calendar published by Dunlop in 1913, manuscripts compiled assiduously by Prendergast, Sir William Betham, Richard Bagwell and others serve as vital substitutes for the volumes which have been lost. These transcripts are the core source materials upon which this study is based. The Carte manuscripts in the Bodleian Library, Oxford, also contain much crucial data for the entire period. For the 1670s the correspondence of Arthur Capel, earl of Essex, preserved among the Stowe manuscripts at the British Library has been extensively employed. The Books of Survey and Distribution, compiled in part under Essex's direction, are also essential to establishing how the transplantation scheme impacted on landownership patterns in the west of the country. In addition, the various precious collections of family papers that have survived enable valuable insights. Together with the relevant works published since the seventeenth century, these extensive and diverse sources provide an ample body of evidence for the history of the transplantation.

The account that follows is arranged into six chapters and seeks to address a number of important questions. First, what were the factors which shaped the formulation of English parliamentarian policy towards Irish Catholics up to 1653? Once the policy of transplantation to Connacht had been finalised in that year, how did the authorities in Dublin go about enforcing it? To what extent did they endeavour to adhere to the harsh terms of the relevant laws passed at Westminster? Furthermore, how effective were the strategies of resistance and obstruction pursued by the many Irish landowners targeted for confiscation and transplantation? Against this background, the practical results of the transplantation up to the end of the 1650s can be explored. In what ways was the shape of Irish society transformed by this episode? Moreover, how many individuals actu-

---

[37] Simington, *The transplantation*, pp. xxvii–xxviii; Smyth, *Map-making, landscapes and memory*, 161, 183–7.

ally received assignments of land, and how did the working out of this process impact on landownership patterns in the west? For the period after 1660 it is most worthwhile to trace the fate of the transplanters within the overall context of the Restoration land settlement, and to investigate the controversy that surrounded the question of whether or not the transplantation should be reversed. Why were some restored to their old estates while others were, as the contemporary poet Dáibhí Ó Bruadair put it, left 'But to gaze at their lands like a dog at a lump of beef?'[38] By 1680 the remaining transplanters had regularised their status as proprietors within the new landed society that had been constructed in Ireland over the previous decades. It is necessary finally to examine the circumstances under which this belated resolution was achieved, and to assess the ultimate consequences of the transplantation to Connacht.

While engaging with these questions, it is also necessary to remember that the events of the 1650s cannot be divorced from previous English policy towards Ireland, both in the 1640s and in the longer term; Cromwell was not a Columbus. Indeed, even the drastic policy of transplantation was very far from being a new departure. The expulsion of the native inhabitants from certain regions and the reallocation of land to those of them considered most deserving had been a feature of English plantation schemes in Ireland since the 1550s. While such earlier schemes had rarely been effectively implemented in practice, the theory behind them was fully developed prior to the 1650s: the destruction or removal of existing residents was often deemed essential to enabling the secure establishment of English or British colonies on Irish soil.[39] Moreover, in the mid-seventeenth century those who supported such harsh measures against the Irish Catholics could point to all sorts of supposed precedents from beyond Ireland: the dispossession of the seven nations by the Israelites; Roman policy towards the Ligurians; the actions of William the Conqueror in England; and the more recent expulsion of the Moors from Spain.[40] The mass exodus of Protestants from Habsburg Bohemia after 1620 was also a familiar subject for contemporaries. In 1662 Roger Boyle, earl of Orrery, would seek to clinch the argument for preserving the transplantation by harking back to the Old Testament and to Joseph's prudent policies as steward to Pharaoh in 'removing, that is TRANS-PLANTING THE PEOPLE from one end of the borders of Egypt, to the other end thereof'.[41]

Twenty years earlier Orrery's father, Richard Boyle, first earl of Cork, had insisted that 'so long as English and Irish protestants and papists live here intermingled together, we can never have firm and assured peace'.[42] He was writing in the aftermath of the 1641 rebellion, in which many thousands of Irish Protestants had been either killed or forced to flee their homes. This rebellion sparked the ferocious conflict which culminated in the Cromwellian conquest a decade later. The English parliament had responded to the news of trouble in Ireland by

---

[38] *Duanaire Dáibid Uí Bruadair*, ed. John Mac Erlean (Irish Texts Society, 1910–17), iii. 17.
[39] Canny, *Making Ireland British*, 60, 78–9, 83, 154, 206, 210, 216, 219.
[40] *The great expedition for Ireland by way of underwriting proposed*, London 1642, 12.
[41] Roger Boyle, earl of Orrery, *The answer of a person of quality to a scandalous letter lately printed and subscribed by P.W. intituled, A letter desiring a just and merciful regard of the Roman Catholicks of Ireland*, Dublin 1662, 93.
[42] Bottigheimer, *English money and Irish land*, 49.

endorsing a massive confiscation and sale of Irish land designed so as to provide funds for a military expedition. This departure, formalised in the Adventurers' Act of March 1642, cut away what little ground there existed for any form of settlement with the Irish Catholics.[43] However, the outbreak of civil war in England shortly thereafter meant that the parliament's preferred outcome, a quick victory in Ireland, also became impossible. By the autumn of 1642 the Catholics had established their own government at Kilkenny. This troubled regime was to control much of the island up to 1649.[44]

During those years the English parliament remained committed to the policy of confiscation and plantation in Ireland. As it sought to negotiate a settlement with Charles I at various times throughout the 1640s, the issue of punishing Irish rebels and planting Irish acres remained always on the agenda.[45] This question was also crucial to the Irish Catholics as they attempted to reach an agreement with the king which would secure for them key religious and political concessions and allow him to unleash large resources of Irish manpower against his English and Scottish enemies.[46] By the time that the royalist marquis of Ormond eventually agreed a treaty with the Irish Catholics in January 1649, their king was on trial and hurtling towards his end.[47]

With Charles finally out of the way, the English parliament could turn its attention to the long-delayed task of conquering Ireland. However, the enemy ranged against it in the neighbouring island now seemed more formidable than ever. The spilling of royal blood had helped to cure the fragile adhesive holding Ormond's alliance together, and only the cities of Dublin and Derry now held out for the parliament. The coming together of confederate Catholics, Protestant royalists and the Ulster Scots certainly rendered more difficult the task of conquest. On the other hand, it also made Ireland potentially a much richer prize for a conqueror. Writing from Dublin in July 1649, Colonel Michael Jones, the parliamentarian commander, reported that 'this may be called a second rebellion, the former was only of Irish, this of Scots and malignant English, so is there in this new rebellion, almost as much land escheated as in the former, and what may alone defray the whole charge of the war'.[48] Jones's words of reassurance echoed the reports that had been sent from Ireland in the aftermath of the outbreak of rebellion in 1641. His estimation would have reassured the various parties awaiting the spoils of war that there would be enough Irish land to satisfy all of their needs.

---

43 Ibid. 30–53.
44 On this Catholic government see Micheál Ó Siochrú, *Confederate Ireland, 1642–1649: a constitutional and political analysis*, Dublin 1999.
45 *The constitutional documents of the puritan revolution, 1625–1660*, ed. Samuel Gardiner, 3rd edn, Oxford 1906, 279, 281, 299.
46 Ó Siochrú, *Confederate Ireland*, ch. ii.
47 Ibid. 185–201.
48 *Memorials of the great civil wars in England from 1646 to 1652*, ed. Henry Cary, London 1842, ii. 153.

1

Conquest and Land in Cromwellian Ireland, 1649–1652

The Cromwellian conquest of Ireland is synonymous with massacre, death and destruction. Inevitably therefore, its more controversial incidents, particularly the mass killing at Drogheda, have been frequently explored by historians.[1] Although the military events which unfolded at Drogheda, Wexford, Scarrifhollis, Limerick and elsewhere were of undoubted importance in shaping the course of the conquest, in this chapter they will necessarily be consigned to the background. Such an approach is adopted not so as to minimise the monumental violence and human suffering which occurred, but because it can enable the shedding of fresh light on other relatively neglected aspects of the history of the conquest. The main focus here will be on the policies proposed and employed by the English leadership in Ireland to foster settled conditions while the protracted military struggle still raged. Alongside their quest for victory in siege and battle, Oliver Cromwell, Henry Ireton and the commissioners of parliament sought both to secure the co-operation of the existing civilian population and to commence the introduction of Protestant colonists as soon as possible.[2] Although the efforts of Cromwell and his immediate successors in these two areas rarely produced the desired results, their policies did gradually evolve into more concrete plans for a lasting settlement. It is essential therefore to examine carefully these wartime measures, because they helped to prepare the way for the schemes of plantation and transplantation which were eventually approved at Westminster.

---

[1] Ó Siochrú, *God's executioner*; James Scott Wheeler, *Cromwell in Ireland*, New York–Dublin 1999; John Morrill, 'The Drogheda massacre in Cromwellian context', in Edwards, Lenihan and Tait, *Age of atrocity*, 242–65.

[2] Cromwell was appointed lord lieutenant of Ireland by the English parliament in 1649. At his departure from Ireland in May 1650, his son-in-law Henry Ireton assumed the leadership of the parliament's forces in Ireland. Early in 1651 he was joined by four commissioners of parliament, Edmund Ludlow, John Jones, John Weaver and Miles Corbet. In September 1652 Charles Fleetwood was also appointed a commissioner and sent over to command the army. In August 1654 he was promoted to lead the Irish government as lord deputy. Following Fleetwood's return to England in 1655, Henry Cromwell became the chief figure in the Irish administration, even more so after his appointment as lord deputy in 1657.

Cromwell in Ireland

Cromwell's political paymasters in London did not demand that he instigate a massacre at the first enemy garrison he encountered in Ireland. Instead, in the summer and autumn of 1649, their main concern was money. Following his departure from London in July, the council of state wrote to Cromwell urging him to 'make the best improvement you can for storing up provisions in Ireland, when God gives you footing and opportunitye there'.[3] By September he was being warned that England could no longer pay for his expedition, because 'the tree which bare this treasure hath no roots'.[4] These messages from London ensured that Cromwell was aware of the urgent need for his new establishment in Ireland to put down roots of its own which would allow it to draw supplies of money and food from the Irish population. It was out of this requirement to protect the inhabitants of captured towns and districts, and to receive taxes and supplies from them in return, that the earliest English initiatives to foster more settled conditions in Ireland emerged. Upon his arrival at Dublin in August 1649, Cromwell moved quickly to issue a declaration promising payment to persons who would bring supplies for his army and protection to persons willing to reside and pay taxes in parliament quarters.[5] However, while some among the local population responded favourably to these initial overtures, they also demanded higher prices for their corn than had been anticipated by the English; Ireland would not be conquered cheaply.[6]

The declaration with which Cromwell introduced himself to Ireland for the first time was not a new tactic. Upon their arrival at Dublin in 1647, the then commissioners of parliament had issued a similar conciliatory declaration in which they insisted that they did not 'intend the extirpation of the Irish nation'.[7] In 1649, however, the bloody episodes at Drogheda and Wexford provided chilling evidence that extirpation might indeed be Cromwell's goal. Indeed, this point was taken up by the Irish Catholic bishops in a declaration issued by them in December 1649. Having surveyed with dread Cromwell's speedy progress southwards to Munster, the bishops appealed to those members of their flock who were co-operating with the enemy to desist at once. After all, they insisted, Cromwell's ultimate purpose was 'the destruction of the lives of the inhabitants of this nation', and any expectations to the contrary represented nothing more than 'a vaine opinion of hopes'.[8] The Catholic bishops would appear to have had a receptive audience for their admonitions. In a letter to parliament which would be censored before publication, Cromwell confessed his difficulties, 'all the

---

3 CSPD, 1649–1650, 245–6.
4 CSPI, 1647–1660, 792.
5 Oliver Cromwell, A declaration by the lord lieutenant of Ireland: concerning his resolutions for the peace and safety of Ireland, and the free injoyment of the rights of the people, London 1649, 1–2.
6 Edmund Ludlow, Memoirs of Edmund Ludlow, Vivay 1698, i. 334.
7 TNA, SP 63/264/132.
8 Certain acts and declarations made by the ecclesiasticall congregation of the arch-bishops, bishops, and other prelates: met at Clonmacnoise the fourth day of December 1649, London 1650, 3–6.

natives, almost to twenty, being friends to them ... the people that are under your contribution, being so daily robbed by their neighbours ... and we cannot be in all places to protect them'.[9] At the same time, Cromwell's direct opponent, the royalist lord lieutenant James Butler, marquis of Ormond, was seeking to ensure the collection of royalist taxes in parliament quarters.[10] All the while, Charles II was in Jersey waiting for an opportune moment to depart for Ireland.[11] Even though the royalists were unable to match his forces militarily, it was apparent that Cromwell still faced great difficulties in protecting conquered land and people.

To address this problem, and to counter the bishops' grim warnings, in January 1650 Cromwell issued a *Declaration for the undeceiving of deluded and seduced persons*. This was a furious tirade against Catholicism, but in its closing passages Cromwell none the less aimed to reassure 'the people of Ireland' of his favourable intentions towards them.[12] The bishops had insisted that Irish Catholics ought to expect no 'assurance concerning their religion, lives or fortunes' from the English parliament.[13] Cromwell now sought to persuade the population otherwise, by insisting that his new regime would judge individuals simply according to 'the nature and quality of their actions' since 1641; 'only the leading persons and principal contrivers of this Rebellion' would face exemplary justice. At the same time, anyone who continued to offer resistance thereafter could expect to be treated with 'utmost severity'.[14] In this rather ungentle effort to win hearts and minds, Cromwell was clearly making use of the powers that he enjoyed as lord lieutenant to offer terms to his enemies in Ireland. He aimed to divide Protestants from Catholics and leaders from followers. Moreover, although the terms he offered in January 1650 were rather vague, they were perhaps the most concrete statement of the intentions of the parliamentarians towards the Irish population to date. In the 1640s the parliament had advocated blanket condemnation to death of all persons associated with the Irish rebellion.[15] Cromwell, however, was now ready to recognise the varying roles and perceived guilt levels of the different categories of participant in the war in Ireland.

The intensity of Cromwell's attack on Catholicism in his *Declaration* probably helped to ensure that the overtures accompanying it would have little impact on Catholic opinion. On the other hand, he fared much better with the Protestant population. Even before his arrival in Ireland, he had won over Roger Boyle, Baron Broghill, a figure of considerable influence in Munster. Through Broghill's influence, many Munster Protestants were persuaded to defect from the faltering

9 HMC, *Seventh report*, ed. George Jessel and others, London 1879, i. 73–4. See also Deana Rankin, *Between Spenser and Swift: English writing in seventeenth century Ireland*, Cambridge 2005, 46–61.

10 HMC, *Manuscripts of the marquess of Ormonde*, ed. John Gilbert and Sidney Ratcliff, o.s. London 1895–1909, ii. 225.

11 James Scott Wheeler, *The Irish and British wars, 1637–1654: triumph, tragedy and failure*, London–New York 2002, 227.

12 *The letters and speeches of Oliver Cromwell with elucidations by Thomas Carlyle*, ed. Sophia Lomas, London 1904, ii. 5–23.

13 *Certain acts and declarations made by the ecclesiasticall congregation at Clonmacnoise*, 3.

14 *The letters and speeches of Oliver Cromwell*, ii. 21–3.

15 *Constitutional documents of the puritan revolution*, 262–347.

royalist cause late in 1649.[16] The generous terms offered by Cromwell to this community, and the guarantees outlined in his *Declaration*, could not have escaped the notice of Protestants elsewhere in Ireland. By the end of April 1650 he had agreed terms with the remaining Protestant forces.[17] Significantly, the promises made by Cromwell to the Irish Protestants concerning their property would later have a major impact on the implementation of the land settlement. More important in the shorter term, the exit of the Protestant royalists from the war served to establish a more distinct ethno-religious divide between the warring parties, thereby setting the scene for further destructive conflict.

Alongside his efforts to win over sections of Ireland's existing population, Cromwell also endeavoured to encourage the arrival of new colonists. As early as October 1649 he asked parliament to arrange for the sending over of families to re-populate the recently taken town of Wexford.[18] Apart from getting the process of colonisation underway, such a settlement would also help to support the town's English garrison. Cromwell also dispatched letters of invitation across the Atlantic to New England. The eventual response from that quarter was marked by caution. Influenced perhaps by their perception of 1641, and by their dealings with Native Americans, the New Englanders requested that in their proposed plantation at Waterford 'noe Irish may inhabite among us, but such as we shall like of'. They also chose to wait until 'the Lord's mind shall clearly appear to give us a sufficient call and encouragement to remove into Ireland'.[19] Yet despite Cromwell's optimistic design to re-establish New England in Ireland, only a handful of people acceded to his invitation to recross the ocean. In the mid-1650s the government eventually reserved a small amount of ground around Sligo town 'for the use and behoof and interest of such English families, as shall come from New England in America'.[20] This represented a rather poor outcome for the ambitious project that had caught Cromwell's imagination some years previously.

Ireton takes over

Cromwell departed from Ireland in May 1650 following a string of military successes, marred only by his failure to take Waterford six months before and his recent embarrassing set back at Clonmel.[21] While he had perhaps broken the backbone of Irish resistance, its flailing limbs still needed to be individually pinned down and smashed. This difficult task fell to Cromwell's successor in Ireland, his son-in-law Henry Ireton. In common with other English officers, Ireton's contribution to the conquest has long been overshadowed by that of Cromwell. Moreover, military historians, working from the improvable assump-

---

16 Wheeler, *Cromwell in Ireland*, 72, 103–4.
17 *A contemporary history of Irish affairs, from 1641 to 1652*, ed. John Gilbert, Dublin 1879–80, ii. 393–6.
18 *CJ* vi. 314–15.
19 *Original letters and papers of state addressed to Oliver Cromwell*, ed. John Nickolls, London 1743, 44–5.
20 *IUC* ii. 499.
21 Ó Siochrú, *God's executioner*, 122–5.

tion that Cromwell would have completed the conquest more quickly, have sometimes been scathing of Ireton's leadership in 1650–1.[22] The tendency to criticise Ireton because he was not more like his somewhat singular father-in-law does little to enable a balanced assessment of his role in Ireland. It is worth noting that the growth of Ireton's reputation in England in the 1640s was based on his use of the pen rather than the sword. Indeed, Ian Gentles has described him as 'the chief theoretician of the revolutionary army'.[23] This circumstance hints at the need to adopt a wider perspective if Ireton's importance in an Irish context is to be fully appreciated. Before his death at Limerick late in 1651, he had devoted considerable energy to the key tasks of winning over the existing population, planning its place in a post-war society, and promoting the arrival of new colonists. Moreover, the policies that he designed to achieve these ends were to have a significant impact on the subsequent settlement of the country.

Ireton's main achievement in 1650 was the capture of the city of Waterford. His impatient approach to this task exhibited some crucial differences from the tactics employed previously by Cromwell. First, he summoned the city to surrender even before he had actually arrived to supervise the ongoing siege. Secondly, rather than engaging in negotiations as was customary, he abruptly sought to impose terms of surrender. In response, the besieged commander, Sir Thomas Preston, rebuked Ireton for his 'unsoldierly' approach, 'against the rules of wars'.[24] Significantly, the unilateral terms proposed by Ireton also contained novel aspects, which reflected some of the main problems now faced by his forces. The loss of walled towns and castles had caused Catholic troops to retreat into the bogs, mountains and woods, from where they repeatedly raided English quarters. Accordingly, rather than allowing the Waterford garrison to march out honourably to continue the struggle elsewhere, Ireton demanded that they dump arms and either return to civilian life or depart the country.[25] It is clear, therefore, that from an early stage Ireton was attempting to use specific terms of surrender to force the conflict more swiftly towards its end game.

Another key challenge which Ireton faced was the task of guarding numerous strongholds while at the same time attempting to extend the conquest westwards. He explained that captured towns required large garrisons 'by reason of the inhabitants being all Irish, or else Old English (made as much our enemies by their religion, and as ill to be trusted as the other)'.[26] This awareness that he might soon be short of men led Ireton to introduce another new measure at Waterford. In the surrender terms, the citizens were warned that they might be expelled from the city at any time upon thirty days notice.[27] Ireton's Waterford proposals, of consequence both to soldier and civilian, represented the begin-

---

22 Wheeler, *Cromwell in Ireland*, 180, 185–6; Ian Gentles, *The new model army in England, Scotland and Ireland, 1645–1653*, Oxford 1992, 379.

23 *ODNB s.v.* 'Ireton, Henry (1611–1651)'.

24 Edmund Borlase, *The history of the execrable Irish rebellion*, 2nd edn, Dublin 1743, appendix, 32–3, 38–43; HMC, *Calendar of the manuscripts of the marquess of Ormonde*, ed. Francis Elrington Ball and Caesar Litton Falkiner, n.s. London 1902–20, i. 225–6, 229.

25 Borlase, *History of the Irish rebellion*, appendix, 32–3.

26 Zachary Grey, *An impartial examination of the fourth volume of Mr. Daniel Neal's history of the puritans*, London 1739, appendix, 78–80.

27 *Several Proceedings in Parliament*, 22 Aug.–29 Aug. 1650, 709–11.

nings of his attempts to develop a comprehensive longer-term strategy for pacifying and settling Ireland. The soldiers of surrendered garrisons were to be removed permanently from the war and, if necessary, civilians were to be evicted from their homes. None the less, the stubborn Ireton did not have things all his own way at Waterford; Preston's garrison was eventually permitted to march away with their arms to the still unconquered west to fight another day.[28] The consequences of Ireton's climb-down on this key issue were surely brought home to him in the final days of his life, at which point he again decided to appeal at a distance for the surrender of a city. The city was Galway and its commander, one Thomas Preston, must have relished the opportunity to rebuke his opponent for yet more 'unsoldierly' behaviour.[29]

In the months following the fall of Waterford in August 1650, Ireton continued to grapple with the problem of consolidating English control over Irish territory. Of particular concern was the south-east of the country, where conditions remained volatile despite the capture of all the main population centres. To address this problem, Ireton decided to extend to the countryside the policy of relocation that he had first designed for the citizens of Waterford. From September 1650 he began to declare hostile regions, such as the Wicklow mountains, to be out of protection. This meant that designated areas were to be laid waste and their inhabitants required to remove to pacified protected districts. Once there, these people would be unable fully to support the Catholic forces and obliged instead to pay English taxes. Any person found in an unprotected area after the stipulated deadline for removal was liable to be executed as a spy.[30] The effecting of this harsh strategy would see large swathes of countryside destroyed by fire and sword over the following years.

Ireton and plantation

By the winter of 1650–1 Ireton had decided to complement this policy of mass destruction with a new scheme of colonisation focused on the towns of the south-east. A regiment of soldier-settlers was to be recruited from England to take the place of the suspect Catholic inhabitants of Waterford and other towns.[31] This would free up garrisoned troops, while also preventing the towns from becoming ruinous as a result of depopulation. The new settlers would also help to offset the inevitable loss of revenue arising from the expulsion of the Catholics. In February 1651 the parliament assented to this design, and Ireton moved to activate the clause in the articles of Waterford which provided for the removal of its citizenry.[32] Yet despite these preparations, this latest colonisation

---

[28] Ibid.

[29] HMC, Ormonde calendar, i. 229.

[30] A Perfect Diurnall of Some Passages and Proceedings of, and in Relation to the Armies of England, Ireland, and Scotland, 28 Apr.–5 May 1651. See Pádraig Lenihan, 'War and population, 1649–52', Irish Economic and Social History xxiv (1997), 1–21.

[31] Propositions approved of and granted by the deputy-general of Ireland to Colonel Richard Laurence, for the raising in England and transporting into Ireland, a regiment of twelve hundred footmen, London 1650; Grey, An impartial examination, appendix, 78–80.

[32] CJ vi. 540–2; Borlase, History of the Irish rebellion, appendix, 101–5.

scheme met with little success. In 1652 one observer lamented that the settlers who came over 'made too much haste, so that many of them for want perished amongst us, others of them lived to be a burthen to us; whilst others returned home impoverisht to discourage others'.[33] The decision to colonise urban centres in the south-east was ambitious, but premature. None the less, these efforts at pacification through relocating sections of the population and introducing colonists in their stead provided further indications of what was to follow.

Because conditions in Ireland were not yet suitable for the reception of new settlers, Ireton remained to some extent dependent on the willingness of sections of the existing population to support his scattered forces. Amidst the uncertainty of war, however, the co-operation offered by many of the inhabitants of parliament quarters was necessarily tenuous, as the Catholic forces inevitably continued to command substantial support. Moreover, the English belief that the Catholics shared blood guilt for 1641 meant that they remained extremely wary of trusting them. None the less, Ireton felt obliged to give careful thought to the treatment appropriate for the Catholic population. This obligation arose from his need to obey the perceived will of God. As noted by Cromwell's chaplain, John Owen, when it came to making decisions, Ireton asked 'not what saith this man, or what saith that man, but what saith the Lord? that being evident; he consulted not with flesh and bloud, and the wisdom of it'.[34] Owen's dramatic appraisal reflected the reality that Ireton often showed himself reluctant to consult with his fellow officers, preferring instead to rely upon his reading of providential signs from God. This tendency rendered Ireton rather sensitive to setbacks, howsoever minor. For example, in June 1651, the loss of a party of men during a failed assault on an island in the River Shannon at Limerick inspired a bout of intense soul-searching, after which Ireton concluded that 'the hand and will of God was eminently appearing against us' because of his own leniency towards an officer who had wrongly executed a group of Irish prisoners a few weeks before.[35] Ireton's reluctance to risk another divine rebuke may in part explain his seemingly lethargic approach to capturing Limerick over the months following.

Negotiations and qualifications

A year earlier, in the summer of 1650, Ireton and his forces had experienced a deeper crisis when, in the aftermath of a substantial loss of men at Clonmel, the plague had begun to spread to the English army. As it appeared that God had withdrawn 'his former distinguishing mercy', Ireton instituted a series of days of fasting and humiliation.[36] In an accompanying declaration, he warned his men that 'none of the works of our God are without their grounds or ends, or without

---

[33] The present posture and condition of Ireland, London 1652, 10.

[34] John Owen, The labouring saints dismission to rest: a sermon preached at the funeral of the Right Honourable Henry Ireton lord deputy of Ireland, London 1652, 6.

[35] Sad newes from Ireland: how the Lord had been pleased to chastize the parliaments forces by a loss from the rebels, London 1651, 1–6; A contemporary history, iii. 241.

[36] Gentles, New model army, 374; Henry Ireton, A declaration and proclamation of the lord deputy-general of Ireland, concerning the present hand of God in the visitation of the plague, London 1650, 3–4; Original letters addressed to Oliver Cromwell, 72.

their speakings or teachings'. In his meditation upon this latest setback, Ireton showed himself willing to consider that God's anger had been aroused by maltreatment of the Irish population, including 'exaction and cruelty towards people in protection (wherever any opportunity with hope of privacy is found)'. He therefore expressed the hope that God would reveal 'what our carriage and dealings should have been, and what he would have it be, towards the generality of the people, and our enemies here, whether in respect of justice (for innocent blood) or of more moderation and mercy towards any'.[37] This declaration of July 1650 provides evidence of a crisis of confidence on the part of Ireton concerning the proper treatment of 'the poor deluded Popish people of this nation'.[38] Were they to be punished severely for the alleged events of 1641, or did God in his mercy favour a more moderate approach?

Ireton's consideration of this key question must have encouraged the development of his thought on how Catholics, the overwhelming majority of the population, were to be accommodated within a post-war settlement. Indeed, the military situation at the end of 1650 made this issue appear even more pressing. With the main Catholic forces largely confined west of the Shannon, a negotiated end to the war was becoming an increasingly attractive prospect for some figures on both sides of the conflict. At Loughrea, Co. Galway, in December, a bloc among the assembled Catholic leadership proposed that a national treaty should be agreed with the English parliament. Their stated aim was to use the inevitably harsh conditions that would be proposed by the parliament as a means to galvanise Catholic resistance. There were, however, strong indications that the fragile unity of the Catholic cause was already fractured beyond repair; in the south-east, the gentry of several counties living under English protection were reportedly preparing to dispatch agents to negotiate with the parliament, thus formally transferring their allegiance from Loughrea to London.[39] In January 1651 a further significant development occurred when the governor of Kilkenny, Colonel Daniel Axtell, sent two Catholic emissaries to Loughrea. Axtell, presumably acting on Ireton's behalf, urged the Catholic leadership to consent to negotiations towards 'an unanimous treaty', promising that 'the more considerable the body [of the] nation shall be that shall treat in that behalf the better and more secure shall their conditions be'.[40] Ireton and his officers may have adopted this strategy in the hope that it would enable them to avoid the difficult task of conquest in the west. At the very least, their invitation was bound to reveal the mood of the Catholic leadership, and possibly to foster further division.

The threat posed to the Catholic and royalist cause by Axtell's overtures was quickly recognised by Ormond's successor, the newly-appointed lord deputy Ulick Burke, marquis of Clanricarde. Determined to preserve royal authority in Ireland, he issued a proclamation forbidding negotiations with, or submission to, the parliament's forces. In addition, the Catholic bishops published an excommunication against collaborators.[41] While these moves appeared to have dashed

---

[37] Ireton, A declaration concerning the plague, 3–10.
[38] Ibid. 9.
[39] Thomas Carte, The life of James, duke of Ormond, London 1735–6, ii. 141–4; History of the confederation and war in Ireland, 1641–49, ed. John Gilbert, Dublin 1882–91, vii. 362–7.
[40] History of the confederation, vii. 362–7.
[41] Bodl. Lib., MS Carte 29, fo. 132; History of the confederation, vii. 362–7.

any hope of a negotiated settlement, Ireton still had reason to expect that the Irish might apply for a treaty. In February 1651 an intelligence report informed him that the city of Limerick intended to make an approach concerning the possibility of obtaining final surrender terms for the country as a whole.[42] Other intelligence, however, painted a very different picture. An intercepted letter written by the Catholic archbishop of Cashel informed Ireton of a design among the Catholics outside of Connacht, 'so gravelled and yoked by the parliament', for 'a general insurrection this next summer'.[43] Other sources indicated that the duke of Lorraine was destined for the coast of Ireland with a substantial military force.[44] From Ireton's perspective, it appeared that crisis was again imminent.

A further cause for concern was the nervousness being exhibited by the Irish civilians resident in parliament quarters. By March 1651 they had begun to petition 'to know what assurance they shall have for the enjoyment of their religion, lives, liberties and estates'.[45] Amidst rumours of plans for general insurrection and invasion, Ireton now feared that a failure to reassure the civilian population would cause them 'to give over tillage and husbandry and join with those forces which keep in the bogs and woods in almost every county'. As a result, 'the war [would] be much lengthened and made very burdensome to England'.[46] In 1650 Cromwell, when faced with adversity, had opted to publish an invective against his enemies. In 1651 the perilous situation in which Ireton found himself required a more considered response. He accordingly decided to formulate a grander strategy, which involved the drawing up of comprehensive terms or qualifications for the pardon and punishment of the parliament's Irish enemies. This exercise was intended to make known the conditions under which the English would be content to end the war. Ireton was determined to let the population know what was in store for it, to 'quiet the minds of many and justify the severity and justice of the parliament against those that embrace not their clemency'.[47]

The qualifications for Ireland

The use of qualifications involved categorising people according to the extent of their involvement in the war and then prescribing an appropriate measure of punishment. Such an approach had been employed by the parliament as it attempted to reach a settlement with the king during the English civil war in the 1640s. Ireton's personal experience of those earlier failed negotiations undoubtedly helped to shape his new Irish policy.[48] His more recent exposure to the problems of Irish warfare and his attempts to discern God's plan for the country were undoubtedly instrumental too. Moreover, Ireton's qualifications, drawn up by March 1651, were to be of lasting significance because, following some amend-

---

42 *The Tanner letters*, ed. Charles McNeill, Dublin 1943, 332–3.
43 *A Perfect Diurnall*, 21 Apr.–28 Apr. 1651, 989.
44 On the duke of Lorraine and Ireland see Micheál Ó Siochrú, 'The duke of Lorraine and the international struggle for Ireland, 1649–1653', *HJ* xlviii (2005), 905–32.
45 *Tanner letters*, 330–1.
46 Ibid.
47 Ibid.
48 *ODNB, s.v.* 'Ireton, Henry (1611–1651)'.

ments, they would eventually be approved by parliament in August 1652 as the Act for the Settling of Ireland.[49] This remarkable legislation provided the mechanism through which the English state sought to deal with those who had opposed it in Ireland. The content of the act has received much attention, perhaps most famously from Samuel Gardiner who estimated that its terms condemned at least 80,000 men to death.[50] Yet the origin of the legislation with Ireton and its immediate purpose in the context of the war in Ireland in 1651 has not been properly recognised.

Ireton's text began with a preamble which explained his intentions: 'that the people of this nation may know that it is not the intention of parliament to extirpate that whole nation'. It also expressed his belief 'that a total reducement and settlement of this nation may, with God's blessing, be speedily effected'. To this end, he proposed to pardon all 'husbandmen, labourers … and others of the inferior sort', persons who currently played an essential role in generating supplies for his army. The preamble also referred those of 'higher rank and quality' to the main text, where their fate, less kind, was outlined.[51]

The qualifications can be subdivided into two groups. The first group, under which Ireton proposed to exempt from pardon five categories of people, can be reasonably labelled his justice qualifications. The first of these terms exempted from pardon all persons who had 'contrived, advised, councelled, promoted … aided … assisted [or] abetted' the rebellion.[52] This severe clause borrowed from the terminology employed by parliament towards Irish rebels during the 1640s.[53] It appeared sweeping, impractical and essentially unenforceable, although Ireton's later efforts to clarify its meaning indicate that he was chiefly concerned to punish those who had taken up arms in the first year of the rebellion. The second qualification comprehended all members of the first general assembly and supreme council of the Catholic confederacy established in 1642, thus revealing Ireton's intention to hold these leading Catholics responsible for carrying on the war post-1642. The qualification following condemned all Catholic priests who had been anyway involved in the rebellion and war. The fourth qualification was also concerned with punishing persons who had enjoyed positions of influence; they were to be listed by name and exempted from pardon. Again, this was a direct borrowing from 1640s England, where the names of leading royalists selected by parliament for capital punishment had been presented to Charles I. Ireton's fifth qualification was aimed at men still in arms but not comprehended in any of the prior clauses. They too were to receive no mercy if they continued to resist beyond a date to be specified.[54] This proposal to set a final deadline for enemy submissions again reflected Ireton's urgency to end the war. Anyone remaining in arms thereafter could be pursued with what he viewed as 'justified severity', their hearts surely hardened by a vengeful God demanding retribution for 1641.[55]

---

[49] *Acts and ordinances of the English interregnum, 1642–1660*, ed. Charles Firth and Robert Rait, London 1911, ii. 598–603.

[50] Gardiner, 'The transplantation', 703–4.

[51] BL, MS Egerton 1,048, fos 123–9.

[52] Ibid.

[53] *Constitutional documents of the puritan revolution*, 279.

[54] MS Egerton 1,048, fos 123–9.

[55] *Tanner letters*, 330–1.

The next four clauses, three of which were aimed at landowners, can be described as Ireton's mercy qualifications. Anyone who had enjoyed a military rank higher than that of captain, and who was not comprehended in the preceding qualifications, faced banishment and the forfeiture of two-thirds of his property. The remaining one-third was to be retained by his family. Other landowners of lower rank who had already submitted or who would do so before Ireton's deadline would avoid banishment and be allowed one-third of their estates. Any further persons who, while remaining militarily inactive, had none the less failed to manifest their 'constant good affection to the interest of the commonwealth of England' were to forfeit one-third of their estates. Finally, the last qualification offered pardon to those persons possessed of personal estates worth less than ten pounds, provided that they would promptly 'lay down arms and submit'.[56] These nine qualifications represented Ireton's framework for extending God's and England's justice and mercy to Ireland.

From Ireton's perspective, the three qualifications relating to real estates represented significant concessions to his enemies. In December 1649 the Catholic bishops had tried to galvanise resistance by arguing that 'the estates of the inhabitants of this kingdom are sold, so as there remaineth now no more, but to put the purchasers in possession'.[57] In 1651 Ireton hoped to hasten the war's end by convincing the Catholics that all was not yet lost. Indeed, the commissioners of parliament subsequently confessed that his seventh qualification, which allowed persons in arms one third of their estates, had been intended as 'an inducement to a general laying down of arms and surrendering of garrisons by the enemy'.[58] Concessions of this kind, made to secure military objectives in a difficult war, were bound to have a bearing on the future land settlement. In fact, they laid the foundations for continued Catholic landownership in post-war Ireland. The extent of English hostility towards Irish Catholics meant that such an outcome had been far from inevitable. In a pamphlet also produced in 1651, Thomas Waring insisted that due to their actions in 1641, the Irish Catholics had rendered themselves 'uncapable of mercie, protections, or safetie from the people of England, therefore none ought to be given them'. Waring quoted the word of God as mediated through the prophet Jeremiah: 'Cursed bee hee that doth the work of the Lord negligently, and cursed bee hee that keepeth back his sword from bloud'.[59] Yet the seeming will of God and the challenges of Irish warfare had led Ireton to a different and more merciful conclusion.

Although Ireton made some concessions on Catholic landownership, he also saw fit to attach one important condition. In the articles tendered by him to the city of Limerick in June 1651, he referred to regions to be 'planted intirely with English, or set apart to be so'.[60] In order to avoid compromising this vision of future English Protestant colonisation in Ireland, it was essential that the

---

56 MS Egerton 1,048, fos 123–9.
57 *Certain acts and declarations made by the ecclesiasticall congregation at Clonmacnoise*, 5.
58 *IUC* i. 28–9.
59 Thomas Waring, An *answer to certain seditious and Jesuitical queres heretofore purposely and maliciously cast out to retard and hinder the English forces in their going over into Ireland*, London 1651, 63.
60 *IUC* i. 106.

conquerors retain some discretion over the location of the estates that would remain in Catholic hands. Consequently, Ireton's mercy qualifications stipulated that the portions of land being promised to Catholics would be located wherever parliament thought fit.[61] Thus, while he proposed to allow a degree of Catholic property-owning in post-war Ireland, Ireton also believed that an associated scheme of transplantation would be necessary in order safely to facilitate it. In this way, the policy of relocation which he had already seen fit to apply to the south-eastern towns and the various unprotected regions was also to be extended to those entitled to land under his qualifications.

Could Ireton's plan have provided a framework to end the war in Ireland? The first obstacle which had to be overcome was that of securing approval from Westminster. Although the qualifications were first discussed by parliament as early as April 1651, they soon fell victim to its apparent lack of interest in this and in other Irish matters.[62] As the qualifications were not finally approved by parliament until August 1652, Ireton was deprived of what he perceived as the means to end the conflict in 1651. Other observers, however, viewed his proposals in a very different light. One individual with Irish sympathies who became familiar with the qualifications in London in April 1651 was convinced that 'here is enough invented, and intended to destroy and root out the whole nation'.[63] Ironically, Ireton's intention had been to assure the people of Ireland that the opposite was the case. Had they been approved and published in 1651, the qualifications may have proven useful to the Irish Catholic leadership in its efforts to unite sections of the population behind it. Overall, the harshness of Ireton's justice qualifications reflected both his and the general English understanding of what had occurred in Ireland in 1641, and this factor helped to ensure that a peace involving substantial compromise remained unlikely.

The campaign of 1651

Having drafted his qualifications and dispatched them to Westminster, Ireton turned once more to the task of prosecuting the war in Ireland. In 1650 Cromwell had left winter camp in January. In 1651 Ireton had to wait for the April grass to grow before he could renew his campaign.[64] None the less, by the end of June, his forces had crossed the Shannon to besiege Limerick. At the same time, Sir Charles Coote had advanced into Connacht from the north, forcing the surrender of Athlone and other key points along the Shannon and opening up English access to the west. Ireton took this opportunity once again to incorporate his preferred new policies into the terms of proposed articles of surrender for Limerick. The occupants of the besieged city were accordingly informed that pardon and protection would be withheld from three categories of persons: anyone who had borne arms in the first year of the rebellion; members of the first

61 MS Egerton 1,048, fos 123–9.
62 CJ vi. 564, 567.
63 MS Carte 29, fo. 416.
64 Bulstrode Whitlocke, *Memorials of the English affairs*, London 1682, 491.

confederate general assembly; and all priests.[65] By seeking suddenly to impose three of his qualifications on Limerick, Ireton allowed the besieged an insight into the heavy judgement that awaited them, a move which presumably reinforced their resolution to hold out. Shortly afterwards, following the receipt of a protest from the leaders of the city, Ireton conceded that the exempted persons would be allowed to live in protection for the time being.[66] However, this limited concession did little to hasten the surrender of the city; instead, the drawn-out siege impacted on Ireton's health and by November he was dead of a fever.

The fall of Limerick rendered the Irish armies even more desperate. Furthermore, the royalist defeat at Worcester in September 1651 removed much of the 'three-kingdoms' justification for prolonging the fight in Ireland. By November Sir Walter Dongan, who had wreaked havoc in Leinster throughout the summer, had indicated his desire 'to lay down arms and get beyond the seas'.[67] Despite these increasingly unpromising circumstances, Clanricarde continued to encourage resistance. He warned those contemplating submission that 'every foot of lande in this kingdome is divided and sold by the pretended parliament of England to Londoners and others, who have paid their moneyes … consequently the nation cannot expect … to be other than tenants at will to those purchasers'.[68] In fact, the terms which Ireton was willing to offer relating to real estates were more lenient than Clanricarde realised. Although his position was becoming hopeless, Clanricarde was still nominally in command of an estimated 30,000 men scattered across the country. Moreover, despite the various English efforts to wean the wider population from the Catholic and royalist cause, it was evident that 'the people [were] ready to join with them upon any occasion'.[69] Thus when the commissioners of parliament and leading army officers gathered for consultations at Kilkenny at the end of the year, the key problems with which Cromwell and Ireton had grappled over the preceding years, advancing the conquest, pacifying territory, controlling the existing population and attracting new colonists, remained high on their agenda.

With Ireton deceased, some in Ireland hoped that Cromwell would return to complete the conquest.[70] Instead, increased responsibility fell on the four commissioners of parliament who had first arrived in Ireland early in 1651. By 1652 one of the commissioners, Colonel John Jones, was becoming ever more pessimistic about Ireland and her people. Writing to a confidant in London, he announced that he was 'persuaded that the Irish will never be brought to cohabit with the English peaceably (except all men of estates be banished, and the labourer admitted to the same immunities with the English)'.[71] As the Irish forces reached breaking point, the existence in government ranks of such views did not augur well for them. Moreover, Jones and his colleagues were unsure of the extent

---

65 IUC i. 104–6.
66 IUC i. 107–9.
67 Inedited letters of Cromwell, Col. Jones, Bradshaw and other regicides, ed. Joseph Meyer, Liverpool 1861, 21.
68 HMC, Ormonde calendar, i. 238.
69 IUC i. 113–14.
70 Colonel John Jones to Thomas Scott, Dublin, 15 Dec. 1651, NLW, MS 11,440D, fos 25–6.
71 Colonel Jones to Scott, Dublin, 5 Feb. 1652, ibid. fo. 38.

of their powers and uncertain over how to proceed in Ireton's absence. It was in this context that several Irish requests for a national treaty, and the offer of 'a voluntary subjection as well of hartes as armes', were rebuffed by the commissioners in the spring of 1652.[72] Edmund Ludlow, the acting commander-in-chief, insisted that 'the settlement of this nation doth of right belong to the Parliament of the Commonwealth of England, to whom we leave the same'.[73] Unfortunately, parliament, distracted by other matters, continued to disappoint.

Meanwhile, the destructive pattern of warfare continued. The fate of the barony of Burren, Co. Clare, provides a useful example of vicious tactics employed by the English at this time. In December 1651 a large Irish force under Colonel Mortagh O'Brien entered the region and the inhabitants ceased paying their taxes of £200 per month to the English. When a force led by Sir Charles Coote and Sir Hardress Waller arrived to address this situation, O'Brien's men retreated to safety in the mountains. John Jones described what happened next: 'They destroyed all that country by burning corn and habitations, and putting to the sword all the inhabitants they could find, whereof many [were] women, and children ... and I believe ... that their cattle were removed to other pastures.'[74] The campaign to destroy any territory which could not be properly controlled ultimately made matters worse by contributing to a decline in food production and tax revenue. As a result of such ferocious measures, by 1652 'very many baronies, and some whole counties, which paid considerable assessments the last year ... [were] now totally wasted'.[75] Moreover, because the money available to pay the army was insufficient, its arrears mounted accordingly. This development would be of considerable consequence for the shape of the subsequent land settlement.

From war to peace

In an effort to address the difficulties which they faced at the beginning of 1652, the commissioners placed their hopes, as Cromwell and Ireton had done, in plantation. In January they proposed to kick-start the recovery of the country by inviting the adventurers for Irish lands to commence their plantation, 'notwithstanding the war is not ended'. In addition, the commissioners planned to create two English Pales in the south-east, using the Boyne and Barrow, and the Suir and Blackwater rivers to create defensible frontiers.[76] This plan was an elaboration of the unsuccessful soldier-settler scheme of the previous year. In addition, soldiers were to be allotted land adjacent to their scattered garrisons and encouraged to support themselves by keeping gardens.[77] Once this latest blueprint for

[72] Sir Richard Barnewall and Colonel Walter Bagenal to the commissioners of parliament, 15 Mar. 1651, NLI, MS 11,959, fos 55–6.
[73] IUC i. 145–6.
[74] Colonel Jones to Scott, Kilkenny, 27 Dec. 1651, NLW, MS 11,440D, fos 33–4.
[75] Colonel Jones to Scott, Dublin, 15 Dec. 1651, ibid. fos 29–30.
[76] IUC i. 120–2.
[77] Ibid.

settlement had been dispatched to London for approval, the commissioners were forced to turn their attention once more to conquest.

In the opening months of 1652 it was evident that many Irish officers were ready to give up their cause for lost.[78] Yet the parliament, contrary to the expectations of its representatives in Ireland, offered no direction on how the war should be brought to a conclusion. In the absence of any alternative proposals, the commissioners clung to the hope that Ireton's qualifications might still be adopted by Westminster as the basis for a speedy settlement. In March 1652 the commissioners, under pressure from weary army officers on both sides, eventually decided to break the deadlock by accepting the surrender in the midlands of Colonel John Fitzpatrick and his forces.[79] Over the following months other surrenders followed countrywide and the Irish armies prepared to take ship. In the absence of any initiatives from parliament, its army officers looked back to Ireton's qualifications of the previous year for some guidance on the terms which might reasonably be offered to the Irish. For instance, in his negotiations with Colonel Edmund O'Dwyer, Colonel Hierome Sankey used 'the late lord deputy's late qualifications' as his benchmark. O'Dwyer, who 'was by necessity driven … to treat and submit', could not afford the luxury of refusing the terms offered to him.[80]

A letter written at this time by Sankey to Cromwell provides some insight into the reservations which God-fearing Englishmen had to overcome in order to face into negotiations with supposedly blood-guilty Irish Catholics. Sankey admitted that the prospect of negotiating had caused him great mental distress, as he 'meditated upon the crying guilt of blood [and] the severe justice of God'. When he considered the alleged crimes of 1641, he remembered the vengeful God of the Old Testament and his 'severity … against Saul and Jesohopat' when they disobeyed his will.[81] Significantly, his experience of tit-for-tat combat against O'Dwyer in the mountains of Tipperary and Kilkenny caused Sankey to perceive a disparity between the popular image of the blood-thirsty murderous Irish rebel and the professional soldier who followed recognised codes of conduct. O'Dwyer fitted the latter description, and Sankey respectfully described his opponent's 'courtesy to some Englishmen and to all prisoners, [his] exact and punctual performance of his word on all engagements … and [his] very honest and friendly demeanour to Cap. Godfrey, Cap. Cuffe and other officers, whom I much respect, that were his prisoners last summer'.[82] When he considered this irreproachable behaviour, he thought of the loving God of Matthew's Gospel and the moral that 'rewards and punishments are for good and evil works, whatever the workers are'.[83] Recognising the essential humanity of his enemies, Sankey felt obliged to respond favourably to overtures for the surrender of an exhausted guerrilla army.

Although Sankey had sought to adhere closely to Ireton's qualifications, others would agree to more significant concessions in the months following. Two

78 *IUC* i. 128–9; *Mercurius Politicus*, 15 Jan.–22 Jan. 1652, 1,358. The letter published in this newsbook was possibly written by the commissioners of parliament.
79 *IUC* i. 155.
80 *Several Proceedings in Parliament*, 8 Apr.–15 Apr. 1652, 2,066.
81 Ibid. 2,066–7.
82 Ibid.
83 Ibid.

sets of articles, for the surrender of the town of Galway in April 1652, and for the surrender of the Leinster army at Kilkenny in May 1652, were of particular importance. Under the lenient terms granted to Galway by Sir Charles Coote, the city's merchants secured two-thirds of their extensive landed estates, as well as their valuable urban property. The commissioners, distant in Dublin, were outraged at this generosity, which seemed to ensure the continuance of substantial Catholic proprietorship in the west of Ireland.[84] A month later a national treaty of sorts was encompassed in the terms agreed for the surrender of the Leinster army. The terms in question were offered to all Irish forces still in arms, provided that they submitted by 1 June.[85] The Leinster articles also impacted significantly on Ireton's scheme of qualifications. With the focus of their attention now shifting towards specific incidents of alleged murder, the parliamentarian negotiators consented to move away from Ireton's view that simply bearing arms before November 1642 should be considered a capital offence. In addition, Ireton's second qualification, which condemned to death all members of the first confederate general assembly and supreme council, was simply abandoned in the course of the negotiations.[86] The prospects for priests were also enhanced as they were permitted under various articles to depart the country, thus escaping the death penalty laid down in the third qualification.[87] Moreover, many of those 106 individuals specifically named for execution in the fourth qualification also improved their position by surrendering under articles. This was so because the various sets of articles at a minimum guaranteed the lives of those comprehended within them, provided that they were not subsequently found guilty of murder.

The concessions made to the Catholic forces in return for their surrender were to have significant implications for the settlement of Ireland. Overall, the number of people liable to execution under the qualifications was substantially reduced, while Catholic entitlements to land became greater than had been anticipated. In the years that followed, the inconsistencies that existed between the qualifications of the Act for the Settling of Ireland and the various promises contained in articles of war would prove to be among the most problematic issues faced by the government. Furthermore, by mid-1652 it was apparent that a method for accommodating a greater degree of Catholic landownership than Ireton had envisaged would now have to be identified. In 1651 he had tied the prospect of a limited Catholic share in the post-war land settlement to the likelihood of transplantation. The concessions made in 1652 inevitably heightened the perceived necessity for a radical solution to the problem of facilitating continued Catholic proprietorship.

Shaping the settlement

The growing acceptance by 1652 that transplantation would be a central aspect of the coming settlement is reflected by a range of evidence. A useful example is

---

[84] *IUC* i. 165–7.
[85] *IUC* i. 197–201.
[86] *IUC* i. 201–2.
[87] See, for example, the articles for the surrender of Galway in *IUC*, i. 163–6.

supplied by the content of an anonymous pamphlet, *The present posture and condition of Ireland*, published in London in the spring of 1652. The author was one thoroughly familiar with the concerns of the Dublin government and the discussions taking place on Irish policy at Westminster; indeed the work may even have been written in Ireland.[88] Having rehearsed England's right to rule Ireland, the author proceeded to set out a blueprint for settlement. At its heart was a proposal to concentrate all English energies on planting the province of Leinster so as to prevent the new colonies from being thinly scattered countrywide. Only when that primary task had been completed could consideration be given to other regions; for instance, Connacht might be made 'all English' by the resettling of people from Virginia and New England.[89] A few months later Samuel Hartlib would propose an even more ambitious design to involve exiled Bohemians and Protestants from the Low Countries in the colonisation of Ireland.[90]

Perhaps the most notable aspect of *The present posture* was the proposals that it contained relating to the existing Catholic population. While the supposed blood guilt of the Catholics was deemed to justify their complete destruction, the Old Testament showed that when God favoured such extreme courses, such as in Canaan, 'his commands [had] ever been solemnly delivered from heaven'.[91] As the voice of God could not be heard emanating from the rain clouds over Ireland in the spring of 1652, it appeared that a more practical course was perhaps permissible. The author therefore highlighted the precedent of the Gibeonites, a section of the Canaanite population employed by the Israelites as 'hewers of wood and drawers of water'. In the short term, however, allowing Irish Catholics to live alongside English settlers was seen as altogether too risky. Instead, in a 'double, interchangeable transmigration' or 'transplantation', Catholics were to be expelled from the envisaged Leinster colony and the Ulster Scots Presbyterians were to be 'displanted' from the north of Ireland into the least fertile parts of Leinster: Wicklow and King's and Queen's counties. In addition, Catholic children were to be shipped to England to be educated and civilised.[92] In light of what was to follow, the prominent position afforded to transplantation schemes in *The present posture* was significant. Indeed, it may have exercised influence over those who were engaged in designing the Irish land settlement. By mid-1653 proposals for the transplantation of both the Irish Catholics and the Ulster Scots were under consideration in Dublin and London.

The concept of transplantation also surfaced in the course of discussions between the adventurers and the parliament in London in April and May 1652. The adventurers had been spurred into action by the plantation proposals sent over from Ireland in January. Although they had been enthusiastic to begin plantations at various points during the 1640s, by 1652 they saw fit to complain that Ireland had become 'the land of desolation', 'a wilderness abounding with nothing but wants and dangers'.[93] They accordingly sought numerous conces-

88 *The present posture*, 10, 13–15.
89 Ibid. 25–9.
90 Samuel Hartlib, 'The epistle dedicatory', in Gerard Boate, *Irelands naturall history*, London 1652.
91 *The present posture*, 19.
92 Ibid. 25–8.
93 MS Carte 67, fos 236, 259.

sions from the parliament so as to maximise the potential return on their Irish investment. Significantly, they proposed to abandon the four-province model of plantation laid down by the original legislation of 1642, and instead to concentrate their allotments of land in Leinster and Munster, the most fertile regions of the country.[94] The author of *The present posture* had already warned his audience against accepting such demands from the adventurers.[95] In common with that pamphlet, the adventurers' proposals highlighted the fact that the overall shape of the planned Irish land settlement was still very much up for discussion in mid-1652.

The adventurers' discussions with the parliament contributed to a revival of interest in Irish affairs in London in these months. On 20 April the parliament passed a number of pertinent resolutions, including a request that the council of state make provision for 'transporting persons from one part of the nation to another'.[96] A short time later a parliamentary committee recommended that the lands to be allotted to the adventurers should be planted solely by Protestants introduced from outside of Ireland.[97] At the very least, this would necessitate the removal of the Catholic population from the plantation zone. The adventurers responded cautiously by stating that they could 'say nothing to the exempting or admitting of the Irish [into plantations] until the Parliament had disposed of them'.[98] In common with the government in Ireland, the adventurers were evidently waiting for the qualifications which would decide the fate of the Irish population to be approved.

The proposal from the parliamentary committee that Irish Protestants as well as Catholics should be excluded from the adventurers' plantation suggests that concerns other than a straightforward fear of future Catholic treachery were being voiced. These probably included the government's financial worries. In Ireland the taxes levied for the support of the army had reached crippling levels by 1652. Inhabited lands in parliament quarters were being taxed at a rate much higher than they were 'generally worth to be let at rack'.[99] None the less, the adventurers expected to avail themselves of generous tax breaks designed to incentivise plantation.[100] If not prevented, many Irish labourers and husbandmen, both Protestant and Catholic, could be expected to flock to the adventurers' tax haven, thus further disrupting revenue generation. This possibility provided some justification for excluding Irish Protestants from the new plantations. It also provided further reason, if any was needed, for the exclusion of Catholics.

The degree of attention devoted to Ireland at Westminster in April and May 1652 seemed to bode well for the passage of the long-awaited Irish legislation.

---

94 Ibid. fos 230–4.
95 *The present posture*, 24–5.
96 CJ vii. 123.
97 MS Carte 67, fos 256–7.
98 Ibid. fos 258–9; HMC, *Manuscripts of his grace the duke of Portland*, ed. F. H. Blackburne Daniell, London 1891, 649–51.
99 IUC i. 116–18.
100 MS Carte 67, fo. 257.

None the less, throughout the summer progress remained slow.[101] Significantly, some important amendments and additions were made to Ireton's qualifications in these months. In line with the concessions made to the Leinster army at Kilkenny, the second qualification concerning the members of the confederate general assembly and supreme council was dropped. In addition, the ninth qualification was altered to lessen its impact for Protestants; unlike Catholics, they would no longer be required to demonstrate 'constant good affection' in order to escape forfeiture and transplantation. Also significant was the addition of a proviso which legislated for the transplantation 'from their usual place of habitation' of persons who had surrendered under articles.[102] This clause represented a rather inadequate effort to reconcile the content of Ireton's somewhat outdated qualifications to an Irish setting which had been substantially altered as a result of the recent surrender negotiations.

While the final surmounting of such complex problems lay in the future, by August 1652 the way seemed clear for parliament to at last approve detailed plans for the settlement of Ireland. On 6 August, after its second reading, a bill which set out the terms of the proposed land settlement was sent back to a large committee, the members of which were ordered to consult further with the adventurers, 'the agents for New England' and other interested parties.[103] Ultimately, this bill would not be passed until thirteen months later. This failure to approve the central piece of the Irish legislative jigsaw which was being put together at this point limited the effectiveness of the other two related bills which were successfully passed. On 25 August a bill authorising the calculation of arrears due to the army in Ireland was accepted by parliament, but the delay in legislating for plantations meant that the process of disbandment would not be commenced for another year.[104] With each day that passed, army arrears, and the amount of confiscated Irish land that would be needed to satisfy them, continued to spiral. More significantly, the Act for the Settling of Ireland, passed on 12 August, received only a muted welcome in Dublin.[105] After all, Ireton's original intention to use the qualifications to bring the war to an end had by then been achieved by other means. In October the commissioners of parliament sent notice to Westminster that until further legislation authorising plantations in Ireland was passed, 'little advantage can be made of the place'.[106] Although the fighting had mostly ceased, food was expensive and scarce; as the commissioners chose to prioritise the procurement of oats for the army's horse, people starved.[107]

---

[101] For a penetrating analysis of the complex politics of these months see John Morrill, 'Cromwell, Parliament, Ireland and a Commonwealth in crisis: 1652 revisited', *Parliamentary History* xxx (2011), 193–214. I am grateful to Professor Morrill for allowing me to consult a copy of this article prior to its publication.

[102] Council of state to the parliament, 3 Aug. 1652, MS Carte 67, fos 278–9; *Acts and ordinances*, ii. 603.

[103] CJ vii. 161–2.

[104] CJ vii. 169; *Acts and ordinances*, ii. 603–12.

[105] IUC i. 268–9.

[106] MS Egerton 1,762, fo. 46.

[107] The commissioners of parliament to the council of state, Dublin, 4 Dec. 1652, Bodl. Lib., MS Firth C5, fos 171–2.

By the autumn of 1652 those Catholics and Protestants who found it possible to remain in Ireland, and who had secured entitlement to land in the post-war settlement, now faced an anxious wait for their exact fate to be decided by fresh legislation from London. Yet much of the groundwork for the settlement which was to follow had already been carried out. Out of the sphere of conflict in Ireland, there had emerged a succession of policies and proposals designed to smooth the path of conquest. Although designed for the most part to achieve immediate ends in a military context, these initiatives would ultimately serve to inform the character of the subsequent settlement. Apart from swiftly winning control of a large number of towns and other strongholds, Cromwell had also worked to fracture the cross-confessional royalist military alliance, to undermine its popular support and to commence colonisation. Ireton was to devote even more energy to the latter two tasks, and by March 1651 he had drafted a detailed programme for settlement. None the less, twelve months later Ireton was dead, large swathes of the country had been destroyed, the Irish armies were still essentially intact and little progress had been made at Westminster with the various proposals sent from Ireland. By the time that Ireton's qualifications were eventually approved in August 1652, the situation in Ireland had been further complicated by the terms of various articles of surrender. This rather haphazard approach to completing the conquest had produced a problematic and incomplete framework for accommodating the existing population in post-war Ireland. With the fighting drawing to a close, the precise shape which the land settlement would take was still unknown, and the army officers who had conquered Ireland were now readying themselves to enter the debate.

2

Towards Plantation and Transplantation, 1652–1654

In October 1652 a London newsbook, *The Faithful Scout*, reported that 'the long-expected news of the Irish calm, is at last blown over to us with a happy gale'.[1] For the conquerors, the question of precisely how this calm should be exploited remained to be decided. A vast confiscation and redistribution of land was imminent, and Irish Catholics and Protestants, adventurers and soldiers, state creditors and other interested parties all expected to be accommodated. This chapter will reconstruct the bargaining process that occurred relating to the design of the settlement from the autumn of 1652 to final approval in the Act of Satisfaction of September 1653. Once that legislation was passed, the Irish government was expected swiftly to oversee the commencement of the land settlement. As during the conquest, however, the pace of proceedings in London had proven altogether too slow for the needs of the authorities in Dublin. In the closing months of 1652, and throughout the first half of the following year, they had already moved to address their concerns around food supply, finance and security through a range of policies, including transplantation. Because these measures helped subsequently to shape the implementation of the settlement approved in London, it is necessary to take account of them here. Ultimately, the Irish government was faced with the task of enforcing the disruptive policy of transplantation to Connacht while at the same time endeavouring to preserve the arrangements that it had already put in place to promote recovery. This circumstance ensured that the former scheme would enjoy a somewhat tentative beginning.

Securing the Promised Land

While a 'happy gale' brought good news from Ireland to the coast of England in October 1652, a melancholy wind filled the sails of ships carrying Irish soldiers into continental exile. The arrival of more settled conditions allowed the parliamentarian army to turn their thoughts from the problems of conquest to the no less considerable challenges of the land settlement, and their considerable stake in it. In September 1652 army officers gathered at Kilkenny to consult with their newly-arrived commander-in-chief, Cromwell's son-in-law Charles Fleetwood.

---

[1] *The Faithful Scout*, 8 Oct.–17 Oct. 1652, 612.

Over the following two years, Fleetwood would also act alongside Edmund Ludlow, Miles Corbet and John Jones as one of the commissioners of parliament at the head of the Irish government. Despite the wasted condition of the country, some of those present at the officers' meeting found reason for optimism. Justice John Cook declared that Ireland was now 'a white paper', supposedly 'ready to have anything writ in it that the state shall think fit'.[2] John Jones painted the situation in even more dramatic terms:

> the lord hath ledd mee, by strange providences into a strange land, and to act in as strang[e] a worke, a worke that neither wee, nor our forefathers knew, or heard off. The frameing, or forminge of a comonwealth, out of a corrupt rude Masse, the deviding of the countrey amongst the servants of the lord, who have passed through the redd sea, and indured heardshipp in the wilderness.[3]

Jones clearly believed that the army's entitlement to Ireland was that of Israel to the Promised Land.

This striking enthusiasm was not shared by all of those present. Reflecting on the state of the country, the Munster Protestant landowner John Percival could 'compare it to nothing but the first chaos, *rudis indigestique moles*'.[4] Jones was not discouraged by this scenario. After all, the Garden of Eden had been formed from such materials. Yet Percival was more pessimistic: 'poor Ireland' only resembled 'a white paper' because it had 'lost much blood and I cannot wonder it shall be pale-faced now'.[5] As the owner of a ruined estate, Percival was perhaps better placed to assess the situation. The difficult process of recovery would entail more than simply parcelling out the land. Among the problems which remained to be solved was the continued presence of Irish Catholic Canaanites on the land promised to the army. It was in this context that the officers worked out their own blueprint for the settlement.

High on the officers' list of concerns were the various conditions laid down by the Adventurers' Act of 1642. These included a provision that the adventurers should be the first group to receive land after the war's end. If this course were followed, the urgent task of reducing of the size of the Irish army would be delayed. The latter process could not take place without the concurrent granting of land for arrears. Moreover, any further delay in cutting military costs would increase the state's financial difficulties unnecessarily. In what was perhaps a veiled threat to the adventurers, the officers pointed out that it would cost less to reimburse their original investment than to maintain the army at its current size for another year. At the same time they proposed 'that one or more counties in each province ... be set apart by lot and reserved for the satisfaction of the adventurers'.[6] The officers also expected that the adventurers would recruit English Protestants to inhabit these counties, although they said nothing about the fate of the Catholics who would have to make way for these new settlers.[7] It is

---

2 HMC, *Manuscripts of the earl of Egmont*, ed. Sophia Egmont, London 1905–9, i. 514.
3 Colonel Jones to Vavasour Powell, Kilkenny, 8 Oct. 1652, NLW, MS 11,440D, fo. 75.
4 HMC, *Egmont manuscripts*, i. 514.
5 Ibid.
6 Egerton MS 1,762, fos 44–5.
7 Ibid.

possible that the officers' views on this matter were transmitted verbally by the three agents sent by them to Westminster at this time. One of the three, Colonel Richard Lawrence, would later be the most vocal supporter of trans-plantation.[8]

Following the arrival of the officers' delegation in London, it would quickly have become clear that the respective self-interested blueprints proposed by the army and the adventurers could not both be implemented. The task of resolving this situation fell to a parliamentary committee charged with preparing the bill for planting Ireland. In December 1652 it proposed a compromise: a joint ten-county adventurer-soldier plantation which would stretch across the three provinces of Munster, Leinster and Ulster, from Waterford in the south, through the midlands to Antrim in the north. This design was intended to ensure that both troop disbandment and the adventurers' plantation could commence soon and simultaneously. By January 1653 the parliament had endorsed the plan.[9]

Karl Bottigheimer viewed the emergence of the three-province plantation scheme as a clear sign that the policy of transplantation to the fourth province of Connacht had been decided upon by the winter of 1652.[10] This point can be reinforced by additional evidence. When the ten-county plan was reported to parliament in January, it was stated that additional army arrears would be satisfied in 'the other counties of Ireland, not excepted by this act'.[11] This may well have been a reference to the counties of Connacht, perhaps already set aside for the Catholic Irish. Since 1642 the adventurers had at different times expressed their desire to settle in all of the provinces except Connacht. In 1644 they had turned their attention to Ulster; in the following year, Munster seemed to offer better prospects.[12] By 1652 Leinster and Munster were clearly the most sought-after provinces. Therefore, when trans-plantation came to be seen as necessary, it can be no surprise that Connacht was selected for that purpose. Such a policy was not officially adopted in London until July 1653. None the less, by that date the policies already implemented by the commissioners in Ireland had provided a strong indica-tion of what was to come.

Leases and transplantations

Understanding of the emergence of transplantation to Connacht as official policy in mid-1653 has been largely shaped by the work of Samuel Gardiner and Robert Dunlop. Gardiner's most notable contribution was his attempt to asso-ciate the adoption of the scheme with Oliver Cromwell, while both historians

---

8 Lawrence was accompanied by Advocate-General Philip Carteret and Sir Hardress Waller.
9 MS Carte 67, fos 253–5; CJ vii. 242–3.
10 Bottigheimer, *English money and Irish land*, 133.
11 CJ vii. 242–3.
12 BL, MS Add. 4,771, fos 5–6v; *The state of the Irish affairs, for the honourable members of the houses of parliament, as they lye represented before them, from the committee of adventurers,* London 1645, 11.

pointed towards the emergence in May 1653 of a proposal to transplant the Presbyterian Ulster Scots as formative in shaping subsequent policy towards the Catholic population.[13] In order to construct a more accurate account of the background to the announcement of the transplantation to Connacht, it is necessary to examine more fully the policies pursued by the commissioners in Ireland between the autumn of 1652 and the summer of 1653. In some respects these crucial months have hitherto existed in a vacuum between histories of the conquest and histories of the settlement.

By December 1652 there remained in Ireland only small pockets of resistance. One of the main areas that continued to pose difficulties was southern Ulster. In an effort to pacify that district, part of the precinct of Belturbet was excluded from protection in December 1652. The local commissioners received orders from Dublin to remove all 'creaghts' and their stock southwards into counties Meath and Westmeath. As this endeavour would inevitably disrupt the local economy and revenue generation, the commissioners at Belturbet were instructed to ensure 'that the state be not damnified by such transplanting'.[14] A year later, the intractable challenge that faced the Belturbet commissioners – how to relocate people without disrupting tax collection – would be writ large for all areas east of the Shannon. Of greater significance was the government's practical usage of the word 'transplanting' for the first time. The policy applied to Belturbet at the end of 1652 had been widespread since 1650, as the parliamentarians attempted first to remove people from unprotected districts and secondly to kill those who disobeyed. The adoption of the word 'transplanting' at this juncture serves to illustrate the continuity of method in time of war and time of peace. It also coincided with the emergence of the three-province plantation scheme at Westminster.

By the spring of 1653 the legislation for the Irish plantations had still not been approved; Westminster was seemingly oblivious to the maxim that there is 'a time to sow and a time to reap'. A year earlier the authorities in Ireland had grown weary of waiting for the qualifications to be endorsed and had instead commenced surrender negotiations. Early in 1653 the commissioners again found it necessary to take the initiative in the absence of timely direction from London. On 3 February they issued a declaration 'for the better improvement of tillage, and advancement of revenue'.[15] This document was in effect a blueprint for a provisional land settlement. The government aimed to boost revenue generation through increased land cultivation. Moreover, it endeavoured to do so in such a way as to avoid compromising the eventual implementation of the terms of the Irish plantation bill.

To achieve these ends, the commissioners decided to engage in the widespread leasing of forfeited land. Civil and military officers, as well as ordinary soldiers, were given the option of taking up leases from the state of waste and untenanted land, of which there was plenty, for terms of up to seven years. Moreover, this property would be free from the burden of the contribution

---

[13] Gardiner, 'The transplantation', p. cxxxv, f.n.

[14] The commissioners of parliament to the commissioners of the precinct of Belturbet, 15 Dec. 1652, KIL, MS Prendergast 1, fo. 33; *IUC* ii. 303. Belturbet precinct was made up of counties Cavan, Monaghan and Fermanagh.

[15] MS Egerton 1,761, fos 65–73.

tax. As the lands in question were not currently generating any revenue, it was envisaged that their tax-free status would not damage existing revenue, while the rents accruing would help to enhance it. At the end of the lease term, the lands in question would be fully stocked and capable of bearing full taxes. Opportunities were also available to those not in the employ of the state. They were to have three-year leases 'of as much of their holdings as they can till or stock'.[16] However, none of the generous tax breaks afforded to the army were offered to the Catholic population. Moreover, the leases granted to Catholics were also to contain an ominous proviso. The commissioners reserved the right '(in order to the more effectual settling of the nation) to remove such person and persons from their respective holdings, upon six months warning given them before any first day of May'.[17] This reference to 'effectual settling' echoed Ireton's provision for transplantation in the qualifications. The commissioners were clearly willing to lease lands to Catholics to stimulate recovery. They were, however, also anxious to avoid agreeing to any measures which would compromise future schemes of plantation and transplantation.

Despite their best efforts, this is precisely what the commissioners did. The main risk inherent in their plan was that tax-free lands would attract tenants seeking relief from high levels of contribution elsewhere. Already in November 1652 the government had issued an order denouncing holders of tax-free lands because the latter had welcomed tenants who had previously been paying taxes elsewhere.[18] Because of this problem, under the scheme of February 1653 army officers were ordered to 'use their own servants and stock … or plant with English tenants'.[19] Tenants and labourers were, however, a precious commodity, and underpaid army officers were unlikely to turn down the prospect of profit by refusing to allow Catholics to reside on their land. Furthermore, once the officers secured Catholic tenants, they were usually keen to hold onto them, thereby complicating subsequent efforts to transplant them elsewhere. The commissioners' scheme also hindered the proposed plantation in some instances. Seven-year leases would run until 1660. Accordingly, in the shorter term the adventurers sometimes struggled to gain possession of their new estates because officers held prior leases on the land in question. In 1655 the Irish government responded to the adventurers' complaints on this issue by arguing that the state of the country two years earlier was so dire that they had had to do something to address it: 'multitudes in all parts through extremity died, and others were necessitated to sustain themselves by the carcasses of dead beasts and of those very bodies of men, who had a little before perished for famine'.[20] In 1655 the Irish government sought to redirect the blame. It pointed out that the commissioners' stop-gap plan would have been unnecessary if the parliament had approved the necessary plantation legislation more quickly.[21]

16 Ibid.
17 Ibid.
18 MS Prendergast 1, fo. 32.
19 MS Egerton 1,761, fos 65–73.
20 IUC ii. 509–13.
21 Ibid.

Although the commissioners' declaration of 3 February 1653 suggests that they were awaiting the imminent approval of the transplantation scheme at Westminster, it did not contain any solid indication that Connacht had been selected for that purpose. Yet other evidence indicates that the Irish government was fully aware of just such a plan. On 23 March 1653 a court-martial sitting in Dublin heard the case of Rowland Eustace of Co. Kildare. Eustace was 'accused for holding correspondency with, and relieving the enemy' in the Wicklow mountains. While the court found 'strong and pregnant presumptions' of his guilt, it proved reluctant to order his execution, perhaps because he was suffering from a mental illness. Instead it resolved 'that the said Rowland Eustace be forthwith removed with his whole family and dependants in Jagogstowne in the County of Kildare in to the province of Conoght, if the right honourable the Commissioners of Parliament shall give their approbation thereunto'.[22] The tenor of this order suggests that the imminent policy of transplantation to Connacht was already common knowledge in official circles in Dublin by March 1653. On 20 May, following his treatment for being 'distracted', the commissioners ordered Eustace to transplant.[23]

Another policy which must be noticed is that which emerged in May 1653 for transplanting the Ulster Scots from counties Antrim and Down to the south of the country. In September 1652 the commissioners for the precinct of Ulster were ordered to 'look narrowly' into the activities of 'the Scotch gentry [who] have their meeting by fifty or sixty at a time together, sometimes under pretence of hunting'.[24] Robert Cunningham, a minister at Broad Island in Co. Antrim, was one of those known to be preaching violently against the English parliament: 'Pray Lord wilt thou be pleased to give the whip into our hands again, and thou shalt see how well we will scourge these enemies of thy people.'[25] The Irish government's concerns grew further in March 1653 when they learned that the earl of Glencairn had sent an agent to the north of Ireland 'to stir up factions in those parts, and to boat over as many men as he can' as part of his preparations for a royalist rebellion in Scotland.[26] The government responded by contemplating the removal 'of all such persons of the Scottish nation as have been officers and commanders in arms against the Parliament'.[27] In Ulster, Colonel Robert Venables and his fellow commissioners responded enthusiastically to this prompt. By 9 April they had decided that it would be necessary to undertake the 'transplanting [of] all popular Scots into some other part of Ireland'.[28] On 23 May Venables issued a

---

[22] Marsh's Library, Dublin, MS Z3.2.17, fo. 90v.

[23] MS Prendergast 1, fo. 137.

[24] The commissioners of parliament to the revenue commissioners of Ulster, Drogheda, 4 Sept. 1652, Russell Library, Maynooth, MS O'Renehan 2, fo. 488.

[25] Ibid.

[26] Scotland and the Commonwealth: letters and papers relating to the military government of Scotland, from August 1651 to December 1653, ed. Charles Firth (Scottish History Society, 1st ser. xviii, 1885), 87.

[27] IUC ii. 325–6.

[28] IUC ii. 329–32.

proclamation which listed the names of 258 Scots who were to be transplanted to Co. Waterford.[29]

Taken together, the commissioners' caution in granting readily voidable
leases to Catholics in February, the sentence imposed on Rowland Eustace in
March and the plan to transplant the Ulster Scots in May demonstrate
several key points. It is clear that, from the perspective of English officials and
officers in Ireland, the eventual announcement of the transplantation to
Connacht by the council of state in London in July 1653 did not come out of
the blue. Furthermore, contrary to Gardiner's influential argument, that
policy did not originate with Cromwell in the period following his expulsion
of the parliament in April.[30] Rather than viewing the proposal to transplant
the Ulster Scots as the inspiration for subsequent policy towards Catholics, it
can be seen as another offshoot of the Irish government's ongoing efforts to
promote security and recovery by relocating sections of the population.
Moreover, this radical strategy towards the Ulster Scots was adopted without
any conferral with London, a point which again highlights the extent to
which far-reaching policies could emerge from within Ireland. At the same
time, however, the parliament's representatives in Ireland expected that the
main outlines of the land settlement would be shaped by the long-anticipated
legislation under preparation in London.

The blueprint for settlement: finalisation and interpretation

By the time of its expulsion on 20 April 1653, the parliament had devoted a good
deal of time to the issue of the Irish land settlement; much of the detail was
hammered out by the committee of MPs charged with preparing the required bill.
The key feature of this document was the three-province plantation and, in light
of the evidence outlined above, it almost certainly made provision for the transplantation to Connacht. In the summer of 1653 the council of state ironed out
some final details before issuing three sets of orders which allowed the commissioners in Dublin to begin implementing the settlement. On 5 May Henry
Scobell, the clerk of the late parliament, was ordered to furnish 'the Bill which
was prepared by the parliament concerning the lands forfeited in Ireland and
such papers as are in the house touching that business'.[31] By 17 May the council
of state was ready to sign off on the provisions of the settlement, and it ordered a
committee to frame a series of instructions based upon the relevant bill.[32] The
first two sets of instructions produced by this committee addressed the
drawing of lots by the adventurers and the surveying of forfeited land for
redistribution to that group and to the army. A third document, dated 2 July
1653, announced the scheme of transplantation to Connacht and ordered its

---

29 The commissioners for settling a securing the province of Ulster, *Whereas the right
honourable the commissioners … Carrickfergus, 23 May 1653*, Dublin 1653 (BL, 816.
m.17(74)).
30 Gardiner, 'The transplantation', 706–8.
31 John Thurloe to Henry Scobell, Whitehall, 5 May 1653, House of Lords Record Office,
London, MS HL/PO/JO/10/1/282.
32 *CSPD, 1652–1653*, 332.

completion by 1 May 1654.[33] By taking these key steps in the interval between parliaments, the council of state had ensured that the commencement of the Irish land settlement would not be any longer delayed. A new parliament met on 4 July. It fell to that body to formally declare the Irish war 'appeased and ended', but even this task took almost three months to achieve, with the so-called Act of Satisfaction being finally passed on 26 September.[34]

With the exception of a strip of land intended to comprise a buffer zone along the Atlantic coast and the river Shannon, the instructions of 2 July and the subsequent legislation designated the territory Connacht and Co. Clare for the settlement of Catholics. The key question relating to these documents is exactly what type of transplantation scheme they provided for. This issue is further complicated by discrepancies between their respective contents. Under the terms of the instructions, 'all persons in Ireland who have right to articles, or to any favour or mercy held forth by any of [the] qualifications' were ordered to transplant.[35] This categorisation was problematic. Many of the qualifications had already been compromised or rendered obsolete, most notably by promises contained in articles of surrender. Therefore, the task of establishing precisely who had secured 'favour and mercy' under the qualifications was far from straightforward. The Act of Satisfaction, with its rather vague reference to the transplantation 'of all the Irish Nation, comprehended in the qualifications', did little to clarify the situation.[36] At the same time, under the 2 July instructions several categories of persons were exempted from the scheme: anyone 'who did not adhere unto or join with the rebels before the fifteenth day of September 1643, and who did at that time and ever since profess the Protestant religion'; Catholic women married to Protestants prior to 1650 who would renounce Catholicism; and boys and girls who had been entertained as servants by Protestants and reared in that religion.[37] These exemptions emphasised that the transplantation scheme was aimed squarely at the Catholic population.

Yet it was unclear precisely what proportion of this majority population group was expected to remove. In his analysis, Prendergast asserted that 'all the Irish ... except those who had adopted the religion of the English nation, were to transplant'.[38] In contrast, Gardiner concluded that the instructions concerned only 'landed men, who were required to make way for the new settlers'.[39] While historians have disagreed, contemporary interpretations

---

[33] The council of state, *Further instructions unto Charles Fleetwood esq., lieutenant general of the army in Ireland, Edmund Ludlow esq., lieutenant general of the horse, Miles Corbet esq., and John Jones esq.*, London 1653. In BL, Thomason E.1062[4], the pagination of this item begins at 23.

[34] *Acts and ordinances*, ii. 722–53.

[35] *Further instructions unto Charles Fleetwood*, 24.

[36] *Acts and ordinances*, ii. 722–53.

[37] *Further instructions unto Charles Fleetwood*, 25–6.

[38] Prendergast, *The Cromwellian settlement*, 99–100.

[39] Samuel Gardiner, *History of the Commonwealth and protectorate*, London 1903, iv. 311; Patrick Corish, 'The Cromwellian regime, 1650–1660', in Theodore Moody, Francis

were in fact closest to the argument made by Prendergast. Before passing the Act of Satisfaction on 26 September, the parliament rejected a moderating proviso designed to empower the Irish government 'to retain any of the Irish in the Provinces of Ulster, Leinster or Munster', if it should 'see it requisite for publick Use, or advantage to the Commonwealth'.[40] The fact that such a proposal was deemed necessary, and then rejected, demonstrates the parliament's apparent intention to legislate for the removal of all Irish Catholics. That this was indeed the ambition of the London authorities is further confirmed by the content of a petition drawn up in February 1655 by a group of army officers stationed in the south-east of Ireland. In their petition, this well-informed group described the 2 July instructions as 'concerning the removing of all the Irish into Connacht, excepting males of 14 years of age and females of 12'.[41]

The transplantation scheme authorised in London in 1653 effectively provided for the removal of the entire Catholic population from three of four provinces. This decision had now to be communicated to government officials and the Catholic population in Ireland. However, some of the immediate steps taken by the council of state indicate that it also had other audiences in mind. Most significantly, it ordered that the instructions for transplantation be printed and sold at three separate locations in London: 'at the Black Spread-Eagle ... the Three Bibles at the West-end of St. Pauls, or at the sign of Sir John Old-castle in Py-Corner'.[42] This circumstance strongly suggests that the harsh terms of the transplantation scheme were also designed for consumption by an English audience. The sector of English society likely to be most interested comprised the adventurers and other potential planters. The instructions fostered the impression that if a planter should arrive in the three provinces after 1 May 1654, he would find that the former Catholic inhabitants of his new estate were either transplanted to Connacht or else recently executed for failing to remove. He would thus be entirely safe from the dreaded Irish tories and the bloody rebels who had allegedly massacred the previous generation of settlers. The land would be vacant, ownerless and awaiting cultivation. Such colonial arguments concerning vacant land were not new, and they had been used to promote the policy of plantation in Ireland since the sixteenth century.[43]

While the target audience in London possibly welcomed the tenor of the instructions issued by the council of state, the reaction of the commissioners and the army officers in Ireland was altogether more important. They would be responsible for deciding how the policy of universal transplantation authorised in London should be implemented in practice. The earliest evidence for the Irish government's reaction is contained in a set of guidelines issued to a standing committee of army officers on 1 August 1653. These officers were asked to

---

Martin and Francis Byrne (eds), *A new history of Ireland*, III: *Early modern Ireland, 1534–1691*, Oxford 1976, 364; Siochrú, *God's executioner*, 235–7.
[40] *CJ* vii. 324–5.
[41] *Mercurius Politicus*, 29 Mar.–5 Apr. 1655, 5,236–8.
[42] *Further instructions unto Charles Fleetwood*, 30.
[43] Canny, *Making Ireland British*, 133–4, 204.

consider what is necessary to be done in order to the settlement of the Irish nation and in case it be advisable to transplant the Irish inhabitants ... whether the said removal be advisable to be made of all Irish and Papists ... or only of all out of some counties and places as the counties of Kerry, Wexford, Waterford &c., and only landed and popular men from other places.[44]

This passage confirms that in Dublin the instructions for transplantation were interpreted as providing for the transplantation of effectively all Catholics. Of greater significance, however, is the fact that the government did not view the instructions as binding it firmly to such an extreme course. The commissioners were clearly not convinced of the need for wholesale transplantation, and they instead sought out an 'advisable' course.

The adaptation of transplantation policy

The commissioners' directions to the committee of officers hinted at two possible strategies for implementing transplantation. The scheme might be applied more extensively in some regions than in others, or else an individual's social status would be used as the key determinant of his fate. In the context of government policy since 1649, both of these options had considerable merit. In certain counties, mountainous terrain or vast tracts of bog and forest made pacification an extremely difficult task. In March 1653 Colonel John Jones had argued that the only way to address this problem was to declare the relevant regions to be out of protection, and to follow this up by laying them waste and planting strong garrisons to keep the peace.[45] Such a policy had already been attempted in many areas from 1650 onwards. The instructions for transplantation provided scope for this policy to proceed on a more formal and large-scale basis, as the Catholic population of entire regions could now be ordered to depart for Connacht. This policy might be particularly appropriate to the south-east of the country, the area most favoured by Ireton and others for the creation of settlements occupied exclusively by Protestants.

The second potential strategy, focused on the removal of 'landed and popular men', reflected the ongoing approach, initiated by Cromwell and Ireton, of linking an individual's potential for past or future delinquency to his or her social status.[46] Moreover, the planned transplantation of the Ulster Scots was also organised on this basis. Again, the correspondence of Colonel John Jones allows some insight into governmental attitudes on this point; in March 1653 he had expressed his conviction that 'there [was] noe way to reduce this land to a perfect and lasting peace, but by removing all heads of septs and priests and men of knowledge in armes, or otherwise in repute, out of this land'.[47] In theory, a strict transplantation policy along these lines would result in the decapitation of Catholic society in the three provinces, clearing the way for the spread of English culture and the Protestant religion.

---

44 *IUC* ii. 370.
45 *A contemporary history*, iii. 370–2.
46 *IUC* ii, 370.
47 *A contemporary history*, iii. 370–2.

Although these two policy options were offered for the consideration of the standing committee of officers, it is unclear if that body ever produced any recommendations. Nevertheless, by early October 1653 the commissioners had become convinced that the council of state's instructions for transplantation were an altogether unsatisfactory basis for future policy. In a letter sent to the parliament on 5 October, they complained of 'the difficulty of pursuing the late instructions according to the letter of them' and set out 'how we intend to proceed until ... [the parliament's] ... further pleasure be made known to us'. The course chosen was, they confessed, 'not pursuant to, nor warranted by the letter of the instructions'.[48] Within three months of the council of state's endorsement of universal transplantation, Irish government policy was seemingly moving in a more moderate and practical direction. This outcome was the result of consultations with 'a Council of officers of the army in Ireland, and several judges, who were called to advise how the late Instructions for Transplantation of the Irish into Connaught and Clare might be put into effectual Execution'.[49] The employment of the judiciary in this matter indicates that the commissioners either encountered some difficulties in interpreting the meaning of the instructions sent from London, or was reluctant to accept their literal meaning; perhaps both.

While the commissioners voiced their complaints to London in early October, in Ireland they had already provided some hint of their favoured strategy when they published the council of state's instructions on 12 September.[50] This move for the first time revealed to the Catholic community what lay in store for it. Significantly, a declaration which accompanied the published instructions empowered regional governors and revenue commissioners in each precinct to grant licences of exemption 'unto such persons whose removal they shall judge necessary to be dispensed with for the plowing ... inning and disposing of such crops or corn, which those who are to be removed shall have sown before the first day of May 1654'.[51] The appearance of this concessionary document alongside the council of state's instructions ensured that the first message sent to the Catholic population concerning the transplantation was a mixed one. While death was threatened on those who failed to abandon their ancestral homes, the government hoped that they would see fit to sow their crops and pay their taxes as normal.

The government's order for the granting of dispensations offered a strong hint of the obvious difficulties that would attend any effort to enforce the sort of scheme approved by the council of state. The production of both food and taxes would be entirely disrupted, many Catholics would again take to the hills and bogs, and what progress had been made to date in promoting recovery would be swiftly undone. As recently as July 1653 the commissioners had informed the parliament that 'many counties [were] without inhabitants and the whole country miserably wasted and destroyed'.[52] For

---

[48] MS Firth C5, fos 234–8.

[49] CJ vii. 335–6.

[50] No copy of this declaration appears to have survived but it was referred to in subsequent declarations. See, for example, Gardiner, 'The transplantation', 715.

[51] Ibid.

[52] IUC ii. 363–5.

landowners, both Protestant and Catholic, trying to repair their estates, the announcement of the transplantation threatened further catastrophe. From Co. Cork, John Percival's agent informed him that 'some of your tenants of the country were once resolved not to plough or sow a ridge of ground till I fed them with sure promises they should not be transplanted. I have assured them you have a toleration to keep all your own tenants, in which assurance they partly confide and go on'.[53] Percival's agent most likely did not know what would happen to these restless tenants but, like the commissioners in Dublin, he was anxious to ensure the continuation of agricultural activity.

Given the Irish government's reservations concerning the character of the transplantation scheme that had been approved by the council of state, it is possible that it was behind the moderating proviso which was rejected by the parliament on 26 September. That proviso, which proposed to allow the Irish government to exempt persons from transplantation as it saw fit, would have given official sanction to the more lenient dispensations policy which it had already announced on 12 September. Despite this setback, by mid-October the Irish government had concluded its consultation process and it moved to confirm its intentions by publishing a further proclamation.[54] This document set out three categories of persons that the government deemed fit to transplant. These were: all persons comprehended under the first qualification of the Act for the Settling of Ireland; Catholic former soldiers; and those Catholics entitled to land under the qualifications.[55] These revised terms, which were not to be found in either the council of state's instructions or in the recently approved legislation, ultimately provided the framework for the transplantation to Connacht.

Unfortunately, this latest statement of the government's intentions was very far from providing full clarity. For example, Ireton's problematic first qualification, which if taken literally condemned all persons involved in any way in the first year of the rebellion, had effectively been laid aside by mid-1652. This particularly bad piece of law was now revived as a rule for transplantation. Moreover, the task of individually identifying and transplanting all former soldiers, while justifiable on grounds of security, was likely to prove impossible to achieve. The third rule for transplantation, encompassing Catholics entitled to land under the sixth, seventh and eighth qualifications, was the most straightforward. Landowners would be easier to identify and examine than anonymous soldiers who had returned to following the plough. Depriving them of their lands and removing them to Connacht was seen as essential to allowing plantations and new proprietors to prosper.

The requirement that all persons comprehended in the three categories outlined above should transplant themselves to Connacht became something of a government mantra over the following years. These terms were recited in repeated declarations as the authorities in Dublin attempted to enforce its will in the localities.[56] Unfortunately, there were ambiguities of language in some of the

---

[53] HMC, *Egmont manuscripts*, i. 533.
[54] This key document is reproduced in full in Gardiner, 'The transplantation', 710–15.
[55] Ibid.
[56] See, for example, a subsequent declaration of the lord deputy and council extending the

government's official pronouncements, but it is none the less possible to establish how contemporaries understood its intentions. There was clearly some scope for confusion. In December 1653 Percival's land agent in Co. Cork claimed that 'this last proclamation of transplanting clearly extends to all papists without exception'.[57] A year later Vincent Gookin would make the same claim.[58] Gookin's argument was, however, politically motivated and the balance of the evidence is very much against such extreme appraisals of the transplantation policy as set out in October 1653. By February 1654 John Percival could report from Dublin that "tis not intended that any should be sent into Connacht but proprietors and soldiers. The rest stay, and I believe for the future will stay'.[59] While this was a source of relief to Percival, three months later some Irish Catholic landowners in London complained about this selective policy: 'farmers and those of inferior qualitie are not to be transplanted though not so innocent as most of those proprietors who are compelled to goe'.[60] Later again, in November 1654, the Irish government wrote to Cromwell to inform him that it was 'endeavouring to carry on the work of transplanting the Irish proprietors and such as have been in arms into Connacht effectually'.[61] This policy was further confirmed by Colonel Richard Lawrence in March 1655, when he explained that the transplantation extended 'only to proprietors and men in arms'.[62]

Although the authorities in London had provided for a radical universal transplantation, the Dublin government had quickly adopted a more moderate line which made some practical concessions to Irish realities. More than a century ago Gardiner located this shift towards moderation as late as the arrival of Henry Cromwell in Ireland in 1655, and his influential account has distorted the subsequent historiography.[63] In fact, the divergence in the policies favoured by the council of state and the parliament on the one hand and the Irish government on the other had emerged almost straightaway. At the same time, the scope of the policy approved in London meant that the Irish government could in future widen the parameters of its transplantation scheme if it so wished. By mid-1654 a scheme for transplanting all Catholics out of five counties in the south-east had emerged, but this policy would never be seriously pursued. For now, the government had more than enough to do in attempting the transplantation of landowners and soldiers. Conscious of the enormity even of this task, and of its centrality to the work

deadline for transplantation: lord deputy and council, *Whereas by an order ... 27 February 1654[5],* Dublin 1655 (BL, 806.i.14(12)).

57 HMC, *Egmont manuscripts,* i. 530.

58 Vincent Gookin, *The author and case of transplanting the Irish into Connaught vindicated, from the unjust aspersions of Colonel Richard Laurence,* London 1655, 25.

59 HMC, *Egmont manuscripts,* i. 535–6.

60 Charles McNeill, 'Report on the Rawlinson collection of manuscripts', *Analecta Hibernica* i (1930), 12–178 at p. 20.

61 Lord deputy and council to Oliver Cromwell, Dublin, 14 Nov. 1654, MS O'Renehan 2, fo. 538.

62 Richard Lawrence, *The interest of England in the Irish transplantation stated,* London 1655, 7.

63 Gardiner, 'The transplantation', 700–34.

of 'laying a foundation for future generations, and repairing many breaches in this poor waste, desolate country', the commissioners turned to God.[64] On 15 November 1653, a day set aside for seeking the Lord, the commissioners contemplated Ireland, an expectant mother whose Siamese offspring, plantation and transplantation, were 'now come to birth and much [was] desired and expected, but there [was] no strength to bring forth'.[65] The labours of a decade of war had exhausted Ireland, and its government now faced another great trial of its own strength in the projected transplantation to Connacht.

Transplanters' certificates and dispensations

The declaration issued by the Irish government on 14 October 1653 marked the official beginning of the transplantation. Thereafter, it moved quickly to put in place the administrative structures deemed necessary to facilitate transplanters in the relocation process. The declaration of 14 October informed transplantable persons of the procedures that they were required to follow. First, they were to deliver 'a particular of their names and of the names of the persons in their respective families, their tenants and other persons that shall willingly move with them ... with the number of cattle, quantity and quality of tillage, and other substance'. The local revenue commissioners were required to check the accuracy of the details provided and to issue a certificate to each transplanter before 20 December.[66] Both local officials and transplanters would have recognised obvious parallels with the ticketing system used during the war to identify individuals and families entitled to protection. The deadline of 20 December was the first of many that would be missed, as the process of issuing certificates continued in some cases until at least February 1654.[67]

The contents of three registers of transplanters' certificates, which were eventually destroyed in 1922, bore testament to the government's efforts at this early stage to micro-manage the process of transplantation. The two volumes relating to the provinces of Munster and Leinster contained details of some 26,324 people, over 15,000 cows, around 142,000 sheep, nearly 14,000 horses, and other animals.[68] The primary purpose of those documents was to ensure that local officials in Connacht would be able immediately to grant provisional assignments of land sufficient to support the persons and animals listed in these documents. They were to have three acres for every cow, four acres per horse, and so on.[69] This was another borrowing from the war years, when persons received into protection were usually assigned waste lands proportionate to their stock. The government hoped that this approach

---

[64] *IUC* ii. 376–8.

[65] Ibid.

[66] Gardiner, 'The transplantation', 312.

[67] William Hardinge, 'On circumstances attending the outbreak of civil war in Ireland on 23rd October, 1641', *Transactions of the Royal Irish Academy, Antiquities* xxiv (1873), 379–420 at p. 415.

[68] Ibid.

[69] *IUC* ii. 407–8.

would minimise the disruption caused to agricultural production by enabling transplanters to resettle as quickly as possible in Connacht.

Whatever the reasoning behind their creation, the transplanters' certificates were to have a profound influence in shaping the historiography of the transplantation to Connacht from the mid-nineteenth century onwards.[70] Most significantly, W. H. Hardinge inflated the numbers of people named in them to 44,210 and he treated these documents as a precise record of a well-managed and swiftly executed transplantation scheme.[71] John Prendergast exploited for their emotive content certificates such as that which described Nicholas Comyn of Limerick as 'numb at one side of his body of a dead palsy, accompanied only by his lady, Catherine Comyn, aged thirty five years, flaxen-haired, middle stature; and one maid servant'.[72] However, the interpretations offered by Hardinge, Prendergast and some subsequent historians are extremely problematic. Although many certificates were compiled and registered with the transplantation commissioners at Loughrea, Co. Galway, in the first half of 1654, there was in fact no corresponding mass movement of Catholics westwards. The remarkable administrative achievement to which the certificates bore testament was not matched by any willingness on the part of the persons named in them to depart from their homes.[73]

By the beginning of May 1654, the official deadline for transplantation, a number of factors had combined effectively to bring the scheme to a halt. One of these was the uncertainty created by the presence of Irish Catholics in London petitioning against the transplantation.[74] In some cases the Irish government showed leniency towards Catholic groups and individuals who had cooperated with its policies over the preceding years.[75] The government was also reluctant to force aged and sick transplanters to undertake the journey to Connacht.[76] Perhaps the most important factor impeding the progress of the transplantation in 1654 was the still perilous economic situation. This reality was reflected in the warning issued by John Lambert to Cromwell in July 1654 that 'our army and inhabitants in Ireland must quit the country, or you must find more treasure'.[77] The public accounts revealed a monthly shortfall of over £45,000 in Ireland, and Fleetwood was as yet reluctant to cut costs by drastically reducing the size of the army.[78] In this context, the £10,000 per month generated by the contribution tax, levied for the most part on the Catholic populace, provided a vital lifeline to the Irish government amid continuous uncertainty over the arrival of subventions from London. Officers and officials in Ireland were well aware of this reality. In

---

[70] For a detailed analysis of this historiography and a reappraisal of the transplanters' certificates see John Cunningham, 'The transplanters' certificates and the historiography of Cromwellian Ireland', *IHS* xxxvii (2011), 376–95.

[71] Hardinge, 'On circumstances', 379–420.

[72] Prendergast, *The Cromwellian settlement*, 104.

[73] Cunningham, 'The transplanters' certificates'.

[74] See chapter 3 below.

[75] MS Prendergast 2, fo. 478.

[76] MS Egerton 1,761, fos 404–9.

[77] *The Clarke Papers*, ed. C. H. Firth (Camden n.s. xlix, lix, lxi, lxii, 1891–1901), iii. 207.

[78] MS Carte 74, fo. 90; *IUC* ii. 457–9.

April 1654 the governor of Drogheda, Colonel Foulke, accordingly advocated exempting Catholics temporarily from transplantation so that 'the contribution and other public taxes will be the better secured and paid'.[79] Such practical necessities, combined with a wave of petitions from the Catholics themselves, led to the appointment of officials in each precinct charged with granting exemptions from the already faltering scheme of transplantation.

A surviving partial record of the proceedings of the dispensation court for the precinct of Trim allows some crucial insight into the dispensations process. Of the 277 cases heard, only seven individuals were refused temporary exemption from transplantation. Among those dispensed were several merchants from Foulke's Drogheda.[80] It can be assumed that other dispensation courts were equally lenient, as additional data allows the identification of numerous certificate-holders remaining outside of Connacht after 1 May 1654. This state of affairs was also commented upon in the pages of London newsbooks. A letter from Ireland published in July 1654 reported that 'the transplanting work moves on but slowly, not above six score from all provinces are yet removed into Connacht'.[81] In the following month another letter revealed that 'the work of transplanting is at a stand'.[82] The likelihood is that the transplantation scheme made very little headway before grinding to a stop in time for the harvest of 1654. If the scheme was to prove anything other than a spectacular failure, the government would have to renew its efforts to enforce it in the ensuing winter.

The period from September 1652 to the summer of 1654 was formative for the design of the Irish land settlement. By the end of 1652 the competing demands of adventurers and the army had been to some extent reconciled, and a scheme of transplantation to Connacht looked increasingly likely. Yet it would take another nine months before a new parliament got around to endorsing the final blueprint for settlement. Under its terms, Ireland was to be divided into two parts: a three-province Protestant zone; and a Catholic reservation in Connacht. This plan was remarkably ambitious, and numerous obstacles threatened to derail its execution. The most important underlying problems were the wasted condition of the country and the lack of money available to the Irish government. These problems were accentuated by the slowness of the London authorities in approving the relevant legislation. In this context, the Irish government saw fit to implement its own provisional arrangements. As a result the eventual enforcement of the Act of Satisfaction was greatly complicated. Over the following years, army officers and other officials would prove reluctant to part both with the land that they had leased and with the Catholic tenants whom they had attracted.

Yet even in the absence of such practical problems, the task with which the Irish government was charged, universal Catholic transplantation, would have

---

[79] IUC ii. 422.
[80] TCD, MS 844, fos 160–70.
[81] Gardiner, 'The transplantation', 718.
[82] Mercurius Politicus, 24 Aug.–31 Aug. 1654, 3,732.

proven extremely difficult, if not impossible, to execute. Catholics inevitably did not want to go, and any use of force was bound to drive them to seek refuge in areas where the conquerors were already struggling to exert control. Therefore the more moderate course adopted by the commissioners, focused on landowners and former soldiers, made sense on a number of counts. Furthermore, they believed that the removal of these people would be sufficient to clear the way for successful Protestant colonisation and the remaking of Irish society. In the winter of 1653–4 the transplantation was diligently administered by the relevant officials, and a large number of transplanters' certificates were issued. None the less, by mid-1654 a range of factors, not least Catholic reluctance to transplant, had combined effectively to bring the scheme to a halt. Moreover, the presence of a cohort of Irish landowners in London was by then causing additional worries for the Irish government.

3

The Land Settlement under Threat, 1653–1655

The approval in September 1653 of the legislation relating to the Irish land settlement saw an intensification of the efforts made by the various groups affected by it to protect and to enhance their prospects. The army and the adventurers both believed that their respective requirements for land should take precedence over all other demands.[1] They would face stiff competition, however, from Irish Protestants and Catholics, both of which groups hoped to retain as much as possible of the land that they had held in 1641. Under the terms of the relevant legislation, both communities stood to lose a great deal. Only eight Protestants were exempted from pardon under the terms of the third qualification of the Act for the Settling of Ireland, and six of these were already dead or in exile by 1652.[2] None the less, subsequent clauses in that act made many other Protestants liable to partial forfeiture of their estates. In May 1653 the Presbyterian Scots of east Ulster learned that their partial forfeitures were to be accompanied by transplantation to the south. For Catholic landowners the outlook was altogether bleaker by the autumn of 1653. In the aftermath of a long and complicated war, few of them could expect to meet the requirement of constant good affection necessary to avoid confiscation and transplantation to Connacht. Moreover, for both Protestant and Catholic landowners, resort to the authorities in Dublin offered little prospect of an improvement in their circumstances. The commissioners of parliament, led by Charles Fleetwood, naturally viewed the Catholics with great suspicion. They also deeply distrusted the Protestant population. As late as November 1654 Fleetwood reported that 'the Scottish inhabitants [were] generally disaffected', while the remainder of the Protestants 'rather choose to associate in a confederacy with bloody Irish rebels, than own the government of the Comonwealth'.[3] Past and present manifestations of royalist tendencies among Irish Protestants continued to colour the government's attitude towards them. This hostility on the part of the Irish government ensured that both Cath-

---

[1] For an example of the adventurers' arguments on this point see *IUC* ii. 483–4.

[2] Ormond, Inchiquin, Bramhall and Sir George Munroe had left Ireland. James Dillon, earl of Roscommon, and Sir James Montgomery were dead. While Roscommon's heir remained on the continent until after the Restoration, Montgomery's son returned from exile in Holland to recover his estate.

[3] Lord deputy and council to the lord protector, Dublin, 14 Nov. 1654, MS O'Renehan 2, fo. 538.

olics and Protestants were forced to look elsewhere for redress of the grievances relating to the land settlement.

In London it was possible that their appeals might receive a sympathetic hearing from the parliament, Oliver Cromwell or the council of state.[4] Moreover, because many landowners had secured promises concerning their estates in the various sets of surrender articles agreed in Ireland between 1647 and 1653, the committee for articles also had a potentially significant role to play. As a result of pressure from parliamentarian army officers, this important committee had been revived in September 1652 to deal with any outstanding cases relating to persons 'who are or shall be arrested, sued, impleaded, imprisoned or sequestered, contrary to any articles given or granted by any commission officer'.[5] At the same time, the committee's remit was extended to include articles agreed in Ireland.[6] Thereafter, the committee for articles would pass judgement on a number of significant Irish cases. For many owners of Irish land, some form of intervention from London on their behalf had the potential to moderate or to overturn the heavy penalties which they faced. The progress of their efforts to secure such intervention, the mixed results obtained and the responses of the Irish government are the subject of this chapter.

The articles of Dublin

The first set of articles which gave rise to controversy in the 1650s was that agreed upon Ormond's surrender of the city of Dublin to the English parliament in June 1647. Ormond's decision to hand over the city was to have a considerable impact on the subsequent course of the war, most notably when his efforts to recover Dublin two year later culminated in the rout at Rathmines.[7] Under the terms agreed in June 1647, Irish Protestants were confirmed in possession of their estates.[8] However, many members of that community subsequently forfeited this benefit by joining Ormond's royalist alliance in 1649. By 1652 some uncertainty still surrounded the fate of a particular group of Protestant royalists who owned land in both England and Ireland. These men had supported the royalist war effort in England, while avoiding involvement in the fight against the English parliament in Ireland. In an English context they were delinquents and they were accordingly required to compound for their English estates. In Dublin the commissioners of parliament were determined that these men should also suffer penalties relating to their Irish estates. This policy quickly met with opposition from the landowners concerned. As a result, the commissioners were, as so often, unsure how to proceed.[9]

---

4   For a detailed analysis and contextualisation of Oliver Cromwell's dealings with Irish landowners in the mid-1650s see John Cunningham 'Oliver Cromwell and the "Cromwellian" settlement of Ireland', *HJ* liii (2010), 919–37.

5   *Acts and ordinances*, ii. 618–20; On the committee's work in an English context see Gentles, *New model army*, 420–2.

6   *Acts and ordinances*, ii. 618–20.

7   Ó Siochrú, *God's executioner*, 71–5.

8   *Articles of agreement, made, concluded, and agreed on, at Dublin, the eighteenth day of June, 1647*, Dublin 1647, 2.

9   *IUC* i. 60, 125–6.

The most notable of the figures in question was Richard Boyle, second earl of Cork. Because of his royalist activities in England, Cork had to pay a fine of £1,631 to secure his estates there.[10] After their arrival in Ireland early in 1651, the commissioners ordered the sequestration of Cork's substantial Irish estates. This move soon drew objections from Cork, who claimed an entitlement to his lands under the articles of Dublin. In the midst of this confusion, the case was referred to London for decision. Meanwhile the influence of his younger brother, Baron Broghill, helped to ensure that Cork was able to win permission to enjoy his estates *pro tem.* in January 1652.[11] The uncertainty which surrounded the status of Cork's Irish estates, and those of other Protestants such as Edward Brabazon, earl of Meath, and Edward Conway, Viscount Killultagh, meant that a speedy decision was not forthcoming from London. On 18 August 1652 the issue was raised in the parliament, only to be referred back again to the council of state.[12] The revival of the committee for articles in the following month at last created the prospect of a final resolution. Early in January 1653 that committee made its first significant intervention in Irish affairs when it ruled in favour of the Protestant landowners concerned. They were to be restored to their estates without any penalisation.[13] From Dublin, the cash-strapped commissioners complained that this ruling had cost '£100,000 at least at one clap', presumably in lost composition fines.[14] Yet they remained confident that the state would derive a considerable benefit from the partial confiscation of other Protestant estates. However, once Cork and those in the same position as him had wriggled free from the net of confiscation, others were bound to attempt to follow.

Irish Protestants and their estates

Despite their involvement in Ormond's royalist coalition and the harsh tenor of the Irish land legislation, most Irish Protestant proprietors had some reason for optimism following the success enjoyed by Cork and some other landowners early in 1653. Of particular significance in this context were the contents of the articles that they had agreed with Oliver Cromwell during the early stages of the conquest. Many Munster Protestants had obtained terms before 1 December 1649, while those elsewhere in the country submitted in April 1650. In both cases Cromwell had made important promises concerning the estates of those surrendering. For example, in November 1649 royalist officers in Cork and Youghal were assured that they would 'be fully indemnified for anything past … as is desired'.[15] Five months later, as Ormond's royalist alliance faltered, Crom-

---

[10] *ODNB*, s.v 'Boyle, Richard, first earl of Burlington and second earl of Cork (1612–1698)'.

[11] *IUC* i. 116, 125–6. Broghill was instrumental in ensuring that the Munster Protestants switched sides to support Cromwell in Ireland from late in 1649. He was one of the leading Irish Old Protestant officers in the Cromwellian army.

[12] *CJ* vii. 165.

[13] SP 63/283/8.

[14] *IUC* ii. 295. In a rare blunder, Dunlop placed this undated letter in November 1652. However, it was written after January 1653.

[15] *The letters and speeches of Oliver Cromwell*, iii. 416–17.

well offered terms to any Protestants who would 'come off ... from the Irish Popish party'. They were to have possession of their estates 'until there be commissioners or rules settled by authority from parliament for fines or composi-tions of persons in their quality of delinquency'. Those who consented to pay such fines were to 'enjoy their lives, liberties, and estates (both real and personal) with the same immunity, protection, and right, as any other people under the authority, not obnoxious for any delinquency at all'.[16] Such concessions helped to ensure that Cromwell was able to make substantial progress in conquering Ireland up to May 1650, but they would subsequently complicate the implementation of the land settlement.

Among the key groups who submitted in April 1650 were the Ulster Scots forces under Hugh Montgomery, Viscount Ards. At that point it seemed that Ards, his fellow nobleman James Hamilton, earl of Clanbrassil, and other Ulster Scots proprietors would have to pay fines in the same way as royalist delinquents in England had been required to do.[17] By mid-1653, however, it was clear that the Irish government had other ideas. The Act for the Settling of Ireland said nothing of composition fines; indeed Ards was exempted from pardon by name. For other Ulster Scots that legislation combined partial confiscation with the prospect of either banishment or transplantation.[18] The scheme which emerged in May 1653 for the transplantation of Ards, Clanbrassil and more than 250 others to the south created further confusion.[19] Amidst these difficulties, the ex-perience of one of their Ulster neighbours, Viscount Killultagh, highlighted a possible way forward. He had recently secured his estate under the judgement on the articles of Dublin.[20] For the Ulster Scots, their best chance of winning a reprieve from confiscation and transplantation appeared to lie also with the committee for articles.

In the case of the Ulster Scots, the main issue to be resolved in London was the clear contradiction between the divergent modes of punishment, fines and forfeitures, laid down by the articles of April 1650 and by the Act for the Settling of Ireland respectively. The Irish government was convinced that the key proviso appended to the latter legislation empowered it to override articles of surrender and to transplant whomsoever it saw fit in the interests of national security. This position was set out in a declaration issued in Dublin in July 1653, in which land-owners were instructed to apply to the commissioners 'for the enjoyment of the benefit of articles, according to the sayd proviso ... [and] ... according to the true intent and meaning of the said act'.[21] In other words, the commissioners were convinced that the Act for the Settling of Ireland empowered them to modify any promises contained in articles. This viewpoint, which surely reaf-

---

16 A contemporary history, ii. 393–6.
17 Although Hamilton was created earl of Clanbrassil by the king in 1647, most docu-ments cited in this chapter refer to him by his former title as Viscount Clandeboye.
18 Acts and ordinances, ii. 598–603.
19 The commissioners for settling and securing the province of Ulster, Whereas the right honourable the commissioners ... Carrickfergus, 23 May 1653, Dublin 1653 (BL, 816. m.17(74)).
20 SP 63/283/3.
21 SP 63/286/66.

firmed the futility of appeals to Dublin, was not shared by any of the landowners concerned.

As might be expected, the two noblemen threatened with transplantation spearheaded the Ulster Scots' opposition to this scheme. While Clanbrassil had returned home to his estate after his surrender, Ards's subsequent activities meant that his circumstances were more complicated.[22] Following accusations that he was covertly encouraging the Catholic resistance, Ards was arrested and brought to Kilkenny. Ireton was anxious to have Ards out of the way and in April 1651 he issued him with a ten-month pass for the continent.[23] The commissioners presumably anticipated that Ards, like many other royalists, would settle for life in exile and in the summer of 1651 they proposed that he be exempted from pardon under the third qualification.[24] Instead, by the end of the year he was back in London petitioning for possession of his lands.[25] In February 1652 a subcommittee of the council of state recommended that he be permitted to travel to Ireland to compound for his estate.[26] However, his name was not removed from the third qualification of the Act for the Settling of Ireland, a circumstance which reflected the haphazardness of that legislation. This meant that Ards's troubles were far from over. Following his return to London, in the spring of 1653 the committee for articles ruled that he should enjoy his estate 'till the parliament legislate in the matter of composition'.[27] In effect, the committee for articles was ignoring the Act for the Settling of Ireland, and signalling its intention that Cromwell's prior promises to Ards and other Irish Protestants should enjoy precedence.

This ruling in favour of Ards only very briefly dispelled the ambiguity that surrounded his position. By the time that he presented himself in Dublin in May 1653 the Ulster Scots transplantation scheme was being finalised. Accordingly, rather than allowing him to recover his property, the commissioners 'ordered that he forfeit two third of his estate and be transplanted as to the other third'.[28] Following their dismay at Cork's success earlier in the year, they were now evidently determined to ignore the wishes of the committee for articles. None the less, by July Ards had undertaken a third trip to London, accompanied this time by Clanbrassil.[29] After their arrival, the latter protested that the proposed transplantation had caused 'his tenants [to] refuse to have any dealings with him', and that its enforcement would lead to his being 'disinherited and destroyed, contrary to the meaning of his articles'.[30] In the following month Ards and

---

[22] MS Carte 74, fo. 119.

[23] SP 63/286/62; *The Montgomery manuscripts, 1603–1706*, ed. George Hill, Belfast 1867, 194.

[24] His name was most likely included in one of the several lists which the commissioners had sent to Westminster by August 1651. See *IUC* i. 28–9.

[25] *The Montgomery manuscripts*, 198–9; *CSPD, 1651–1652*, 99; SP 63/286/61. This last document stated that Ards had arrived in England 'ten weeks since'.

[26] *CSPD, 1651–1652*, 147; SP 63/286/61.

[27] SP 63/286/64, 65.

[28] SP 63/286/68.

[29] *Calendar of the Clarendon state papers*, ed. Octavius Ogle and others, Oxford 1869–1970, ii. 240.

[30] MS Carte 74, fo. 119.

Clanbrassil succeeded in obtaining further rulings in their favour; due to the protection afforded by their articles, they were to be 'subject to no further transplantation'.[31]

In an effort to ensure that these latest rulings from the committee of articles would at last be taken seriously in Dublin, Ards and Clanbrassil moved to enlist the vital support of Oliver Cromwell. Because the Ulster Scots had submitted directly to Cromwell, he was inevitably concerned with their fate. Moreover, he was already familiar with the various problems that had resulted from apparent contradictions between the content of articles granted to English royalists during the civil wars and the terms of legislation passed by the parliament. In the early 1650s, as the parliament made decisions which seemed to impinge upon the honour of its army, this problem had contributed to the growing political tensions in England.[32] In the summer of 1653 Cromwell sided with the Ulster Scots against the Irish government headed by his son-in-law, thus helping to rescue that community from the proposed transplantation. Determined to avoid a breach of faith, he wrote a blunt letter to Fleetwood concerning the proposed transplantation of Clanbrassil and requested 'a stop thereof'.[33] This request was duly obeyed and the planned scheme was soon abandoned. However, as long as the parliament failed to pass judgement on the issue of composition fines, the position of the Ulster Scots remained uncertain. There was as yet no way of knowing how onerous the anticipated fines might be, or indeed how much time landowners would be given to pay them. Any hopes that the parliament would deal quickly with these issues were dashed on 12 December 1653 when it suddenly resigned its powers.

Clanbrassil's anxiety at this turn of events was perhaps reflected in his decision to seek another letter from Cromwell, also on 12 December.[34] His wife too was active in petitioning Cromwell.[35] The latter's appointment as lord protector a few days later boded well for Clanbrassil and the Ulster Scots, as he was clearly sympathetic to their plight. Furthermore, the Instrument of Government under which Cromwell was appointed empowered him and his council 'to make laws and ordinances for the peace and welfare of these nations where it shall be necessary' until the meeting of the next parliament, scheduled for 3 September 1654.[36] This nine-month period would prove to be the main spell of crisis for the Irish land settlement, as both Protestants and Catholics sought to extract concessions from Cromwell over the head of the Irish government.

The greatest success was that enjoyed by the Munster Protestants who had submitted to Cromwell in October and November 1649. In June 1654 their agent at Westminster, Vincent Gookin, petitioned the lord protector for an 'Act of Oblivion'.[37] Gookin duly drafted the relevant ordinance and it was approved by

---

31 Ibid.; SP 63/286/68.

32 Gentles, New model army, 420-2.

33 The Carte manuscripts in the Bodleian Library, Oxford, ed. John Prendergast and Charles Russell, London 1871, 137. Although this letter dates from December 1653, in it Cromwell made extensive reference to the previous letter which he had written in July 1653.

34 Ibid.

35 Ibid. 137-8.

36 Constitutional documents of the puritan revolution, 405-18.

37 HMC, Egmont manuscripts, i. 544-5.

Cromwell and his council on 1 August. All Munster Protestants who had been instrumental in the 'voluntary rendition' of various towns and forts before 1 December 1649 were fully pardoned 'as if they had made no defection, or committed or done any crime', while other Munster Protestant landowners who had surrendered subsequently were permitted to compound for their estates.[38] A month later, a further ordinance confirmed that the remainder of the Irish Protestants, including the Ulster Scots, would have to pay fines of not less than two years value to secure their lands.[39] These measures, which were based firmly on the promises made by Cromwell in 1649 and 1650, paved the way for a remarkable recovery of economic and political power by the Irish Protestants.

Due to the opposition voiced by soldiers and adventurers, this process would not be entirely smooth. On the other hand, Fleetwood was soon reconciled to this new more lenient policy towards Irish Protestants, perhaps because of its potential for raising badly needed revenue. In February 1655 he informed Thurloe that 'wee have many difficulties upon us betwixt the adventurers, souldiers, and the English protestant compounders'.[40] The adventurers asserted their right to all land earmarked for them in the ten counties, and they and the army believed that their entitlements under acts of parliament should override the claims of Irish Protestants, which rested only on the subsequent ordinances approved by Cromwell.[41] None the less, Fleetwood and his council ignored the agents sent to Dublin by the adventurers and proceeded to agree composition fines with individual Protestant landowners. They commenced with the case of Henry Moore, Viscount Drogheda, permitting him two years to pay a fine of £7,000.[42] On 1 March 1655, after two weeks of negotiations, Clanbrassil was ordered to pay just over £9,400.[43] The inclusion of Ards's name in the Act for the Settling of Ireland continued to present problems for him, and his case took somewhat longer to resolve.[44] Both his and Clanbrassil's rights to enjoy their lands were keenly contested by the well-connected adventurers Erasmus Smith and Henry Whalley. The matter was even debated in parliament in December 1656.[45] None the less, just three months later Ards's composition of £3,000 had

[38] Ibid.; *Acts and ordinances*, ii. 933–7. This and other sources have mistakenly identified 27 June, the date of Percival's letter cited above, as the date upon which the ordinance was passed. According to the contemporary printed version of the ordinance, its final approval actually took place on 1 August 1654.

[39] *Acts and ordinances*, ii. 1015–16.

[40] *TSP* iii. 145.

[41] Ibid.

[42] Ibid.; *The Carte manuscripts*, 139.

[43] Viscount Ards to Colonel Edward Conway, Dublin, 14 Feb. 1655, SP 63/286/4; John Lodge, *The peerage of Ireland*, London 1789, iii. 4.

[44] The ordinance of 2 September 1654 did not allow those who had been exempted from pardon to compound for their estates. Such a clause was necessary to guard against the unlikely event that figures such as Ormond and Inchiquin would seek to regain their estates under its terms. As Ards had also been exempted from pardon this clause, while not necessarily aimed at him, made his circumstances more difficult.

[45] *The diary of Thomas Burton*, ed. John Towth Rutt, London 1828, i. 2–5; For Whaley's claims and Ards's counter arguments see SP 63/286/71.

been agreed upon.[46] Despite drawing a lot for 6,000 acres belonging to Ards and Clanbrassil, Henry Whalley was forced to petition his cousin the lord protector for satisfaction elsewhere.[47]

While the Irish Protestants would have welcomed the apparent willingness of the Irish government to defend their interests against newcomers, the problem of finding the money to pay their composition fines was a significant one. Almost half of Clanbrassil's fine remained unpaid in 1660, even after he had obtained a remission of £1,500.[48] Although two declarations ordering Irish Protestants to pay their fines were issued in 1655, many of them seem to have ignored the wishes of the government.[49] Having previously been threatened with transplantation, the Ulster Scots proved to be more co-operative than others. Ards was among a small group of Irish Protestants referred to as 'the jovial compounders'.[50] Toby Barnard credited Henry Cromwell with quietly dropping the composition scheme altogether; 'faced with almost total non-compliance, he did not squeeze the money from the owners'.[51] Despite the soft approach taken by Henry Cromwell, there were at least some efforts made to collect the monies in question. In July 1657 exchequer affidavits were issued against a group of seventeen Protestants 'for not compounding'.[52] However, such proceedings had no serious implications for Irish Protestant efforts to retain control of their estates.

Although the finer details remained to be ironed out, by September 1654 the Irish Protestants had essentially managed to circumvent the penalties laid down for them in the Act for the Settling of Ireland. The success of the Ulster Scots in securing the benefit of a 'Cromwellian settlement' as opposed to an 'Iretonian settlement' was particularly notable. Barnard rightly highlighted the roles played by Oliver and Henry Cromwell in creating the circumstances which allowed Irish Protestants to recover and enhance their position as the decade progressed. However, his main focus was on the years after 1654.[53] Thus, the extent to which the eventual Irish Protestant recovery was rooted in concessions initially made by Cromwell in 1649 and 1650 has not been properly recognised. The complex and crucial role played by the committee of articles as it upheld Cromwell's earlier promises against the weight of parliamentary legislation and pressure from Fleetwood's government has also received insufficient notice from historians.

---

46 SP 63/286/77; Ards to the Irish council, Dublin, 2 Mar., 20 Apr. 1657, NAI, MS Ferguson 13, fos 95–8.

47 SP 63/286/74. A bill permitting Whalley and Smith to have lands elsewhere was approved by parliament on 27 Dec. 1656: CJ vii. 476.

48 The original fine totalled £9,435 2s. The sum actually paid was £4,677 11s. See Lodge, *Peerage of Ireland*, iii. 4; SP 63/286/92; SP/63/303/74.

49 *IUC* ii. 586–7.

50 Ibid.; *The Montgomery manuscripts*, 211.

51 Barnard, 'Planters and policies', 37–8.

52 Those summoned included: from Co. Roscommon Tirlagh O'Brien; from Co. Galway Francis Foster of Fedda, John Morgan of Kilcolgan and Walter Taylor of Ballymacrahe; from Co. Sligo John Crofton of Longford: MS Prendergast 2, fo. 927. See also MS Ferguson 9, fos 272, 278.

53 Barnard, 'Planters and policies', 36–9; Karl Bottigheimer, 'The restoration land settlement in Ireland: a structural view', *IHS* xviii (1972), 1–21 at pp. 4–6. See also Clarke, *Prelude to Restoration*, 10–13.

The incorporation of these significant aspects allows a deeper understanding of the Irish Protestant struggle for their estates in the aftermath of conquest. It also creates space for an exploration of the parallels between the respective experiences of Protestant and Catholic landowners at this time. The removal of Protestant estates from the store of land available for redistribution meant that the success of the land settlement became even more dependent on forfeited Catholic acres. Some among that community were to prove both willing and able to go to the same lengths as their Protestant counterparts in an attempt to maintain a grip on their lands.

Irish Catholics and their estates

The Catholics of Ireland were believed to be guilty of committing widespread massacres in 1641, and they were held responsible for the long and costly war that had ensued. By 1653, in the face of schemes of confiscation and transplantation, it appeared unlikely that they would be able to win any significant concessions. Although Fleetwood was willing to lend assistance to his own Catholic relatives in England, he harboured no sympathy for their Irish coreligionists.[54] However, the avenues successfully pursued by the Protestants to secure their lands were also open to some Catholics. Most of the Catholic forces who surrendered in 1652 had obtained promises concerning their estates. The fifth article agreed between Colonel Sankey and Colonel O'Dwyer is representative: 'as to the real estates of any of this party, they shall have equal benefit with others under the like qualification in any offers that shall be hereafter held out from the parliament'.[55] The passing of the Act for the Settling of Ireland in August 1652 appeared to confirm the fate of landowners who had obtained such a guarantee. There were, however, two important exceptions to this rule. The townsmen of Galway who had surrendered in April 1652 and the officers of the Leinster army who had surrendered at Kilkenny in the following month had secured somewhat more concrete promises in their articles.[56] The committee for articles, established to safeguard the 'justice and honour' of the army, could be expected carefully and fairly to consider any claims entered before it by these Irish Catholics.[57]

Prior to the announcement of the proposal to transplant the Ulster Scots in May 1653, the Irish Catholics were most likely unaware of the existence of any such monumental schemes. The revelation of the fate in store for their northern counterparts evidently inspired some anxiety. As soon as it became public knowledge, several officers of the Leinster army sought clarification of the commissioners' intentions towards them.[58] The declaration issued by the commissioners on 27 July 1653 was a direct response to these requests. This document spelled out the commissioners' belief that the proviso contained in An Act for the Settling of Ireland empowered them to transplant Catholics regardless of any promises

---

[54] Thomas Fleetwood to Edward Montagu, Dublin, 6 Apr. 1655, MS Carte 74, fo. 41. In this letter, Fleetwood requested Montagu's assistance for the English Catholic Sir Thomas Fleetwood, whose estate had been confiscated.

[55] *A contemporary history*, iii. 295.

[56] *IUC* i. 163–6, 197–201.

[57] *Acts and ordinances*, ii. 148–51.

[58] MS Carte 63, fo. 634.

made to them in articles of surrender.[59] As they remained unaware of the Catholic transplantation scheme recently approved by the council of state, the Leinster officers expressed satisfaction with the declaration, perhaps because it restated their right temporarily to receive the rents of their estates. This apparent satisfaction evaporated rapidly in September 1653 when they became aware of the proposed transplantation to Connacht.[60] While the Leinster officers presumably were taken by surprise when the transplantation scheme was announced, the Galway townsmen had already been at work to secure the promises contained in their articles.

The case of the Galway townsmen

The extensive estates built up by the merchant townsmen of Galway since the late sixteenth century had already been seriously threatened once before, by Strafford's proposed plantation of Connacht in the 1630s.[61] The conquest of Ireland meant that their lands were in danger once again. Although Galway held out longer than any other major urban centre, Sir Charles Coote granted relatively lenient terms to the town on 5 April 1652. The townsmen were guaranteed two-thirds of their extensive lands, most of which lay in the province of Connacht. They also obtained what appeared to be fairly watertight guarantees concerning the retention of their property and their right of residence in the strongly fortified town of Galway and its liberties. Under the articles, individuals could only forfeit their urban property through 'future misdemeanour'.[62] Five days passed before the commissioners at Dublin received notice of the articles agreed. By then the Irish garrison had left Galway and the preparations for its occupation by the parliamentarian army were at an advanced stage. Therefore, while the commissioners felt that Coote had been altogether too generous, they 'thought it not advisable in honour and justice to make any further alterations or diminutions of the terms granted'. Their uneasiness at Coote's actions was illustrated in letters dispatched both to the council of state and the parliament in which they denied any responsibility for the outcome: 'we do hope it will appear that no act done by us hath given any ground to those concessions now given to those of Galway'.[63] The commissioners' letters ensured that the articles of Galway would not be presented to the parliament for ratification.

Almost immediately, both Coote and the commissioners began to investigate ways to override the promises made to the Galway townsmen. Their primary aim was to find a way legitimately to remove the suspect Catholic population from the strongly fortified town. Coote suggested that if the parliament issued a declaration forbidding Catholic residence in garrisons, the Galway townsmen would 'conceive themselves bound to observe such a law' and depart the town.[64] At the same time the commissioners and a group of army officers drew up a list of 'qualifications and limitations' designed to negate significant aspects of the articles. In

59 SP 63/286/66.
60 MS Carte 67, fo. 634.
61 Breandán Ó Bríc, 'Galway townsmen as owners of land in Connaught, 1585–1641', unpubl. MA diss. NUI Galway 1974.
62 IUC i. 163–6.
63 IUC i. 167–71.
64 IUC i. 92.

particular, they wished to reserve the right to remove 'such inhabitants and citizens in Galway, who shall be thought fit'.[65] However their attempts to have the townsmen agree to these new terms proved rather unsuccessful. In November 1652 only eight individuals signed a certificate assenting to the alterations proposed by the commissioners, while 104 townsmen flatly refused to sign the document. A further group of around eighty were noted as being absent from the town during these proceedings. Significantly, not one of the seven men who had negotiated the articles on behalf of the town agreed to the commissioners' alterations.[66] This level of concerted resistance undoubtedly made it difficult for the commissioners to enforce their will.[67]

Apart from the doubts surrounding their articles, the Galway townsmen also faced considerable day-to-day difficulties. In August 1652 'some gentlemen of the County of Galway' presented a list of grievances to the commissioners. Among the problems cited by them was the taking of free quarter by soldiers. Moreover, garrisons were refusing bulk deliveries of hay; the inconvenienced inhabitants were instead forced to bring it in 'as they spend it'. The inhabitants of some baronies beyond the town were also unhappy that they had to maintain their local garrisons as well as sending supplies into Galway to support the large force stationed there.[68] High levels of taxation were exacerbating the problems that existed in the west. After the surrender of Galway, a tax of £2,300 per month was laid on the county, while the town was required to pay £400 per month.[69] In November 1652 the monthly assessment tax for the precinct of Galway was set at £3,200; only Dublin and Belfast paid more. While the task of supplying hay to garrisons had previously proven problematic, the new demand for almost £800 per month of 'forage payments in money and not as formerly in kind' on top of the assessment tax probably only made matters worse.[70]

Because of these high levels of taxation, by March 1653 'many of the inhabitants and proprietors' had fled the town 'whereby the public contribution falling upon them is wholly lost, and the burden falling upon the remaining inhabitants becomes the more heavy and intolerable'.[71] This situation had already been hinted at in the high number of townsmen marked absent in October 1652.[72] It can be assumed that many of those who left the town had retired to begin the repair of their estates in the country. The commissioners were anxious to seize deserted properties and to lease them out for the benefit of the state so as to compensate for any shortfall in the taxes paid by the town.[73] However, the townsmen would have viewed such a move as a breach of the articles which had guaranteed them possession of their urban property. Unfortunately for them, a

---

65 IUC i. 165–7.
66 IUC i. 272; James Hardiman, The history of the town and county of the town of Galway, Dublin 1820, appendices xxxii–xxxiii.
67 IUC i. 272.
68 IUC i. 270–1.
69 Mary O'Sullivan, Old Galway, Cambridge 1942, 339.
70 IUC ii. 288.
71 IUC i. 326–7, 371. The assessment levied on the town was eventually reduced in September 1653.
72 Hardiman, History of Galway, appendix xxxiii.
73 IUC ii. 326–7.

loophole in their articles allowed the commissioners to circumvent such objections. In April 1652 it had been agreed that property in the town would only be seized in the event of a 'future misdemeanour'.[74] To achieve their ends, the commissioners chose to portray the partial desertion of the town over the following months as precisely such an event; they claimed that those who left had done so solely because of 'their disaffection to the parliament and their forces'.[75] This alleged evidence of hostility to the government provided them with grounds sufficient to authorise the seizure of houses in the town.

The commissioners' strategy, which involved both an attempt to alter the articles and to avail of loopholes in them, gave the townsmen considerable cause for alarm. The articles of Galway were evidently under sustained attack. Given the degree of hostility that they experienced at the hands of both the commissioners and local officers and officials, it can be no surprise that the townsmen decided to take their case to the committee for articles. In fact, they did so even before the planned transplantation to Connacht was announced.

At some point around May 1653 Geoffrey Browne, a lawyer and former leading confederate, travelled to London to plead the case of his fellow townsmen.[76] During his visit to Galway in 1635 as a prelude to plantation, Strafford had knighted Browne's father Sir Dominick, the mayor of the town in that year.[77] A few years later, Geoffrey Browne formed part of the Irish parliamentary delegation which travelled to London to present evidence against Strafford at his trial. After the establishment of the Catholic confederation in 1642, Browne played a leading role. Along with serving on the supreme council, he was appointed a member of the delegations sent to negotiate with Henrietta Maria and the duke of Lorraine in 1648 and 1651 respectively.[78] This prominent role helped to ensure that Geoffrey Browne was exempted from pardon by name in the third qualification, along with his uncle and fellow townsman Patrick Darcy.[79] However the lives of both men were secured by the articles of Galway. Other members of the Browne family were also involved in important matters. Geoffrey's daughter Julian was accused of having 'performed the part of Rahab' during the siege of the town.[80] In November 1652 his father was one of the few men who accepted the commissioners' alterations to the articles of surrender. Geoffrey himself was noted as being absent from the town at that point.[81]

Geoffrey Browne's activities during the 1640s helped to ensure that he would not receive a warm welcome in London. In fact he soon found himself locked up

---

[74] *IUC* i. 163–6.

[75] *IUC* ii. 326–7.

[76] *CSPD, 1652–1653*, 387.

[77] Lord Oranmore and Browne, 'The Brownes of Castlemacgarrett', *Journal of the Galway Archaeological and Historical Society* v (1907–8), 48–59, 165–77, 227–38 at p. 167.

[78] Ibid. 165–77; *ODNB, s.v.* 'Browne, Geoffrey (c.1608–1668)'. Neither of these sources contains any account of Browne's mission to London in 1653.

[79] *Acts and ordinances*, ii. 598–603.

[80] Roderic O'Flaherty, *A chorographical description of west or h-Iar Connaught*, ed. James Hardiman, Dublin 1846, 244. According to the Book of Joshua, Rahab was a prostitute who sheltered Israelite spies in Jericho prior to the destruction of the city.

[81] Hardiman, *History of Galway*, appendix, p. xxxiii.

in the Gatehouse at Westminster.[82] The council of state appears to have been suspicious of him and to have had some doubts regarding his entitlements to the articles of Galway. Furthermore, his journey had evidently not been approved by the commissioners as they immediately insisted that he be sent back to Dublin to stand trial for his alleged role 'in contriving and carrying on of the Rebellion, before and in the first year ... in order to the appeasing of the wrath of God'.[83] Apart from Browne's personal history, several other factors worked against him. Perhaps most significantly, the council of state was in the process of finalising the details of the scheme of transplantation to Connacht at this time. Its instructions of July 1653 stipulated that no Catholics were to be allowed to 'live in, or enter into, any Port, Town, or Garrison' in Connacht.[84] Browne had travelled to London precisely to seek confirmation that the Galway townsmen could remain resident in their town, being both a port and a garrison. Therefore any arguments which he might have put forward in June 1653 were very much against the tide of the Irish policy then being discussed in London.

Despite these inauspicious circumstances, Browne did make some progress. From the Gatehouse, he petitioned the council of state for release. On 6 June 1653 it ordered him to be freed 'for prosecution of his business depending before the Court of Articles sitting in Westminster'. However, he was required to give himself up as a prisoner to the council in the event that the committee for articles should rule against him.[85] Within a short time, Browne was back in prison. On 4 July the council of state issued a warrant for his release so that he could be returned to Ireland to stand trial and a party of horse was appointed by Cromwell to convey him to Chester. He was to be accompanied on the journey by another 'popish lawyer' who had been arrested along with him, William Brent.[86] These developments suggested that Browne's mission had ended disastrously, but it was not yet over. Browne was to remain in London, albeit imprisoned in the Gatehouse, until November 1653. By then, the parliament's approval of the proposal to transplant Catholics to Connacht meant that the articles of Galway had assumed even greater significance.

After July 1653 the case of the Galway townsmen became inseparable from the overall policy of transplantation to Connacht. The success of the latter scheme was dependent both on there being enough land available for transplanters and on the transfer of all strongholds in the province into Protestant hands. The articles of Galway concerned much of the land of the province as well as its major urban centre.[87] Therefore the articles, if confirmed, posed a direct threat to the success of the scheme and indeed to the overall land settlement. These circumstances meant that a speedy resolution of this complex case was most necessary. The Galway townsmen could expect no favours from the commissioners in Ireland and they instead pinned their hopes on Browne's endeavours in London. Despite being imprisoned, Browne managed to present to the committee for articles a petition drawn up by the mayor and corporation of

[82] *Clarendon state papers*, ii. 217.

[83] *IUC* ii. 342.

[84] *Further instructions unto Charles Fleetwood*.

[85] *CSPD, 1652–1653*, 387.

[86] *CSPD, 1653–1654*, 6.

[87] *IUC* i. 163–6.

Galway.[88] This ensured that their side of the argument would receive at least some notice at Westminster. On 22 August 1653, in response to Browne's petition, the committee for articles wrote to the commissioners in Dublin seeking further information on the articles of Galway.[89] Given that committee's track record to date in dealing with owners of Irish land, this move must have appeared to the townsmen as a very positive development.

In Dublin, the commissioners viewed the matter in a rather different light. The request of the committee for articles for further information about the Galway case came on the same day as they ruled in favour of the earl of Clanbrassil.[90] From the Irish government's point of view, it must have appeared that both schemes of transplantation were now coming under attack from the same quarter. They accordingly chose simply to ignore the committee for articles' letter. Rather than risking the possibility that that body might rule in favour of the Galway townsmen, the commissioners focused their energies on influencing opinion in both the council of state and the parliament. On 5 October they wrote to the former requesting 'their pleasure how far the Articles upon the surrender of Galway are to be made good' and enclosing 'seven papers' which outlined the details of the case from their point of view.[91] The committee of parliament for Irish affairs was informed that

> much of this work of removal will depend thereupon; for, if the articles be confirmed, all the forfeited lands in the County of Galway, and two-third parts of the forfeited lands in the province at large will thereby be given to the Irish and other delinquent proprietors, most of the proprietors of that province being included (as is conceived) in those articles; and if so, the lands in the Commonwealth's dispose will probably fall much short of giving satisfaction to the Irish proprietors of the other three provinces.[92]

The commissioners were evidently keen to press their point that the success or failure of the transplantation hinged on the manner in which the articles of Galway would be implemented. Eventually, on 21 October 1653, they responded to the request sent by the committee for articles two months before. In their letter to the committee, the commissioners merely announced that they had elected to bypass it and instead to trust the resolution of the matter to the council of state and the parliament. Rather than furnishing it with the relevant documents which it needed to enable it to reach a decision on the Galway case, the commissioners curtly informed the committee for articles that 'we shall not need to enlarge at present'.[93]

The papers sent to Westminster by the commissioners in October 1653 were designed solely to undermine the claims of the Galway townsmen. At the heart of the matter was a fundamental conflict of interpretation; the commissioners and the townsmen could not even reach agreement on which text actually constituted the articles of Galway. The townsmen, through Geoffrey Browne, pressed for the ratification of the articles to which they had initially signed. The commis-

---

88 *IUC* ii. 374.
89 Ibid.
90 MS Carte 74, fo. 119; *IUC* ii. 374.
91 *IUC* ii. 372–3; *CSPD, 1653–1654*, 234.
92 *CSPD, 1653–1654*, 234.
93 *IUC* ii. 374.

sioners argued that Sir Charles Coote had not been empowered to grant those articles and sought to amend them significantly. Coote, caught in the middle, struggled to find a way to satisfy both sides. By 16 November 1653 the council of state had reached its verdict. The articles were to be confirmed 'only so far as the said commissioners have, in their resolves and exceptions touching the same ... consented and agreed to, and no further'.[94] The council had come down firmly on the side of the commissioners in Dublin against the claims of the Galway townsmen.

This decision was guided largely by the commissioners' arguments concerning the circumstances in which Coote had negotiated the surrender of Galway. In backing the alteration of the articles of Galway, the council of state found that 'the public faith is not herein violated, as Sir Charles Coote was not empowered to grant the said articles without consent of the said commissioners'.[95] The root of this matter could be traced back to 1651. In June of that year the town of Limerick had refused the surrender terms offered to it by Ireton. In November 1651, after the fall of Limerick, Ireton offered these same terms to Galway in the hope that it might submit. Following Ireton's death a few weeks later, the commissioners instructed Coote to break off his negotiations with Galway if the town had not surrendered by 10 January 1652. When Coote recommenced the surrender negotiations in March 1652, he continued to use the articles offered to Limerick in June 1651 as a basis for agreement. Given the reduced circumstances of the Irish forces by April 1652, the commissioners believed that Coote had been altogether too generous in his dealings with the townsmen.[96] While their initial reaction had been to respect the proceedings out of consideration for 'the honour and service of the parliament', they had quickly changed their minds.[97]

The notion that Coote had acted without authority in April 1652 had opened up another useful line of attack for the commissioners in their effort to undermine the intent of the Galway articles that he had granted. Yet at no stage were questions raised about the other instances where articles had been agreed without the commissioners' knowledge.[98] Significantly, the council of state, sufficiently impressed with the importance of 'the great work of transplanting', proved itself acquiescent to the commissioners' demands.[99] On 16 November 1653 it entrusted Henry Cromwell with the task of winning the parliament's approval for its proceedings.[100] Meanwhile, the Galway prisoner in the Gatehouse remained an inconvenient presence. On 19 November the council again turned its attention to Geoffrey Browne. It once more ordered Browne and William Brent to be sent to Dublin to the high court of justice to be 'proceeded against or acquitted, as their case shall be found to be'. Another petition from Browne reached the

---

94 *CSPD, 1653–1654*, 236–7, 254–5.
95 Ibid.
96 *IUC* i. 167–9.
97 Ibid.
98 For example in March 1652 Colonel Sankey simply convened a council of war at Cahir and drew up articles of surrender for Colonel O'Dwyer without any consultation with the commissioners. In July 1652 the commissioners wrote to Cromwell recommending O'Dwyer as an 'eminent officer' and asked him to mediate for O'Dwyer with the Spanish ambassador: *IUC* i. 240.
99 *IUC* ii. 374.
100 *CSPD, 1653–1654*, 254–5.

council on 28 November, perhaps his final attempt to press the strong claims of the townsmen.[101] Within days Browne and Brent had at last been transported under guard to Chester at a cost of ten pounds.[102] The commissioners would have welcomed Geoffrey Browne's eventual forced return to Ireland. With the ultimate failure of his mission to London, it appeared that a serious obstacle to the success of the transplantation scheme had been removed. However, despite appointing a morning for a debate on the issue, the parliament did not get around to discussing the articles of Galway before 12 December 1653.[103] This meant that the matter was not fully closed after all.

The resignation of the parliament helped to renew the uncertainty that had existed concerning the articles of Galway. Although the council of state had backed their stance, for some six months afterwards the commissioners made no attempt to enforce its decision. Eventually, in June 1654, a petition from the governor of Galway, Colonel Peter Stubbers, forced them to address the issue. At that point, Stubbers was empowered to remove 'dangerous and active persons from the town'. Any persons removed were to be allowed to lease their property to others for one year.[104] This order reflected how unsure the commissioners were about the situation in which they now found themselves. Despite their previous attempts to alter the articles of Galway, they were still anxious to keep up some pretence of respecting them. The provisional measures which they suggested to Stubbers were designed to meet his needs until the articles were 'considered, and a determination given thereunto'.[105] The Galway case was clearly still open.

In the following month, July 1654, the commissioners requested the lord protector's 'resolution touching the articles of Galway'. John Jones was entrusted with the task of briefing Cromwell on the case.[106] Cromwell had been absent from the council of state meeting on 16 November 1653 at which it had given its verdict on the articles of Galway.[107] There is no evidence of what opinion, if any, he expressed on the matter in the summer of 1654. Nevertheless it is possible to discern a clear change of direction in subsequent policy towards the case of the Galway townsmen around that time. The highly questionable notion that the articles were void because Coote had not been authorised to grant them was quietly laid aside. Henceforth the authorities in Ireland accepted the validity of the original articles agreed by Coote with the townsmen in April 1652. Yet this did not mean that the struggle was over. The Irish government now concentrated its energies on the task of discovering loopholes in the existing articles which would allow them to remove the townsmen from their homes. Thus, although the government's attempts to alter the articles of Galway ceased after 1654, the townsmen were still not fully secure in the possession of their valuable homes. More worryingly for the Irish government, Geoffrey Browne's treatment in London had done nothing to deter other Catholics from making the same trip.

---

101 *CSPD, 1653–1654*, 260, 272, 276, 427–9.
102 *CSPD, 1653–1654*, 450–60.
103 *CJ* vii. 358.
104 *IUC* ii. 431–2.
105 Ibid.
106 *IUC* ii. 436.
107 *CSPD, 1653–1654*, 36–40.

The case of John Grace

From 1653 onwards the Irish government also had to pay increasing attention to the efforts being made by individual Catholic landowners to secure concessions in London. While Browne awaited his release from the Gatehouse in 1653, the case of another Catholic, John Grace of Courtstown, Co. Kilkenny, was being considered by the council of state. Grace was one of a number of landowners whose claims to favour were based on individual circumstances, as opposed to agreements enshrined in articles of war. In January 1651 Grace had been dispatched to Loughrea by Ireton to investigate the prospect of a settlement between the opposing forces in Ireland.[108] In the same year he was deputed to treat with parliament on behalf of the landowners of Co. Kilkenny, although it is not clear if he went to London at that stage.[109] As a result of his services, he obtained 'an assurance under the hand of the late lord deputy Ireton, that he should be admitted to a composition for his estates, at an easy rate, and that he would recommend him to parliament in that particular'.[110] This was essentially the same guarantee which Cromwell had given to the Irish Protestants upon their surrender. Unfortunately for Grace, Ireton died before fulfilling his promise. Moreover, his activities during the 1640s, both living in rebel territory and sitting in the confederate general assembly, meant that he came some way short of the required standard of 'constant good affection' necessary to avoid confiscation.[111] Like Browne, Grace elected to pursue his entitlements even before the transplantation was announced, with the council of state noticing a petition from him as early as February 1653.[112] With only one estate at stake, this case was of far less significance than that of the Galway townsmen. None the less, in its dealings with Grace, the Irish government would again exhibit its customary lack of sympathy.

On 11 October 1653 Grace's case was considered by the council of state for the second time.[113] Two weeks earlier the parliament had rejected a legislative proviso which would have allowed the government to exempt more deserving Catholics, including perhaps John Grace, from transplantation.[114] This hard line stance effectively ensured that the issue would have to be revisited. On 18 October Colonel Sydenham read Grace's petition in parliament and moved the house 'that Power may be given to such as they shall think fit, to dispense with the late Act, injoining the transplanting of those of the *Irish* Nation, in *Ireland*, from the Places of their present Abodes, into *Connacht*, in certain particular Cases where it shall be found necessary to dispense with the said Act'.[115] This time the parliament did not display the same degree of resolve. Instead of again

---

[108] *History of the confederation*, vii. 362–7.
[109] Sheffield Grace, *Memoirs of the family of Grace*, London 1827, 11.
[110] William Shaw Mason, A *statistical account, or parochial survey of Ireland*, Dublin 1814–19, iii. 586.
[111] Ó Siochrú, *Confederate Ireland*, 257.
[112] SP 25/39/37.
[113] *CSPD, 1653–1654*, 198
[114] *CJ* vii. 324.
[115] *CSPD, 1653–1654*, 198; *CJ* vii. 336.

rejecting the suggestion that the transplantation scheme might be moderated, it referred the issue to the consideration of a committee.[116] Although there was no guarantee that he would manage to avoid transplantation, the fact that Grace's petition was read in parliament showed that his case was at least being treated seriously. However, the parliament failed to reach any decision in his case before it resigned its powers.

Fortunately for Grace, Ireton's recommendation of favour ensured that Cromwell would be sympathetic to his plight. The latter's elevation to the position of lord protector therefore boosted Grace's chances of securing permission to compound for his estate, even though he was a Catholic and the law required that he be transplanted. The events of December 1653 presented Grace with the same nine-month window of opportunity that was available to Irish Protestants. Eventually, on 27 July 1654, the council of state consented 'as to suspending his transplantation until further order'.[117] In the following month it endorsed the passing of 'an ordinance to admit John Grace, of Ireland, to a composition and exemption from transplantation'.[118] On 30 August Cromwell approved the relevant ordinance.[119] Despite being an Irish Catholic, Grace was in effect being allowed to avail of terms equivalent to those which would shortly thereafter be granted to Irish Protestants. Sheffield Grace, one of John Grace's descendants and the family historian, claimed that his 'fearlesss, generous, and spirited conduct, combined with extraordinary personal beauty, had acquired the particular favour of Cromwell'.[120] The ordinance in favour of Grace recited the case more plainly: he was 'no way accessary to any of the murders, massacres, or robberies, committed by the rebels', and since April 1650 he had 'been faithful to the English interest, and done many acceptable services'.[121] In a subsequent letter Cromwell explained that Grace was 'I think, the only person that the late lord deputy [Ireton] did soe particularly recommend to favour, upon account of his forwardness and readiness to assist the English forces, and interest.'[122] Yet despite Grace's triumph in London, he would still face considerable difficulties in reclaiming his lands.

Having apparently fallen ill, Grace did not depart for Ireland until the summer of 1655. He took with him a letter from Cromwell urging Fleetwood to grant him 'a speedy and favourable dispatch' of his business.[123] By this time Grace's lands had been surveyed for distribution to the army and he was ordered to conform to the rules for transplantation and to apply for land in Connacht.[124] By November the Irish government, following a judicial review of the case, had decided to back down.[125] Any remaining uncertainty was dispelled by another letter from London

---

116 CJ vii. 336.
117 CSPD, 1654, 268.
118 Ibid. 325–50.
119 Shaw Mason, Statistical account, iii. 585–6.
120 Grace, Memoirs of the family of Grace, 11.
121 Shaw Mason, Statistical account, iii. 585–6.
122 Grace, Memoirs of the family of Grace, 39.
123 Ibid.
124 NLI, MS 11,961, fo. 43.
125 Ibid. fos 250–1, 91–2.

in December 1655, which ordered that Grace should have the benefit of his ordinance.[126] Thereafter a composition was agreed but, as in the case of many Protestants, the size of the fine was a cause of some distress. On 23 October 1656 Cromwell again intervened to order that the fine be reduced and the term of payment extended.[127]

John Grace's experience in London showed that Cromwell could be just as instrumental on behalf of Irish Catholics as he was for Irish Protestants. Because of Grace's activities in the 1640s, he had no prospect of satisfying the requirements of constant good affection which would have entitled him to be permanently exempted from the transplantation scheme. From a moderate viewpoint, one which Cromwell apparently held, Ireton had set the bar for constant good affection somewhat too high. Grace's particular circumstances made even the council of state realise that the laws which governed the transplantation were somewhat too strict and inflexible. As Vincent Gookin was soon to argue, 'the fair vertue of justice (overdon) degenerates into the stinking weed of Tyranny'.[128] Gookin's pamphlets would not appear until 1655. Before then, another important group of Irish Catholic landowners, the officers of the Leinster army, would attempt to secure for themselves the same favourable outcome obtained by both the Irish Protestants and John Grace. The latter's triumph demonstrated that Irish Catholic hopes of avoiding transplantation through resort to Westminster could not be dismissed as incidents of misguided optimism.

The case of the Leinster officers

The efforts made by the Leinster officers from 1654 onwards to avoid transplantation would represent the most substantial Catholic challenge in the decade to the policies of the Irish government. Prendergast described this group as 'the lords and gentlemen of the Pale, the Barnewalls, the Nettervilles, Bellews, Plunkets, and others'.[129] It included former leading confederates and highly experienced military commanders, prime candidates for transplantation. If such a potentially dangerous cohort was allowed to retain and reside upon part of its old estates, the scheme's justification could be seriously undermined. However, any attempt to transplant the Leinster officers was bound to be complicated by the terms of their articles of surrender. Most significant was an undertaking given by the parliamentarian army officers 'faithfully and really to mediate with the parliament to our utmost endeavours … that they may enjoy such moderate part [of their] estates as may make their lives comfortable who live amongst us, or for the comfortable maintenance of the families of such of them as shall go beyond the seas'.[130] In May 1652 the Leinster landowners believed that this promise would enable them to retain at least part of their hereditary estates. By the end of 1653 therefore, the scene was accordingly set for yet another conflict between the Irish government and a group of discontented landowners.

---

126 Shaw Mason, *Statistical account*, iii. 587; *CSPI, 1647–1660*, 820.
127 Shaw Mason, *Statistical account*, iii. 588.
128 Vincent Gookin, *The great case of transplantation in Ireland discussed*, London 1655, 14.
129 Prendergast, *The Cromwellian settlement*, 115–16.
130 *IUC* i. 202.

In March 1654 the committee for articles heard the case of 'the Earle of Westmeathe, Sir Richard Barnwall, and others'.[131] Westmeath and the other Leinster officers put forward a number of strong arguments. They insisted that the promised mediation with the English parliament had never taken place, and that therefore the intentions of that body towards them were as yet unknown. The Act for the Settling of Ireland was dismissed as irrelevant to their circumstances; only a subsequent parliament, properly informed on the matter, could pass judgement. The legislative proviso, which the Irish government believed empowered it to transplant whomever it pleased, also came under attack. The whole issue could be reduced to a basic question of justice, and 'justice required that private or publicke faith agreements grounded upon good considerations be performed'.[132] The committee for articles was suitably impressed by these arguments. It ordered that the Leinster officers should 'have their estates until a future Parliament in England shall declare what part of their estates they shall enjoy, and that they ought not to be transplanted into Connacht in the mean time'.[133]

The favourable ruling obtained by the Leinster officers at Westminster in March 1654 ensured that they would be allowed at least temporarily to live in a legal limbo in Leinster, rather than as transplanters in Connacht. However, they were determined not to trust their fate to the vagaries of an English parliament. In common with the Irish Protestants, the Leinster officers now focused their attention on Oliver Cromwell. On 29 March 1654 Cromwell sent a letter to Dublin on behalf of the earl of Westmeath in which he warned the government about the extent to which 'the faith of the army and our own justice and honour is concerned in the just performance of articles'.[134] This letter helped to alert the commissioners to the growing threat to the land settlement posed by the presence of Irish Catholics in London, and to convince them of the need for a firm response.

The commissioners' reaction

From April 1654 the Irish government adopted a strategy designed to undermine the position of the Irish Catholics in London. First, because Cromwell now occupied such a key position, it was necessary for the government to win him over to their point of view on articles of war and other issues affecting the land settlement. Secondly, although Fleetwood and his colleagues were seemingly unable to prevent landowners from travelling to London, they would subsequently make a greater effort to discredit the Irish Catholics and to block their access to the corridors of power. On 18 April the commissioners dispatched a lengthy letter to

---

131 MS Carte 63, fo. 634.
132 NLI, MS Bellew of Mountbellew 31,966. Although this document dates from March 1655, it can be safely assumed that the arguments contained in it were largely the same as those presented by the Leinster officers to the committee for articles a year earlier.
133 The commissioners of parliament to the lord protector, Dublin, 18 Apr. 1654, MS Prendergast 2, fo. 177. Dunlop's transcript of this same letter does not contain the significant wording 'in the mean time': IUC ii. 421.
134 IUC ii. 414.

Cromwell justifying their opposition to the work of the committee for articles and to the claims of the Leinster officers. Shortly afterwards, two agents were sent to London to reinforce these points.[135] In their letter of 18 April, the commissioners depicted the success of the entire land settlement as hinging on the case of the Leinster officers. Any concessions to the latter group would derail the plantation and set a precedent for 'all the Rebells of Ireland' to enjoy their lands until a new parliament should find time to devote to the matter.[136] Neither rulings from the committee for articles nor letters from Cromwell were deemed to provide sufficient grounds for permitting such a supposed disaster to unfold. The commissioners instead requested that a separate committee for articles be established in Dublin, where 'the truth with much lesse trouble and charge' could supposedly be arrived at. They also signalled their intention to disregard Cromwell's earlier letter on behalf of the earl of Westmeath.[137] This boldness exemplified the Irish government's determination to defeat the ambitions of the Leinster officers.

Two documents dating from May and June 1654 epitomise the fierce struggle which was ongoing in those months. In a petition which they drew up in London in May, the Leinster officers sought to assert their Englishness dating back to the Norman conquest of Ireland in the twelfth century. They claimed that they 'and their progenitors have since there arrival there affected and continued the Civility, breeding, landguage, lawes, and manners of the English ... who now to be proscribed to a wilderness devoid of all accomodation is to diswont them from there accustomed Civilitie and betray the same to barberties, Custome being a second nature'.[138] A few weeks later, Fleetwood wrote from Dublin to voice a very different perspective. He warned Thurloe that 'these people are an abominable false, cunning, and perfidious people; and the best of them to be pitied, but not to be trusted'.[139] This claim was made as part of Fleetwood's efforts to drive a wedge between Cromwell and the Irish Catholics. Moreover, the recent discovery of John Gerard's plot to assassinate the lord protector provided Fleetwood with further scope for scaremongering. His letter to Thurloe also revealed that

> We have ground to believe, that the Irish have some desperate thing in design to execute speedily, and to believe, that the late bloody intentions to my lord's own person was part of this design ... I therefore beg, you will suffer no Irishman, under what pretence soever, to come near my lord's person ... and that you would remove the Irish from about London.[140]

Fleetwood warned in particular about 'one Segrave, a notable Jesuited papist' and Sir Richard Barnewall, one of the leading Leinster officers.[141] It is extremely

---

135 *IUC* ii. 421; the commissioners' instructions to Captain Richard Kingdon and William Rowe, Dublin, 18 May 1654, MS Carte 63, fos 632–6.

136 *IUC* ii. 421; the commissioners' instructions to Captain Richard Kingdon and William Rowe, Dublin, 18 May 1654, MS Carte 63, fos 632–6.

137 *IUC* ii. 421; The commissioners' instructions to Captain Richard Kingdon and William Rowe, Dublin, 18 May 1654, MS Carte 63, fos 632–6.

138 McNeill, 'Report on the Rawlinson collection, 20.

139 *TSP* ii. 343.

140 Ibid.

141 Ibid.

unlikely that the Leinster officers were scheming to kill Cromwell, as an ordinance from him appeared to offer the best prospect of their avoiding transplantation. Yet the Irish government's effort to ensure the survival of the transplantation scheme by damaging Irish Catholic links with the lord protector would none the less prove successful.

One of those who observed the events to which Fleetwood's intervention must have contributed was Peter Talbot, an Irish Jesuit who fled London for Antwerp in June 1654.[142] Talbot's elder brother Sir Robert Talbot was among the Leinster officers who had been active in London over the previous months. In a letter written in early July Peter Talbot reported a sharp decline in the fortunes of the Leinster officers. Although 'a promise was made to Sir Robert Talbot and the other Irish agents that ... [the transplantation] ... would not be proceeded with', that guarantee had subsequently been overturned and Cromwell was 'now busy imprisoning the Papists and the priests. Of the latter, four have been arrested, and a vast number of the former, twenty of whom were Irish, all of them being quite guiltless of any conspiracy'.[143] Another observer, John Percival, claimed that 2,000 people were arrested and that 'many Irish likewise are seized, amongst which McCarty Reagh, Fagan of Feltrim, Lord Barnewall and his son and many others'.[144] This number also presumably included some of the Leinster officers, whose prospects of obtaining an ordinance from Cromwell now appeared lost. They could only stand by as Cromwell fulfilled the desires of the Irish Protestants, John Grace and some other Irish landowners. None the less, the Leinster officers remained hopeful that the next parliament might grant them a sympathetic hearing.

Back in Dublin the Irish government moved to reassert its authority by announcing a plan to transplant the entire Catholic population out of five counties in the south-east.[145] Ultimately, no serious attempt would be made to implement this scheme, but its announcement did signal the commissioners' intention to press ahead with their agenda for the settlement of Ireland. At the same time, they had still to pay some attention to events in London. By the summer of 1654 plans were afoot to re-establish the traditional mode of government in Ireland by a lord deputy and council. One of the four commissioners, Edmund Ludlow, had refused to recognise the protectorate, while another, John Jones, was also reportedly discontented.[146] In August the traditional post of lord deputy was revived and conferred on Fleetwood. These changes again raised hopes of some alteration

---

142 Talbot had arrived in London from Spain in April 1653 with royal letters enjoining the Spanish ambassador to help him to secure toleration for Catholicism in Ireland. He journeyed to Ireland before again returning to London. See *ODNB*, s.v. 'Talbot, Peter (1618/1620–1680)'.

143 Patrick Moran, *Historical sketch of the persecutions suffered by the Catholics of Ireland under the rule of Cromwell and the puritans*, Dublin 1862, 297–8.

144 HMC, *Egmont manuscripts*, i. 542–3.

145 MS Prendergast 1, fo. 206. While no copy of this declaration appears to have survived, its content was cited at length in a subsequent declaration issued by the lord deputy and council on 27 Feb. 1655: *Whereas by an order of 30 November last ... 27 February 1654[5]*, Dublin 1655 (BL, 806.i.14(12)).

146 During a brief trip to Ireland on behalf of his father in March 1654, Henry Cromwell reported that both Jones and Ludlow were dissatisfied with the establishment of the protec-

in transplantation policy. On 24 July John Percival reported his belief that 'when our new council goes over ... they will give some stop to the transplantation; it being one of their instructions to moderate it as they shall think fit'.[147] Indeed, the instructions issued to Fleetwood and his new council on 17 August permitted them

> so far as they judge fit and to be for the public service, [to] dispense with the Orders and Instructions made and given by the late Parliament or Council of State for the transplantation of the Irish natives ... and likewise with the penalties and forfeitures set and imposed by the authority aforesaid upon such persons as shall not transplant themselves accordingly.[148]

This clause did not, however, signal a change in the direction of transplantation policy. Rather it simply conferred *post facto* legitimacy on the steps towards moderation taken by the commissioners over the past year in exempting the lower orders from the scheme and in permitting widespread dispensations. This new instruction relating to transplantation went some way towards closing the gulf between the legislation of September 1653, which had made no provision for such a flexible approach, and the policy which the Irish government actually wished to implement. This meant that once the harvest of 1654 had been gathered, Fleetwood and his new government were able to move swiftly to reactivate their transplantation policy.

Carrying on the work

November 1654 brought the clearest statement yet of Fleetwood's intentions. Writing to Cromwell around the middle of the month he informed him that 'we are endeavouring to carry on the work of transplanting the Irish proprietors and such as have been in arms into Connacht effectually'.[149] This letter to Cromwell was followed two weeks later by another declaration on the subject of transplantation. Unfortunately, no copy of this declaration appears to have survived, but much of its content can be reconstructed from citations in subsequent documents. The same three categories of people identified in October 1653 were again singled out for transplantation in November 1654; those involved in the first year of the rebellion; those who had borne arms at any time during the conflict; and landowners entitled to land under the qualifications.[150] It was clear that this formula quite simply meant that landowners and soldiers were to be transplanted. Moreover, in one important respect the 30 November declaration on transplantation was more practical than the former edicts on the issue. The penalty stipulated for those who would ignore the new deadline of 1 March 1655

---

torate. See *TSP* ii. 149; *IUC* ii. 436. Although it was expected by some that Jones would be arrested on his arrival in London, he subsequently married Cromwell's sister.

[147] HMC, *Egmont manuscripts*, i. 550–1.

[148] *IUC* ii. 437–43.

[149] *IUC* ii. 457–9.

[150] The lord deputy and council, *Whereas by an order of 30 November last ... 27 February 1654[5]*, Dublin 1655 (BL, 806.i.14(12)).

was not execution but instead the confiscation of their 'corn, gardening, and planting'. The funds derived from the sales of these goods were to be used to provide support in Connacht for those who would actually obey the order to transplant.[151] The aftermath of their latest declaration was to prove more encouraging for the Irish authorities. On 21 December 1654 an observer in Ireland noted that 'the transplantation is now far advanced'.[152] This optimistic appraisal contrasted sharply with several reports made earlier in the year.

Despite these signs of progress, Fleetwood still had much to be concerned about at the end of 1654. The complicated cases of the Galway townsmen and the Leinster officers had yet to be finally resolved. By this stage the former group had appointed Sir Richard Blake as their agent in place of Geoffrey Browne. Significantly, following Browne's forced departure in November 1653, the Galway townsmen had had no representative in London in the crucial period during which other groups and individuals managed to secure important concessions. In November 1654 Blake attempted to make up lost ground when he petitioned the lord deputy and council and requested that steps be taken to have the articles of Galway ratified by an act of parliament.[153] A week later the Leinster officers appointed Sir James Barry as counsel to represent them while Fleetwood and his council deliberated on their articles.[154] The Irish government was determined that both groups should be transplanted as soon as possible. However, the Leinster officers continued to maintain a presence in London in the hope that the first protectorate parliament might deal sympathetically with their plight.[155] This was just one of the factors which ensured that the Irish government would once more have to focus its attentions closely on London in the opening months of 1655.

In his speech at the opening of the new parliament in September 1654, Cromwell had drawn the attention of its members to Ireland: 'You have great works upon your hands. You have Ireland to look unto. There is not much done to the planting of it, though some things leading and preparing for it are.'[156] This invitation suggested that the parliament would at some point give some thought to the Irish settlement. This was certainly the expectation of Vincent Gookin, the member of parliament for Bandon and Kinsale and the author of a controversial pamphlet published anonymously in London around 3 January 1655. Gookin's *The great case of transplantation in Ireland discussed* was ostensibly concerned with the policy of transplantation, but it also incorporated a scathing critique of the Irish government.[157] Fleetwood appeared fairly certain concerning the identity of

---

151 The lord deputy and council, A *declaration for making sale of the corn ... 7 March 1654[5]*, Dublin 1655 (BL, 806.i.14(13)).
152 Prendergast, *The Cromwellian settlement*, 127.
153 *IUC* ii. 461.
154 *IUC* ii. 462–3. As Catholics were not permitted to practise law, the Leinster officers were obliged to choose a Protestant to plead their case. Barry had formerly held a number of important legal posts in Ireland. See *ODNB*, *s.v.* 'Barry, James, first Baron Barry of Santry (1603–1673)'.
155 *TSP* iii. 139.
156 *The letters and speeches of Oliver Cromwell*, ii. 359.
157 Cunningham 'The Gookin-Lawrence pamphlet debate', 63–80.

the author of this surprise attack, and he reacted angrily to what he saw as Gookin's attempts to 'verie falsely and unworthily asperse those, that did and now doe serve the state heere'.[158] For the lord deputy, the appearance of Gookin's pamphlet was further confirmation of the 'bloody confederacy' that Irish Catholics and Protestants were supposedly engaged in.[159] While Colonel Richard Lawrence was commissioned to respond to Gookin, Fleetwood's attention was soon drawn once again to the problematic presence of Irish Catholics in London.

Despite the recommendation made by Cromwell in his speech to parliament in September 1654, that body never got around to considering Irish affairs. Instead it was dissolved at the earliest possible opportunity on 22 January 1655. In the first instance, this development appeared as a blow to lingering Irish Catholic hopes for leniency. A letter written from Dublin two weeks later reported that 'the Irish are much troubled to hear of the dissolution of the late parliament, in whom they had great hopes, but blessed be God their hopes are prevented'.[160] Sir Robert Talbot and his colleagues had failed to win any concessions, but they were not yet ready to concede defeat. Fleetwood expected that the Catholics would again focus their attentions on Cromwell. Moreover, some uncertainty existed regarding the precise powers now enjoyed by Cromwell in the aftermath of the dissolution of parliament. In an effort to block potential concessions, Fleetwood recommenced his attempts to discredit the Catholic lobby in London. In a letter to Thurloe early in February 1655 he insisted that the Catholics were once again involved in conspiracies against the state and he expressed the hope that 'the Lord will discover and blast their designes'. Fleetwood identified six Irish agents and advised that 'it were well an eye were had on those persons in London, especially mr. Seagrave and Grace, who are men of parts and interest; and so is sir Robert Talbot'.[161]

Fleetwood's fresh concerns regarding Cromwell's intentions were soon assuaged. According to the Instrument of Government under which Cromwell had been appointed, his right to pass legally binding ordinances had terminated once parliament convened on 3 September 1654. In February 1655 Fleetwood accordingly welcomed the news that, after dissolving the parliament and in line with the terms of the Instrument of Government, Cromwell 'hath declined the legislative power'.[162] This meant that there was now no way that Irish Catholics could obtain ordinances as their Protestant counterparts had done some months earlier; it may have been this circumstance to which Fleetwood was referring when he suggested to Thurloe that 'those thinges, which we heare are attempted to be done in England concerninge Ireland, will be prevented through the want of power'.[163] The lord deputy was now at last satisfied that the transplantation of Catholic landowners and soldiers could go ahead unhindered, as any change in the law, he explained, 'must be the exercise of the legislative power'.[164] Once the

---

[158] *TSP* iii. 139.
[159] Lord deputy and council to the lord protector, Dublin, 14 Nov. 1654, MS O'Renehan 2, fo. 538.
[160] *Mercurius Politicus*, 15 Feb.–22 Feb. 1655, 5,136–7.
[161] *TSP* iii. 139.
[162] *TSP* iii. 183.
[163] Ibid.
[164] *TSP* iii 196.

first protectorate parliament had been dissolved, that power did not exist; parliament would not meet again until September 1656. Sir Robert Talbot remained in London for much of the rest of the decade, but after February 1655 there was little that he or indeed any other Irish Catholic could do to overturn the official policy of transplantation to Connacht.

Between 1653 and 1655 an intense struggle was played out in London between the Irish government and many of the country's landowners. The government was determined to maximise the amount of land available for adventurers and soldiers, while existing Protestant and Catholic proprietors were even more anxious to hold onto their estates. The controversy essentially hinged on the discrepancies which existed between articles of war and parliamentary legislation, but it was exacerbated by the uncertainties of the constitutional situation in these years. Fortunately for the landowners concerned, the influential committee for articles provided a seemingly impartial platform for them to rehearse their objections to the policies favoured in Dublin. When Cromwell threw his weight behind the rulings of that committee, the Irish government was obliged to pay even more attention to events in London. While the Irish Protestants achieved notable successes, Fleetwood's efforts to block further concessions helped to ensure that most Catholic hopes would ultimately be frustrated. From his perspective, the challenges mounted by Irish landowners, combined with Gookin's intervention, were both unjustifiable and dangerous. By February 1655 he was content that the storm had passed. None the less, the character of the land settlement which he worked so energetically to protect had undergone important alterations. Most notably, the existing Old Protestant landowners had seen off the threat to their estates and stabilised their position, thereby establishing a base from which to rebuild their political power. Fleetwood would himself be the most notable casualty of this development, as his days in Ireland were now numbered. At the same time, he had already done enough to ensure the continuity of policy towards Catholic landowners after his departure. With the exception of John Grace and a few others, every Catholic landowner in Ireland would have their estates confiscated. Moreover, the transplantation of landowners and soldiers remained a key priority for the government. The extent to which this policy would actually be implemented in practice over the years that followed remained to be seen.

4

Enforcing Transplantation, 1655–1659

By the spring of 1655 the Irish government was at last ready to attempt the full implementation of its transplantation policy. Following its uncertain beginnings in the previous year, the effort to transplant former landowners and soldiers was carried out with some degree of success up to the end of the decade. This chapter will explore several key aspects of that process. It is necessary to set the scene by outlining the range of punishments that persons refusing to transplant were liable to. The government's attempts to enforce the transplantation in Dublin and the south-east, the region where it had the most direct involvement, will then be assessed. Here as elsewhere, Fleetwood and his successor Henry Cromwell were largely dependent on the co-operation of local officers and officials. Some insight into the extent to which the members of this vital group went about fulfilling their duties can be pieced together from the surviving sources. The most important of these officials, the two teams of commissioners appointed to oversee the resettlement of the transplanters in Connacht, merit particular attention. Finally, some further account must be taken of Catholic responses to the policy of transplantation from 1655 onwards, particularly those of the Galway townsmen and the Leinster officers. The examination together of these various elements should make it possible clearly to discern why the transplantation scheme ultimately assumed the form that it did.

The punishment of non-transplanters

The instructions for transplantation issued by the council of state threatened the death penalty upon any transplantable Catholic who remained east of the Shannon after 1 May 1654.[1] Although this threat was not carried out, by 1655 those individuals who refused to transplant still ran the risk of subjection to a range of punishments. These included the confiscation of crops, imprisonment, transportation to Barbados and execution.[2] The limited success of the transplantation was at least partially due to the Dublin government's extreme reluctance to endorse the latter strategy. In March 1655 an observer in Co. Kildare reported

---

[1] *Further instructions unto Charles Fleetwood*, 24.
[2] A declaration issued on 30 November 1654 stated that those who did not transplant by 1 March would have their crops seized. Another declaration to this end was published in March 1655: *A declaration for making sale of the corn … 7 March 1654[5]*.

that 'the officers [were] resolved to fill the gaols … we shall be very tender of hanging any except leading men'.[3] The first wave of arrests duly took place a few weeks later, but the officers in charge of courts martial were instructed by the government not to carry out executions at this point. They were instead advised to accept bonds and to set a time limit for the individuals concerned to transplant.[4]

Despite the overall trend towards moderation, more severe punishments were sometimes inflicted. Edward Hetherington was executed on 3 April 1655, but only after the Dublin administration had satisfied itself that he was responsible for the murder of several Protestants in Co. Kildare in 1643. He was hanged in Dublin wearing placards that communicated a clear message to passersby: 'for not transplanting'.[5] Three months later, in the same city, Peter Bath's death sentence was commuted to transportation to Barbados and he was delivered to a Mr Mouldsworth for shipping.[6] In other cases a more lenient approach was sometimes adopted. In Wexford in August 1655 one Edmund Furlong was sentenced to transportation 'for not transplanting' and placed in the custody of agents for Mr Mouldsworth and a Mr Boyd. However, he was subsequently released and dispensed from transportation upon swearing an oath that he was seventy years old.[7] Had Furlong made it to Barbados, he would presumably have been of little use to anyone there.

Over the following years, many of those who refused to transplant were repeatedly arrested and some were sent to Barbados as punishment for their recalcitrance. In October 1658 the Irish government reprieved a number of people who had been sentenced to death at the assizes for not transplanting and ordered that up to 100 of them should be transported instead.[8] In the same month, Francis Cole, sheriff of Co. Monaghan, was rebuked for 'contrary to law set[ting] at liberty divers persons who were convicted at the last assizes for not transplanting'. His actions were viewed as 'of dangerous consequence and a breach of trust'.[9] Cole and his Protestant neighbours had evidently overcome their recently expressed fears of a repeat of 1641; 'a second eruption of the malice of our cruel enemies'.[10] The tactic of convicting non-transplanters at the quarterly assizes was continued into 1659.[11] The fact that such measures were still deemed necessary at that point indicates that various pressures applied over the preceding years had in many case proven ineffective in persuading some Catholics to remove.

3 Prendergast, *The Cromwellian settlement*, 134–5.
4 MS Prendergast 1, fo. 298.
5 Ibid. fo. 304.
6 MS Prendergast 2, fo. 315.
7 NLI, MS 11,961, fos 110–11.
8 MS Prendergast 1, fos 542–4.
9 Lord deputy and council to Francis Cole, high sheriff of Co. Monaghan, 8 Oct. 1658, ibid. fo. 542.
10 Robert Blayney, Francis Cole and others to Henry Cromwell, Monaghan, 6 Oct. 1657, BL, MS Lansdowne 822, fo. 198.
11 MS Prendergast 1, fos 446–9, 547–8.

Transplantation in Dublin and the south-east

Despite the very public threat conveyed by the execution of Edward Hetherington, as well as by the transportation of Peter Bath and others, the lord deputy and council still faced considerable difficulties even in removing Catholics from Dublin and its vicinity. At one point around the middle of the decade, it was even deemed necessary to issue an order for the removal of Catholics from the seat of government at Dublin Castle.[12] It would appear that repeated government orders for Catholics to depart the city were largely ignored.[13] This reality reflected in many ways the situation across the three provinces. By July 1655 the government was attempting to lease out houses in the city formerly belonging to transplantable Catholics, but they were still in residence and refusing to yield.[14] Thereafter, the mayor of Dublin was asked to provide a progress report.[15] His inquiries led eventually to the identification of just fourteen Catholics, including 'Philip Strong, an antient man' and eleven women.[16] These were evidently not the persons whose presence threatened the success of the transplantation. Over the following years, the Catholic problem persisted. In November 1656 the Protestant shoemakers of the city called for the expulsion of their Catholic counterparts, a move replicated by Protestant coopers five months later.[17] To make matters worse, a number of people, including Lord Strabane, an Ulster Scots Catholic, were arrested at mass in Dublin in February 1657.[18]

In the midst of their anxiety over the presence of Catholics in Dublin, the lord deputy and council also paid intermittent attention to the planned creation of a five-county zone of Protestant settlement in the south-east of Ireland. This scheme had first been announced in July 1654 but no effort had been made to implement it at that point. However, a petition which emerged early in 1655 from among army officers stationed in the south-east called for the full enforcement of the scheme. By then the Protestant landowners in the region had organised themselves in an effort to prevent the removal of their Catholic servants and tenants. On 19 February their agent, Arthur Annesley, was permitted to attend a committee which had been appointed to consider the issue.[19] Some discussions took place over the following months before the government's intentions were revealed in a declaration published on 21 May 1655. This document described how 'the practice, connivance, or remissness of other of the Irish papists' had enabled tories to commit murders in counties Wicklow, Wexford and adjacent areas. In an effort to deal with this problem, it was deemed prudent to remove all

---

[12] MS Egerton 212, fo. 73.
[13] MS Prendergast 1, fo. 289; Lord deputy and council, *Upon consideration had ... 12 February 1654[5]*, Dublin 1655 (BL, 806.i.14(11)) and *A declaration that all Irish papists remaining within Dublin ... 18 May 1655*, Dublin 1655 (BL, 806.i.14(19)).
[14] MS Prendergast 1, fos 335–6.
[15] Ibid. fos 340, 362–3.
[16] Ibid. fos 372–3.
[17] Ibid. fo. 402; for similar petitions from other towns see MS Egerton 1,762, fos 175–8.
[18] MS Prendergast 1, fo. 515.
[19] Ibid. fos 295, 297–8.

Catholics. At the same time the government saw fit to reach a compromise with the Protestant proprietors of the region; it was agreed that they could retain their Catholic tenants until 20 October 1655.[20]

As this deadline approached, a notable development occurred. On 3 October the recently demobilised officers and soldiers who had been granted land in Co. Wexford requested permission to retain Irish labourers, husbandmen and servants 'untill they were better enabled to plant without them'.[21] These were presumably some of the same men who just eight months previously had demanded the 'rooting out' of all the Catholics in their midst. As they metamorphosed from English army officers into Irish landowners, the practical difficulties likely to be posed by the absence of tenants and servants had seemingly become apparent to them. Thus on 19 October 1655 the expulsion of the Catholics was again postponed.[22] The government may have had second thoughts when within days two Protestants were murdered at Lackagh in Co. Kildare.[23] Once the chief perpetrators had been executed and some others had been dispatched to Barbados, attention turned to proposals for 'reducing the said Papists into the true worship of God and the English manners and customs'.[24] The drive to remove all Catholics from the region had gradually evolved into an effort to ensure their conformity to Protestantism. A sumptuary declaration was accordingly issued ordering all Catholics who wished to remain to take an oath abjuring Catholicism, to attend religious services regularly, to forbear from speaking Irish and to adopt English modes of dress.[25]

This shift in policy was not without its critics, the most outspoken of whom was Colonel Richard Lawrence. In 1656 he published *England's great interest in the well planting of Ireland with English people discussed*. This pamphlet elaborated upon some of the ideas that Lawrence had set out in a previous pamphlet, in particular the need for 'considerable intire plantations together' from which Irish people should be excluded. The south-east of Ireland seemed best suited to such a scheme as 'the inlargement of the English nation so near itself, would add much to its strength, riches and reputation, much more than the West Indian Plantations'. Lawrence first claimed that 'the Irish [were] generally removed' from the region, before then admitting that 'much of what is planted in those counties are Irish people, brought in by the proprietors out of other planted counties where they lived'.[26] In other words, rather than becoming a no-go area for Catholics, the five counties had instead become something of a haven for them. They had been transplanting eastwards rather than westwards. Nevertheless,

20 Lord deputy and council, *Whereas the late commissioners … 21 May 1655*, Dublin 1655 (BL, 806.i.14(21)).
21 MS Prendergast 1, fo. 353. For details of the regiments which were assigned land in Co. Wexford in August 1655 see Prendergast, *The Cromwellian settlement*, 216–17.
22 MS Prendergast 1, fo. 358.
23 Ibid. fos 360–1, 363.
24 Ibid. fo. 386.
25 The council, *Whereas by a declaration … [1656]*, Dublin 1656 (BL, 806.i.14(31)); the second page of this declaration containing the date of its issue has not survived. The available evidence suggests that it was probably published around mid-1656.
26 Richard Lawrence, *England's great interest in the well planting of Ireland with English people, discussed*, Dublin 1656, 3, 8–9, 22, 30.

Lawrence persisted with his optimistic arguments, insisting that the area could be 'well planted' with English people within a year if suitable tax breaks and other incentives were offered. He even suggested that the good reputations of Cromwell, Ireton and Fleetwood were dependent on the implementation of such radical initiatives: if the scheme were not enforced 'it [would] be said of them in after ages, they conquered much, but secured little'.[27]

Lawrence's suggestion that Catholics were moving to the south-east appears to be confirmed by a government order dating from June 1656. This recited how 'divers of the said Irish nacion (as is credibly informed) have of late removed themselves and also their families and substance out of the neighbouring counties into the said County of Wicklow'. The area was likely to become 'a nest and sheltering place of loose and dangerous persons'. This was contrary to the government's hope that Co. Wicklow would be 'thoroughly and seasonably planted and inhabited by Protestants of this and the English nation'.[28] The '1659 census' provides further indication that the proposal to transplant all Catholics out of the five counties made little headway. In Co. Kildare Catholics outnumbered Protestants on a ratio of fifteen to one.[29] Nevertheless, throughout the decade some Protestant proprietors remained fearful lest their Catholic tenants would be removed.[30] Such fears were perhaps grounded on an overestimation of the diligence and effectiveness of the officers and officials in the region. In 1659, for example, Robert Thornhill was cashiered from the army for, amongst other offences, 'receiving transplantable papists into the militia' in Co. Wexford.[31] Elsewhere in the same year, the government found it necessary to order the disarming of the Catholic inhabitants of Co. Wicklow.[32] The fact that Catholics had remained in the region and had also kept their weapons helped to lend credence to rumours such as that which emerged in Co. Wicklow in October 1659 of 'some design in hand to massacre the English inhabitants'.[33] Neither the initial plan to transplant all Catholics nor the subsequent proposal to induce their mass conformity to Protestantism had produced any substantial results.

The phenomenon described in both Lawrence's pamphlet and the government's order of June 1656 whereby Catholics were moving into the region, Co. Wicklow in particular, was perhaps attributable to the fact that that county was in effect something of a tax haven. It had been taxed for the first time as late as July 1654 when a levy of £30 per month was imposed.[34] This sum was subsequently reduced to £20, thereby ensuring that the county remained by far the lowest taxed in the country as a whole. Dublin city and county paid taxes of approximately £600 per month; Kildare £233; Wexford £183; and Carlow £83.[35] In this context, despite the poorer quality of much of its land, Wicklow evidently

---

27 Ibid. 30, sig. A2.
28 MS Prendergast 1, fos 494–6.
29 A census of Ireland, circa 1659, ed. Seámus Pender, Dublin 1939, 409.
30 Arthur Annesley to H. Cromwell, London, 22 Mar. 1659, MS Lansdowne 823, fo. 259.
31 MS Prendergast 2, fos 457–8.
32 Ibid. fo. 464.
33 Ibid. fos 453–4.
34 NLI, MS Gilbert 857, fo. 51.
35 The council, A declaration and commission for three months' assessment of £10,000 ... 6 September 1655, Dublin 1655 (BL, 806.i.14(4)), 1–5.

proved attractive to Catholics. It may even have had greater appeal than the fertile plains of Co. Meath. By 1656 the heavy tax burdens imposed on that county were allegedly causing people to flee from there. Catholics, both those transplantable and those not transplantable, and Protestants had reportedly taken themselves and 8,000 cows out of the county 'by reason of the height of the contribution in Meath, and the lowness of it (in comparison) in other places'. The monthly taxes levied on the county had increased sharply, rising from £561 in 1654 to £1,068 in 1656.[36] In this context, the adoption of Lawrence's proposal substantially to reduce taxes in the south-east would probably have encouraged further inward Catholic migration and undermined even more his hopes of attracting English people into the 'empty prepared hive [ready] to receive its swarms'.[37]

Transplantation in the localities

The apparent energy and persistence displayed by the Dublin government between 1655 and 1659 can be contrasted with the seemingly more lethargic approach of many of its officials and officers elsewhere. Even the common policy of imprisoning individuals who refused to transplant was of limited effect because many such people were being protected by Protestants in the localities. From 1655 onwards, the government viewed this phenomenon as one of the major obstacles to the success of the transplantation scheme. In May 1655 it issued a declaration denouncing those Protestants who had leased land from the state and who were retaining 'not only Irish tenants but also several persons that have been active in the first year of the rebellion, and that have been in arms and are proprietors'. In this way, the 'acts of state for removing such persons into Connacht [had] been rendered ineffectual'.[38] Early in the following month, while on a progress to Munster, Fleetwood found that numerous persons in the precincts of Limerick, Cork and Kerry had tenanted their estates with transplantable Catholics. Had he visited other parts of the country, he would no doubt have discovered the same problem elsewhere. This led him wryly to observe that 'the greatest want this nation hath, is a better people'.[39] In July 1655 another declaration threatened court martial proceedings against officers and soldiers who neglected to give up their Catholic servants and tenants.[40] Nevertheless, petitions from Protestants seeking to have Catholics exempted from transplantation continued to be presented. In Ulster, Lord Annandale needed Catholics to work on his estate; elsewhere Philip Bigoe was dependent on Catholic labour to maintain a glasshouse; Captain Staples required twenty Irish men for an iron mill; Thomas Tomkins sought permission to retain forty labourers at his silver mines; and Sir

---

36 Ibid. 2; TCD, MS 844, fos 171–2.

37 Lawrence, *The interest of England*, 3.

38 The lord deputy and council, A *declaration, that all persons holding custodiams, or leases from the state ... 21 May 1655*, Dublin 1655 (BL, 806.i.14(20)).

39 *TSP* iii. 558–9.

40 The lord deputy, *Whereas in pursuance of ... 14 July 1655*, Dublin 1655 (BL, 806.i.14(25)).

Charles Coote needed men for his iron works. Some requests for leniency also came from farther afield; the Bristol merchant Richard Christmas was reliant on the services of Edward Browne, his Irish Catholic servant in the city of Waterford.[41] Evidently, these individuals did not share Fleetwood's concern to 'make this nation of much happyness to future generations' through the removal of Catholics.[42]

The government's correspondence with the governors of the various precincts also sheds some light on the implementation of the transplantation. It would appear that some of these individuals were either totally lacking in initiative or rather simply reluctant to enforce the removal of Catholics. Numerous lists of queries were sent up to Dublin, the contents of which suggest that in many cases the excuses furnished by Catholics for not transplanting were being passed on to the government for resolution. Thus it was forced to consider issues such as 'weak cattle', the fate of 'the very aged and impotent', the 'inconsiderable copyholders' and persons comprehended in various other categories.[43] At the same time, official efforts to measure the overall progress of the transplantation proved ineffective. In August 1656, following an apparent increase in the number of tories, 'to the disturbance of the soe much desired peace and settlement of this nacion', the government ordered all sheriffs and justices of the peace to compile lists of the names, descriptions and places of abode of those transplantable persons who had not yet removed themselves.[44] By the end of the year, the local authorities in many counties had neglected to send in the requested reports. A new deadline of 1 February 1657 was announced, but presumably this too was ignored by some.[45]

One of those who did comply with the government's orders was Lieutenant-Colonel John Hewetson in Co. Kildare. On 6 February 1657 he sent to the council 'a list of such as were proprietors or in arms according to the best of my knowledge ... and many of them dangerous persons'.[46] Unfortunately, Hewetson's list does not survive. However an extant specimen relating to the barony of Orrery and Kilmore in north Co. Cork can perhaps be taken as representative of efforts to identify transplantable persons remaining in the three provinces. This brief list of 'non-transplanters' contained the names and addresses of ten Catholics. Six had been soldiers; the names of the officers under whom they had served were also noted in some cases. All six were noted as having 'never removed'. Two of the four former landowners listed, Francis Stapleton of Faronemaghery and John Lacy of Broghill, had also 'never removed'. The former was now resident at Buttevant, while the latter was reported to be living a short distance away in Co. Limerick. Another former proprietor, John Lombard, had apparently transplanted but had then returned home again. The grounds upon which he had been allowed to do so were unknown to local officials in Co. Cork. The only individual on the list who was described as both a landowner and a

---

[41] MS Prendergast 1, fos 635, 652; MS Prendergast 2, fos 328, 376–7, 279, 399; IUC ii. 371, 456.

[42] TSP iii. 566–7.

[43] MS Prendergast 1, fos 488–92; MS Egerton 1,762, fos 175–6; Prendergast, The Cromwellian settlement, 119–20, 130–1.

[44] MS Prendergast 1, fos 500–1.

[45] Ibid. fo. 503.

[46] John Hewetson to H. Cromwell, Kildare, 6 Feb. 1657, MS Lansdowne 821, fo. 276.

soldier was Robert Magner of Castlemagner. He was noted as having served as commissary-general under Viscount Muskerry in Munster. Magner had reportedly 'removed according to order, but returned with a pass' and was 'now resident at Newtown in the barony of Kilmore'.[47] This was about ten miles north of his former home. There is no evidence to suggest that any of the persons identified in this precise list were afterwards compelled to transplant.

Magner's continued residence in Co. Cork, and the presence of other former soldiers, exemplified the shortcomings apparent in official efforts to implement the transplantation. A separate inquiry conducted by John Read in the precinct of Belturbet led to the identification of three transplanters there who had returned from Connacht with passes. His efforts to identify other transplantable persons were obstructed by local Protestants. Read reported to Henry Cromwell that 'some fewe of mean quality, I am informed there is, but under the notion of servants, and so kept as yet from my knowledge'.[48] It is significant that these inquiries conducted both in north Co. Cork and in south Ulster identified persons who had gone to Connacht and had then returned home again. This is evidence of the government's inability to regulate the granting of dispensations to transplanters by officials located at key crossing points on the Shannon, such as Athlone and Limerick.[49] Moreover, the policy of appointing specific individuals to oversee this process proved unsuccessful, as lower-ranking officers and other individuals regularly issued licences to transplanters.[50] It may be safely presumed that this process involved bribery. An attempt was also made to ensure that transplanters who obtained passes would quickly return again to Connacht by having them enter bonds. This mechanism too proved somewhat ineffective; in March 1656 the substantial sum of £1,623 paid in by transplanters that had crossed into Leinster and had not returned was sent by convoy from Athlone to Dublin.[51]

Another obvious and important factor which deserves some consideration is the understandable reluctance of Catholics to transplant. In July 1655 an observer in Dublin noted that 'the Irish chuse death rather than remove from their wonted habitations'.[52] A year later, the government noted that many Catholics were refusing to transplant; 'some of them out of their desperate and malicious designs [had] taken occasion to run out again into the boggs and wood'.[53] At the same time, petitions for dispensations continued to swamp the government. In certain cases individuals claimed to have conformed to Protestantism; others complained that they were aged, ill, mad, innocent or pregnant. Some sought and obtained the intervention of Oliver Cromwell on their behalf. Vincent Gookin's observation that the Irish were unlikely to transplant 'like geese at the wagging of a hat upon a stick' was correct.[54] This factor combined with those already outlined above to ensure that the government remained

47 BL, MS Egmont 46,937, fos 58–59v.
48 John Read to H. Cromwell, Belturbet, 25 Feb. 1656, MS Lansdowne 821, fo. 101.
49 MS Prendergast 1, fos 222, 227–8, 529–30.
50 Ibid. fo. 449.
51 Ibid. fo. 482.
52 Prendergast, The Cromwellian settlement, 133.
53 MS Prendergast 1, fos 500–1.
54 Gookin, The great case of transplantation, 25.

always dissatisfied with the progress of the transplantation scheme. Nevertheless, their efforts did produce substantial results. These can best be understood by an examination of the work carried out by the transplantation courts at Athlone and Loughrea.

The Athlone court

The Athlone court for hearing and determining the claims of transplanters to land in Connacht was established on 28 December 1654. In the previous month a separate court had been established in Dublin to hear all claims for land in Ireland and it seems likely that some transplanters from counties Dublin, Meath, Kildare and Wicklow did enter claims there.[55] Once the Athlone court had been set up, the transplanters were expected to make their claims before it, and many did so between March 1655 and August 1657. The government initially appointed eight commissioners to the court. These included John Santhy, a judge, and the army officers Lieutenant-Colonels Alexander Brayfield and Robert Doyly. Brayfield was also the governor of Athlone. William Halsey, second justice of Munster, was later added to the commission. The other two commissioners were Thomas Hooke, an alderman of Dublin, and the New Englander Edmund Leach. The latter was also actively involved in a project to settle families from New England in Sligo. The regicide Judge John Cooke was subsequently appointed to the commission in July 1655. Cooke's involvement in official deliberations relating to the Leinster and Galway articles and his role as a commissioner in the court of claims in Dublin meant that his appointment to Athlone added considerably to the level of expertise available. It appears that the three judges, Cooke, Santhy and Halsey were ultimately responsible for over-seeing most of the court's proceedings.[56] In this task they were assisted by a team of at least fifty-five additional clerks and officials.[57]

Although the commissioners were first appointed in December 1654, the preparations for their work did not begin in earnest until some months later. On 1 April 1655 the governor of Athlone was ordered 'to prepare a convenient place in Athlone Castle' for storing the records which were to be sent down from Cork House in Dublin.[58] These records would subsequently become known as the 'Black Books of Athlone'. They included extensive documentation relating to the 1641 rebellion and the Catholic confederation.[59] The findings returned by the delinquency commissioners appointed to each precinct in November 1653 were presumably employed as well. However, as late as February 1656, it was noted that the latter records in respect of ten counties had still not been received at Athlone.[60] The commissioners had also to be furnished with the details of various relevant land surveys. As early as August 1653 a committee had been

---

55 IUC ii. 455–6.
56 MS Prendergast 1, fos 436–41.
57 MS Gilbert 857, fos 90–1, 107.
58 NLI, MS 839, fo. 196.
59 Prendergast, The Cromwellian settlement, 156–7.
60 NLI, MS 11,959, fos 349–51; MS Prendergast 1, fos 397–8.

instructed to seek out 'maps of Connacht and Clare and all other places taken in or since the time of Queen Elizabeth'.[61] It was not until May 1655 that the government became aware that Sir William Parsons had 'perfect surveys of the province of Connacht' in his custody.[62] Parsons's grandfather and namesake had been surveyor general of Ireland in the 1630s and it appears that he kept the Strafford Survey in private custody during the 1640s.[63]

The instructions issued to the Athlone commissioners in December 1654 reflected the haphazard and difficult legislative background to their work. According to the various declarations that had been issued by the government, transplanters' entitlements to land were based either on the terms of articles of surrender or on one of the respective qualifications contained in An Act for the Settling of Ireland.[64] Remarkably, the Athlone commissioners were instructed by the government to determine an individual's right to land by reference to 'the crimes, offences, and misdemeanours' mentioned in the Adventurers' Act of 1642. That legislation had declared forfeit the lands of all those who were or 'shall be in Rebellion, or levie War against the Kings Majestie within his Realm of Ireland, or shall willing aid, assist or countenance any person or persons in rebellion'.[65] By contrast, under the terms of An Act for the Settling of Ireland, involvement in the rebellion was stated to be a capital offence.[66] Had the commissioners been required to judge transplanters by that severe standard alone, they would necessarily have found many people liable to execution rather than adjudged them entitled to life and land in Connacht. Perhaps surprisingly, there is no record of any individual being refused an assignment of land in Connacht on the grounds of involvement in the rebellion. Instead, the criteria laid down in the Adventurers' Act could be employed to find simply that an individual had forfeited their land due to rebellion. The focus then switched either to articles of surrender or the relevant qualifications of An Act for the Settling of Ireland, in order to establish whether the transplanter was entitled to the equivalent of either one-third or two-thirds of his former estate.

The transplanter was first required to prove title to his land and other property, including houses, orchards, outstanding mortgages and fisheries. His claim for land usually concluded with an assertion to the effect that he 'had never acted anything to the prejudice of the English interest'. The commissioners would then assign the case to one of its team of investigators for examination, a process which sometimes took several months. Both the size and value of the transplanters' former estates and their role in the war, if any, had to be established.[67] After all the necessary data had been gathered, the claimant's case came to a 'final hearing'. There were several possible outcomes. Very occasionally, an individual succeeded in establishing their 'constant good affection'. In order to

---

61 MS Prendergast 1, fos 162–3, 172.

62 Ibid. fo. 314.

63 Ibid. fos 325, 329, 337; MS Prendergast 2, fos 421–2; NLI, MS 839, fo. 197.

64 Gardiner, 'The transplantation', 710–15.

65 A collection of acts and ordinances, ed. Henry Scobell, London 1658, 26–31.

66 Acts and ordinances, ii. 598–603.

67 These observations are based upon NLI, MS Pakenham-Mahon 10,125, the most extensive extant collection of documents relating to the claims entered by transplanters. See also NLI, MS Westport 40,893/5(3).

do so, they had to provide 'an account or series of their carriadge or behaviour since the breaking out of the late rebellion until the total reducement of Ireland unto its due obedience'.[68] It appears that having lived and paid taxes in territory under rebel control was a bar to obtaining such a decree. For example, Hugh Wyre of Co. Westmeath had assisted Protestant refugees in 1641 and had been 'plundered by the enemy several times for his adherence to the English'. As 'nothing of delinquency [was] proved against him', Wyre was adjudged to be comprehended within the eighth 'qualification' and he received a decree for two-thirds of his estate 'according to the mercy held forth to recusants not in arms nor otherwise aiding in the late rebellion'.[69]

Perhaps the best known instance of a failure to prove constant good affection was in the case of the Catholics of the southern port towns of Cork, Youghal and Kinsale. These individuals had played no part in the war and had served alongside the Protestant inhabitants in defending their towns. In July 1656 Cooke, Halsey and Santhy travelled to Mallow, Co. Cork to deal with their claims. At Mallow, the claim of Thomas Toomey, a shipwright from Kinsale, was treated as a test case for all of the Catholics concerned. Because Toomey had 'contributed money or victuals not levied by actual force' for the support of Baron Inchiquin's forces after the latter had returned to the royalist side in 1648, he could not be given a decree for constant good affection. The Catholics concerned were appalled by this judgement, declaring that 'they had rather be sent to the Barbados' than Connacht. A compromise was eventually agreed whereby the townsmen of Cork, Youghal and Kinsale were instead granted lands in the nearby baronies of Muskerry and Barrymore in Co. Cork.[70]

Despite the evident strictness of the rules in question, a number of Catholics did manage to prove their constant good affection. William Petty later claimed that twenty-six proprietors had retained a total of 40,000 acres on this account.[71] In January 1656 Colonel John Hewson was obliged to surrender 238 acres to John Connell of Ashtown, Co. Dublin, after the latter had demonstrated his constant good affection.[72] A few months later, Luke Hussey was successful but he was 'left to course of law' to recover his land.[73] The case of Thomas Wallis was somewhat more complicated. After he had obtained his decree of constant good affection at Athlone, 'much of delinquencie hath appeareth' against both his father and his grandfather. Therefore, in June 1656, the Athlone commissioners sought an injunction to prevent Wallis from using his decree as a pretext to recovering his lands.[74] The eventual outcome of this case is not clear. In some other instances the Athlone commissioners dealt sympathetically with cases where they found 'manifestation of a good, but not constant good affection'. In July 1656 the government agreed with their recommendation that four individuals in this cate-

---

[68] MS Prendergast 2, fo. 823.
[69] MS Pakenham-Mahon 10,125.
[70] IUC ii. 604–7; Prendergast, *The Cromwellian settlement*, 164–76.
[71] William Petty, *The political anatomy of Ireland*, London 1691, 3.
[72] MS Prendergast 1, fo. 636.
[73] Ibid. fo. 407.
[74] MS Ferguson 9, fo. 74.

gory should be permitted to reside east of the Shannon while also retaining their transplanters' assignments of land in Connacht.[75]

When the commissioners found that a landowner was transplantable, they proceeded to establish his or her entitlements either under articles of surrender or under the qualifications. Claims under articles of surrender were relatively straightforward because the relevant articles usually stipulated the proportion of land involved. For example, the articles granted to the towns of Limerick and Galway guaranteed two-thirds of their estates to those comprehended therein. Where an individual was not entitled to land under articles, the commissioners had to decide within which of the qualifications they were comprehended. Transplanters who had not played any part in the war were decreed the equivalent of two-thirds of their former estate, while those who were found to be delinquents were decreed the equivalent of one-third. The Athlone court also dealt with widows who were entitled to jointure lands of a certain value during their lifetimes, although the cases of more prominent widows were frequently dealt with by the government itself. The usual outcome here was an order for the widow to have lands in Connacht equal in value to two-thirds of her jointure lands.[76]

The government also found it necessary to intervene on a regular basis to ensure the smooth running of the Athlone court. By May 1655 it had become apparent that among transplantable Catholics 'there [was] not that conformitie and obedience yielded as ought to be'. This led to the first of a number of orders extending the time period for which the commissioners were to sit.[77] The government sought further to expedite proceedings by mitigating the legal fees which transplanters were expected to pay and by permitting impoverished transplanters 'to sue in formê pauperis'.[78] The case of William Kelly of Ballymanagh, Co. Galway, provides a useful example of the costs involved. His Catholic attorney and fellow-transplanter John Hearne obtained an Athlone decree in April 1656 and a final settlement of seventy acres at Loughrea in June 1657. The prosecution of Kelly's case by Hearne cost £7. In February 1658 Kelly sold his assignment to Hearne. As well as clearing his debt, he received an additional £13 for seventy acres of land.[79]

In August 1655, as part of a further effort to speed up proceedings, the Dublin government instructed the commissioners to divide themselves into two teams, to be led by Cooke and Santhy respectively. They were also instructed to allow only one claim per transplanter; claimants had reportedly been 'spinning out the time' by submitting claims for their estates piece meal.[80] Despite these various initiatives, progress was still frustratingly slow and in April 1656 the government saw fit to issue a declaration denouncing 'the backwardness and dilatoriness of

---

75 MS Prendergast 2, fo. 391.

76 See, for example, the documents relating to the case of Ormond's sister Elizabeth Purcell, 1655–6, RIA, MS Purcell 4 A 42.

77 *Whereas by a commission … 23 May 1655*, Dublin 1655 (NAI, M3, 159); MS Prendergast 1, fos 452, 483; *His highness council having taken … 7 April 1656*, Dublin 1656 (BL, 806.i.14(29)).

78 MS Prendergast 1, fo. 270.

79 MSS Hearn of Hearnbrook, James Hardiman Library, Galway, LE 26/65.

80 MS Prendergast 1, fos 341, 367, 380, 395.

the transplantable persons, in entering and prosecuting their claims'. Because of this circumstance, a 'multitude of claims [were as] yet undetermined'.[81] Proceedings were impeded again when Cooke, Halsey and Santhy travelled to Mallow in July 1656 to examine the claims of the Catholic inhabitants of the towns of Cork, Youghal and Kinsale.

The work of the Athlone court can also be assessed through a brief examination of some of the available evidence relating to the number of decrees issued by them. Using the Ormond List, it is possible to date each Athlone decree which was subsequently satisfied by the Loughrea commissioners. The earliest decree recorded was that issued to Hugh and Rose Keogh from Co. Roscommon on 28 March 1655. By the end of that year, around 162 decrees had been issued. However, this was only a fraction of the anticipated number and it is little wonder that the government was dissatisfied at the rate of progress. Progress was much swifter in 1656, with well over 600 decrees being issued in the month of May alone. Numbers were down again in June to around 440, and the departure of the commissioners for Mallow in the following month meant that only seventy more decrees were issued before the end of the year. Approximately thirty further cases were decided in 1657 as the court brought its proceedings to a close.[82] Each transplanter was required to submit the decree which he had obtained at Athlone to a second team of commissioners sitting at Loughrea.

The Loughrea commissioners

In January 1654 the government appointed five commissioners to sit at Loughrea to deal with the expected arrival of large numbers of Catholics bearing transplanters' certificates. They were instructed to assign temporary grants of land to transplanters.[83] Once transplanters began to obtain Athlone decrees in 1655, the Loughrea commissioners were charged with assigning 'final settlements' of land in Connacht. To this end, the government issued a new set of instructions in June 1655. Four of the six men appointed at that time, William Edwards, Charles Holcroft, James Shaen and Henry Greenway, had also been members of the previous commission. The two new members were Sir Charles Coote and Stephen Squibb. At least five of these men were former or current army officers. James Cuffe was initially employed as secretary at Loughrea before he too was subsequently added to the team of commissioners. Staffing levels were much lower at Loughrea and the commissioners were not paid as well as their counterparts in Athlone.[84]

In the course of their work, the Loughrea commissioners pursued a number of strategies designed to simplify the enormous task of land redistribution across a wide area.[85] Yet their job remained a difficult one. Perhaps the greatest challenge that they faced was the inevitable shortage of land available for redistribution.

---

81 *His highness council … 7 April 1656.*
82 'Ormond list'.
83 IUC ii. 387–9.
84 IUC ii. 522–3; MS Gilbert 857, fos 95–6.
85 IUC ii. 522–4, 531, 563, 609–11.

This was caused for the most part by a gradual and substantial reduction in the area designated for transplanters as counties Leitrim, Sligo and part of Mayo were excluded from the transplantation zone.[86] In July 1656 the government attempted to make more land available by reducing the Shannon and Sea Line from three miles to one and reducing the number of garrisons around which land was to be reserved. A previous proposal to establish English plantations in towns such as Gort, Shrule and Ballintobber was also abandoned. Transplanters were to have land around these towns on condition that 'the walls must be pulled down and the places rendered untenable'.[87] A further problem was posed by those individuals who had been leasing formerly reserved lands directly from the state; these proved reluctant to make way for transplanters and refused to pay any rents to them.[88] By July 1657 the number of garrisons in the transplantation zone around which lands were reserved had been reduced to seven. While these alterations did make some more land available, there was still not enough to satisfy all of the decrees which had been issued by the Athlone commissioners, and many transplanters had reportedly been reduced to 'a starving condition'.[89]

In this context, official criticism gradually became focused on the proceedings of the Athlone court and its perceived over-generosity to war-guilty Catholics. They had reportedly 'either through inadvertency or supposing that there would be forfeited lands to spare', decreed 'great stopes of land' to individuals 'who ought not to have [had] any land at all'. In order to address these difficulties, the government proposed that a commission be set up to review the proceedings of the Athlone court and to rectify or reverse its proceedings where necessary.[90] This proposal was not followed through. Simington's analysis of this problem was misguided, as he did not realise the significance of articles of surrender in ensuring that individuals exempted from pardon by the Act for the Settling of Ireland were actually entitled to assignments of land. He cited the cases of a number of Leinster officers and Galway townsmen as examples of land being misappropriated and speculated that some 'secret compromise' had been made with these leading Catholic delinquents.[91]

The scarcity of land in Connacht, their non-judicial backgrounds, and their distance from government supervision together fed into the corruption historically associated with the Loughrea commissioners. Some transplanters, desperate for land or money, either resorted to bribery or consented to sell their entitlements to land at a low price. In November 1656 Robert Mason, one of the clerks at Loughrea, was dismissed and ordered to repay the sixty pounds 'expedition money' which he had accepted from transplanters.[92] Another clerk, Christopher Ormsby, acted as attorney for several transplanters and then subse-

---

86 *IUC* ii. 589, 601, 608; Robert Simington, *The transplantation to Connaught, 1654–1658*, Dublin 1970, p. xxi.
87 *IUC* ii. 609–11; MS Prendergast 1, fos 540–1.
88 MS Prendergast 1, 485.
89 Ibid. fos 540–1; *IUC* ii. 555.
90 *IUC* ii. 647–8.
91 Simington, *Transplantation*, pp. xxiii–xxv.
92 MS Prendergast 1, fo. 482.

quently bought their assignments of land from them. His employment at Loughrea undoubtedly helped to ensure that his clients' decrees were satisfied ahead of others.[93] Most of the Loughrea commissioners were involved in buying land from transplanters.[94] Both James Shaen and Captain Stephen Squibb were dismissed from their posts early in 1656, apparently for granting land to themselves and for oppressing transplanters. Squibb had been able to arrange a seven-year lease for himself of the castle and lands at Glinsk in east Galway, while Shaen was involved in the seemingly common practice of buying unsatisfied Athlone decrees from transplanters and then attempting to ensure that the entitlement would be satisfied with lands of good quality.[95] It would have been relatively easy for an official such as Shaen to block a transplanter's claim from proceeding at Loughrea until he agreed to sell his entitlements at a low rate. In the 1970s Timothy Cronin found that 'the bribery was such that three hundred years later, it [was] still being talked about in Roscommon folklore, and an O'Hanly still points to a bit of land which he lost to an O'Connor "who bribed the official in Loughrea"'.[96]

Despite the level of corruption, the Loughrea commissioners did make considerable progress in assigning land and their success can be gauged using evidence from the Ormond List. This source lists only two final settlements made in 1655. Substantial proceedings finally got underway in April 1656 when around eighty-seven grants were made. In both 1656 and 1657, the vast majority of grants were made in the summer and early autumn. In August 1657 alone, close to 100,000 acres were disposed of.[97] In order to establish reasonably accurate figures for the number of transplanters who received land and the total quantity of acres assigned by the Loughrea commissioners, it is necessary to consolidate the data in the Ormond List and also to incorporate some additional information relating to transplanters not included in that source. The Ormond List contains approximately 2,025 entries. However when duplicate entries and multiple final settlements to single individuals are accounted for, the number of transplanters who received land can be estimated at around 1,815. In the 1670s William Petty estimated the amount of land assigned to transplanters at 700,000 acres. Simington provided a figure around 701,000.[98] The use of technology that was not available either to Petty or Simington confirms that their total figures are essentially accurate; the amount of land recorded as assigned to transplanters by the Loughrea commissioners was approximately 700,000 acres.

Simington's breakdown of the total acreages granted to transplanters from east and west of the Shannon respectively is also generally accurate. Transplanters from within the four-county transplantation zone acquired 38 per cent of the

[93] Ormsby's dealings are detailed in the Ormsby of Ballinamore papers, private collection, NLI Microfilm P. 8,502.

[94] MS Prendergast 2, fos 421–2; *Blake family records, 1300–1700*, ed. Martin Blake, London 1902–5, ii. 214; IRC, *Fifteenth report*, London 1825, 102, 189, 203, 233.

[95] IUC ii. 569–70; MS Prendergast 2, fos 368–9, 418–19, 934–6.

[96] Timothy Cronin, 'The foundations of landlordism in the barony of Athlone', unpubl. MA diss. NUI Galway 1977, 271.

[97] 'Ormond list'.

[98] Ibid; Simington, *Transplantation*, p. xvi; Petty, *The political anatomy of Ireland*, 3.

land redistributed. The inclusion of transplanters from counties Sligo and Leitrim brings the percentage of land assigned to proprietors from west of the Shannon to 40 per cent of the total; approximately 280,000 acres. These local transplanters numbered around 1,025 and received an average of almost 275 acres each. Approximately half of these transplanters originated in Co. Galway alone; individuals originating in that county acquired around 171,000 acres. The roughly 790 transplanters from east of the Shannon were on average assigned estates of around 530 acres. All counties except Donegal and Fermanagh were represented. The province of Ulster produced just twenty-five transplanters. These were assigned almost 34,800 acres. The 395 transplanters from Munster acquired around 178,500 acres, while 379 individuals from Leinster were assigned some 210,000 acres.[99]

An understanding of the transplantation can perhaps be improved by a brief overview of some figures relating to the sizes of the estates created under the scheme. Approximately 397 transplanters received fifty acres or less. This group made up around 22 per cent of the total number of transplanters but they acquired only 2 per cent of the land redistributed. Over 80 per cent of these small grants were assigned to transplanters originating within the four counties of the transplantation zone. Indeed, local transplanters predominated among the large numbers of people granted estates of 200 acres or less. Estates of between 201 and 500 acres were granted to 393 individuals; these grants represented almost 133,500 acres. Here the balance shifted decisively in favour of the newcomers; they were assigned two-thirds of these medium-sized grants. At the top end of the scale were the 139 individuals who received more than 1,000 acres. This group, around 7 per cent of all transplanters, acquired half of the land assigned under the scheme. Fifty-one of these substantial proprietors originated within the four counties of the transplantation zone. Inevitably, the merchant townsmen of Galway who had acquired extensive estates in Connacht before 1641 were predominant within this group of locals.[100]

This pattern of land redistribution reflected several circumstances. There had been a large number of small Catholic proprietors in Connacht before 1641, Gaelic Irish and Old English, with many holding less than 100 acres.[101] Landholding in the west was far more fragmented than in areas east of the Shannon where plantation schemes and various other historic factors had produced both a much greater degree of estate consolidation and a generally lower level of Catholic proprietorship. Kevin McKenny has calculated that, in 1641, 2,519 of Ireland's 6,756 Catholic landowners held land in the four counties later designated for transplanters.[102] Had the Strafford plantation of Connacht gone ahead as proposed in the 1630s, all proprietors of less than 100 acres would

99   'Ormond list'; Simington, *Transplantation*, p. xvi.
100   'Ormond list'.
101   For landholding in Connacht see *Books of survey and distribution*, ed. Robert Simington, Dublin 1949–67.
102   Kevin McKenny, 'The restoration land settlement in Ireland: a statistical interpretation', in Coleman Dennehy (ed.), *Restoration Ireland*, Aldershot 2008, 40–3. McKenny's total figure of 7,798 landowners in Ireland in 1641 is presumably somewhat inflated by the fact that numerous individuals held land in more than one county.

have lost their lands.[103] In the 1650s these numerous individuals on the spot in Connacht were understandably keen to enter a claim at Athlone in the hope of retaining at least part of their old estates. Many of them evidently did so successfully. A proprietor of an equivalent estate in the other three provinces most likely did not have to bear the brunt of government attempts to cajole Catholics into transplanting. Instead, much of its attention was focused on significant proprietors who had played leading roles in the war, such as the Leinster officers. An individual who could expect to obtain an assignment of perhaps only fifty acres in Connacht might have preferred to stay at home and to attempt an accommodation with the new owner of his former estate.

The redistribution of 700,000 profitable acres under the transplantation scheme represented a substantial achievement, even within the context of what was attempted in Ireland in the 1650s. The number of acres involved was greater than that granted in either of the previous plantations of Munster or Ulster.[104] However, while the amount of land assigned by the Loughrea commissioners is obviously an important gauge of the scope and effect of the transplantation, some other relevant figures have been generally overlooked. The most significant shortcoming in the total figures available relates to the number of Athlone decrees left unsatisfied and the quantity of acres involved here. It is important to note that the shortage of land in Connacht ensured that not every transplanter who obtained an Athlone decree actually received an assignment of land at Loughrea. After 1660 Catholics estimated that transplanters had experienced a shortfall of 156,000 acres.[105] It is impossible to determine how much of this land was due to transplanters whose decrees were partially satisfied and how much of it was claimed by unidentifiable individuals who received no land at all. It may not be unreasonable to estimate that the addition of these proprietors would have brought the number of transplanters close to the figure of 2,000. If the post-1660 figure of a deficiency of 156,000 acres is accepted, it can be estimated that transplanters claimed roughly 850,000 acres of land in Connacht in the 1650s. This figure equated to a fraction of their pre-war estates, which can hardly have been less than 2,000,000 profitable acres in extent.

Two groups which featured prominently, first in the sights of the government as it sought to implement the transplantation and then as recipients of land in Connacht, were Sir Robert Talbot and his fellow Leinster officers and the townsmen of Galway. The significant feature common to both cases was the disputes with the government relating to their respective entitlements under articles of surrender agreed in 1652. From the point of view of the authorities, these groups posed contrasting but equally serious difficulties. The Leinster officers were substantial landowners with significant military experience and therefore they could not reasonably be permitted to reside east of the Shannon. The Galway townsmen were already west of the Shannon but their continued residence in a strongly fortified port on the Atlantic coast would pose a considerable

---

103 HMC, *Egmont manuscripts*, i. 105–6.
104 Canny, *Making Ireland British*, 208–9.
105 MS Gilbert 198, fo. 226.

threat to the security of the country. The government's attempts to resolve these issues merit some further examination.

The Galway townsmen and transplantation

Following the abject failure of Geoffrey Browne's mission on their behalf to London in 1653, the Galway townsmen sought to reach a satisfactory accommodation with the authorities in Dublin. In July 1654 their agents, Sir Richard Blake and Patrick Kirwan, were granted permission to reside in Dublin while the articles of Galway were under consideration.[106] Eventually, in February 1655, the government approved the appointment of three lawyers to act as counsel for Blake: Sir James Barry, John Bysse, the recorder of Dublin, and Blake's fellow Galway man Patrick Darcy.[107] This may be the only instance of a Catholic being officially appointed to act as legal counsel in Ireland during the 1650s. A few months later, in June 1655, the government refused to permit another Galway lawyer, Christopher French, to represent transplanters in the transplantation court at Athlone.[108] Despite these preparations, the government did not devote any great attention to the issue of the Galway articles until the summer of 1655.[109]

The fate of the Galway townsmen hinged on the fifth article of the surrender terms negotiated in April 1652. This clause guaranteed to them two-thirds of their extensive lands beyond the town and all of their real and personal estates within the town itself. It also stipulated that

> in case any part of their said real estates shall happen to be contiguous to any castle, fortification, or straigth within this Dominion conceived to be necessary for any particular plantation, that then such person or persons (proprietors of the same) shall be satisfied and paid (in case there be castles and houses upon the land so taken from them) shall be paid the full value of such castles and houses.[110]

As early as May 1652, in response to government dismay at his perceived generosity, Sir Charles Coote had suggested that the townsmen might be willing to give up their homes if a declaration were issued forbidding Catholic residence in garrisons, of which Galway was one.[111] However this recommendation was not adopted and instead the terms of the fifth article remained at the core of the dispute between the government and the townsmen up to 1655.

Something of the townsmen's outlook is revealed by the content of a surviving undated draft petition which may be a copy of that presented by Sir Richard Blake on their behalf in 1655.[112] This recited how the inhabitants of the town of

---

106 NLI, MS 11,959, fos 396–7; IUC ii. 461.
107 MS Prendergast 1, fo. 331.
108 Ibid. fo. 267.
109 Ibid. fos 331–2.
110 IUC i. 163–6.
111 IUC i. 192.
112 NAI, MS Blake of Ballyglunin M6,935/64. The content of this manuscript indicates that it relates to proceedings in 1655. However, as it was addressed to 'the commissioners'

Galway had for 'upwards of four hundred years performed the English interest in this corporation, not withstanding the several rebellions in this nation, till the late general defection'. The townsmen also confessed to 'being totally destroyed, in our personal fortunes, caused by the length of the warres, decay of trade, the present pestilence and so many late payments by us made'. In such difficult and unrelenting circumstances, it is perhaps not surprising that the townsmen announced that they were prepared, upon certain terms, to surrender their 'houses, house rooms, lands, mortgages and interest within the town of Galway, liberties and fishing thereof'.[113] Their main demand was for grants of profitable land in full compensation for their urban property, 'or monie in lew thereof at election of the person'. This land was to be located adjacent to their existing estates. They also expressed the hope that 'the cheerful submission of ours in that which is most dear to us' would ensure favourable treatment in the future.[114]

The government's response to these requests was contained in a declaration issued on 23 July 1655. It invoked clauses in the fifth article and declared that the town of Galway was for the future to be both a garrison and 'a plantation for persons of the English nation'. Therefore the Catholic population was to remove from the town by 1 November. The town was to be surveyed and proprietors were to be compensated with 'other houses and lands of equal value and goodness with their own ... or otherwise satisfied for the same'. Both the government and the townsmen were to appoint 'indifferent men' to conduct the required valuation.[115] The townsmen's readiness to comply with these conditions is suggested by the fact that, within a month, they had nominated two men for the task of surveying.[116] Two further months passed before the government nominated the then governor of Galway, Colonel Richard Lawrence, and Thomas Richardson as its surveyors. On 30 October they were instructed to allow a period of one year during which any townsmen who desired to sell their houses privately to Protestants would be allowed to do so.[117] At the same time Sir Charles Coote was ordered to oversee the clearance of the town.[118] By mid-November Henry Cromwell could report to Thurloe in London that 'Wee have cleared the towne of Galloway of the Irish; and shall have a speciall care of that place.'[119]

In another letter to Thurloe, in January 1656, Henry Cromwell returned to the issue of Galway, describing it as 'the strongest towne in the 3 nations'. He lamented that 'at present there [were] not six familyes in it' and recommended that some London merchants should be granted property in the town, rent free if necessary.[120] Thereafter, Major Anthony Morgan was dispatched to London to inform Oliver Cromwell that 'the houses [were] likely to drop down for want of

---

rather than to the lord deputy and council, it may have been drawn up no later than August 1654.

113 Ibid.
114 Ibid.
115 *IUC* ii. 534–5.
116 NLI, MS 839.
117 *IUC* ii. 543–6.
118 *IUC* ii. 546–7.
119 *TSP* iv. 198.
120 *TSP* iv. 483.

inhabitants'.[121] Henry Cromwell's search for a solution to the Galway problem led eventually to the granting of property in the town to the corporation of Gloucester. In 1653 the parliament had provided for the grant of Irish land worth £10,000 to Gloucester in compensation for the loss of property which had been destroyed during a royalist siege in 1642.[122] In promoting the proposal to satisfy this entitlement with property in Galway, Henry Cromwell argued that

> there never was a fitter time than now for such an undertaking. And forasmuch as the plantation and settling manufactures in that town is not a work for any private interests, but a society to undertake; considering likewise of what publick advantage Londonderry was, not only to the civilizing and securing Ulster, but the whole nation, when in the late rebellion only that place and Dublin stood free from the power of the Irish rebels.[123]

As Henry Cromwell recognised, the precedent set by the granting of Londonderry to the London companies as part of the Ulster plantation seemed particularly pertinent to the case of Galway in the 1650s. That Protestant bastion had held firm against all assaults during the 1640s, and it would do so again more memorably in 1689. On the other hand, Reuben Easthorp, a Protestant settled in Galway, was lukewarm about this plan as he expected that very few people from Gloucester would actually move to Galway. He painted a gloomy portrait of the town: 'Galway sitteth in the dust and no eye pittieth her, her merchants were princes & great among the nations, but now the city that was full of people is solitary & very desolate'.[124] The prevalence of Baptists and Quakers also perturbed Easthorp: 'I do believe men will as soon choose to live under the Turcks as under the power of these.'[125] Despite this pessimism on the spot, by February 1658 houses in Galway worth over £1,500 per annum, over 750 acres adjacent to the town and further land in Co. Mayo had been assigned to Gloucester.[126] By April 1658 a further proposal from the Irish government to grant yet more Galway property to the inhabitants of Liverpool had been approved by Oliver Cromwell.[127] In 1661 it was reported that 'there are about 200 English families, Protestants, planted in Ballinrobe, Galway and Mayo, from Gloucester and Liverpool'.[128] At the same time, some Catholics continued to reside in the town of Galway throughout the decade. As late as August 1659, amidst growing fears of military unrest, the governor Colonel Thomas Sadlier was ordered to remove all Catholics.[129]

121 MS Prendergast 1, fo. 467.
122 Acts and ordinances, ii. 722–53; Hardiman, History of Galway, appendix vii, pp. xxxvi–xlii.
123 TSP vi. 208–9.
124 Reuben Easthorp to H. Cromwell, Galway, 17 July 1657, MS Lansdowne 822, fos 154–6.
125 Easthorp to H. Cromwell, Galway, 11 June 1657, ibid. fo. 86.
126 Hardiman, History of Galway, appendix vii, pp. xxxvi–xlii.
127 The lord protector to the lord deputy and council, Whitehall, 20 Apr. 1658, MS O'Renehan 2, fo. 626.
128 CSPI, 1660–1662, 325.
129 MS Prendergast 2, 450; MS Prendergast 1, 498.

By that date, many of the Galway townsmen had been assigned land as transplanters. The data available in the Ormond List reveals just under 140 transplanters from Galway, 7 per cent of the total number. These were assigned around 112,000 acres. Numerous Galway merchants had acquired large estates in Connacht before 1641 through purchase and mortgage transactions. The considerable size of some of those estates is indicated by the fact that twenty-six townsmen were assigned more than 1,000 acres. Perhaps more remarkably, five Galway townsmen were among the ten transplanters who acquired above 5,000 acres. Most of the acres assigned to the townsmen were given in satisfaction of the two-thirds of their individual landed estates to which they were entitled under the articles of Galway. Some also presumably received lands in lieu of the urban property which they had surrendered. However, more than twenty years later, several of the transplanted townsmen were still complaining that they had never received any land or compensation for what they had lost in the town. In 1676 Marcus Browne petitioned the English privy council on this issue.[130] There was most likely not enough Connacht acres available to recompense Browne and his fellow townsmen for the surrender of their strong stone houses.

Among those required to surrender their property in the town was the lawyer Patrick Darcy. In November 1656 Darcy availed of the opportunity given to the townsmen to sell their urban property to Protestants. He conveyed 'his late mansion stone house' and other property to Arthur Jones, Viscount Ranelagh. Two contradictory pieces of evidence relating to this transaction have survived. An entry in a calendar of deeds enrolled during the 1650s records that Ranelagh paid Darcy £300 for his property. The content of another indenture of the same date suggests that Ranelagh simply agreed to hold the property in trust for the Darcys. Patrick's only daughter Claire was assigned the profits accruing from the property towards her marriage portion of £100. However, if she married in accordance with the wishes of her father, Ranelagh, and the Protestant Sir Maurice Eustace, her portion was to increase to £500. Once these obligations had been satisfied, the profits from the property were to be assigned to other members of the Darcy family.[131] While Patrick Darcy was presumably forced to quit his residence in the town, this neat arrangement allowed his family to continue to derive some benefit from it. Some other townsmen probably reached similar arrangements with co-operative Protestants. One possible example of such an arrangement was the sale by Sir Roebuck Lynch of his house on High Street to Sir Charles Coote, also for £300.[132] The strategy employed by Darcy prefigured that which would be employed by many Catholics in the eighteenth century as they sought to circumvent the penal laws concerning Catholic proprietorship.

The quantities of land assigned to the former inhabitants of Galway ranged from the two acres granted to Katherine Quirke to the 10,393 acres assigned to the former leading confederate Sir Richard Blake. Blake was the second most substantial transplanter overall.[133] While active in Dublin as agent for the townsmen in 1654–5, he had also pursued his own private interests. In a petition

---

130 'Ormond list'; BL, MS Stowe 210, fo. 358; Blake of Ballyglunin papers, M6,935/73(2).
131 NAI, D 20,681; NAI, MS 1A 52 42, fos 21–2.
132 NAI, MS 1A 52 42, fo. 31.
133 'Ormond list'.

which he presented to the government in July 1655, Blake requested a grant of the lands of Ardfry on the coast south of Galway, the 'inheritance of his family since Edward I', as well as Tirellan castle and lands close to Galway which had been formerly leased to him by the marquis of Clanricarde. He produced certificates which recited how he had been 'very serviceable unto the English' in 1641 and that 'his carriage hath been very well to the English since his submission'. It was also reported 'that when he was in the town of Gallway att the time the same was besieged, that he desired to come out of the town of Galway by attempting to leap over the wall to the English but it was thought adviseable to continue longer in that place that he might be the more serviceable to the Commonwealth interest'. Blake also professed himself willing to plant 'with English and Protestants' any lands which might be granted to him within the reserved areas along the coast or around the town of Galway. A high-powered committee of five army officers, suitably impressed by Blake's apparent enthusiasm for high-jumping and Protestant plantations, approved his request for land. The five included Sir Charles Coote, who was presumably able to confirm Blake's instrumental role in the surrender of the town.[134]

It is evident that the Galway townsmen maintained their prominent position as proprietors in Connacht by securing a considerable quantity of land under the transplantation scheme in accordance with their articles of surrender. The estates assigned to them represented 40 per cent of all the land granted to proprietors from west of the Shannon and two-thirds of the total granted to individuals from Galway town and county.[135] During the 1650s and after the Restoration the Catholic townsmen continued as before to acquire land from others through mortgage and purchase.[136] A further set of articles of surrender, those negotiated with the Williamite forces in 1691, ensured that transplanted families such as Blake, Lynch and Martin would prevail as substantial landlords in the west of Ireland over the following centuries.

The Leinster officers

In common with the Galway townsmen, the Leinster officers had initially placed their hopes in the authorities in London. Back in Dublin, towards the end of 1654 the government's determination to transplant them intensified. Early in 1655 it announced what it considered to be the final verdict on the issue. Those Leinster officers exempted from pardon by name in An Act for the Settling of Ireland were to transplant to Connacht by 14 April, after which time they would receive lands equivalent to one-third of their former estates.[137] While Sir Robert Talbot continued his endeavours in London on their behalf, four other former officers, Sir Richard Barnewall, John Bellew, Patrick Netterville and Laurence Dowdall, reacted by petitioning both the Irish government and the English army

---

134 NLI, MS 11,961, fos 99, 170–1.
135 'Ormond list'; Simington, *Transplantation*, p. xvi.
136 See, for example, the various deeds and conveyances in Blake of Ballyglunin papers, M6,931.
137 MS Bellew of Mountbellew 31,966.

officers with whom they had negotiated at Kilkenny in 1652. In March 1655 they quoted chapter and verse from the Old Testament in an effort to persuade the army officers in question to intervene. They invoked Psalm xv which taught that those who desired to live in the sanctuary of the lord were required to keep their oaths and promises. More significant was the Leinster officers' attempt to portray themselves as the Irish equivalent of the Gibeonites. The Gibeonites had tricked Joshua into agreeing to a treaty which allowed them to remain in residence in Canaan, subsequently becoming 'hewers of wood and drawers of water' for the Israelites. This metaphor implied recognition of the English conquerors of Ireland as its rightful proprietors. When Joshua's successor Saul had broken the agreement with the Gibeonites, God had severely punished his people. The inference was clear: God would inflict dreadful punishments on the English for forcing the Leinster officers into the wilderness of Connacht. They insisted that 'your petitioner's removall from their habitations, being a people consumed and reduced to that extremitie and want, as if driven they may say from the coast of Isarell (Samuel 2 Chapt 21 verse 5) must of necessitie perish'. An endorsement on this petition noted only that the officers being addressed did 'not think fitt to take any further notice thereof'.[138] The Leinster officers' foray into biblical exegesis had failed dismally. Other petitions submitted to the lord deputy and council also had little effect.[139]

The increasing likelihood that the Leinster officers would have little option but to transplant served to undermine their previously united approach. Their former commanding officer, the earl of Westmeath, eventually broke rank and resorted to an individual plea for clemency. In a petition to the government he presented his case as 'so different from all other Catholics of this nation'. He emphasised that he had been underage and out of the country in 1641, that he had 'attended to the advancement and interests of England', and that he had been strongly opposed to both to the Ulster commander Owen Roe O'Neill and the papal nuncio GianBattista Rinnucini.[140] There was some logic to Westmeath's arguments. His elderly grandfather had been mortally wounded by the rebels in 1642 and his grandmother's 1641 deposition reported losses of £20,000. Westmeath himself had not returned from England until after the first cessation of hostilities between the royalists and the Irish Catholics in 1643.[141] However, his protests too were in vain. On 17 May 1655 the government gave Westmeath licence to travel to Connacht with two servants, horses and travelling arms 'in order to his transplantation'.[142]

By June 1655 the Leinster officers had accepted their fate and had proceeded to Athlone. The evident need to ensure that they were suitably accommodated in Connacht was perhaps the primary reason why Fleetwood also made the same journey west from Dublin in that month. Conscious of Cromwell's particular

---

138 Ibid.
139 Ibid.
140 John Ainsworth and Edward MacLysaght, 'Nugent papers', *Analecta Hibernica* xx (1958), 126–215 at p. 148.
141 ODNB, *s.v.* 'Nugent, Richard, second earl of Westmeath (1626–1684)'; TCD, MS 817, fos 22–3.
142 MS Prendergast 1, fo. 320.

interest in the case of the Leinster officers, he reported back to Thurloe on proceedings at Athlone: 'The earle of Westmeath and most of the considerable gentry of Lemster were there; and that done by us in order to theire settlement will, I hope, (for the future, as well as it seemed to doe for the present) give them satisfaction.'[143] On 19 June a number of the leading Leinster officers were granted estates 'de bene esse', that is, on a provisional basis until their actual entitlements to land were established. During his time at Athlone, Fleetwood also dealt with a number of other outstanding issued relating to the Leinster officers, including a request from Baron Trimleston, John Bellew and Patrick Netterville for permission 'to pass and repass the bridge' at Athlone.[144]

Over the following years, many of the Leinster officers were granted considerable estates in Connacht; around twenty of them acquired more than 1,000 acres. The earl of Westmeath secured the largest estate granted to a transplanter at 11,574 acres. Sir Robert Talbot and Henry O'Neill joined him among the ten most substantial transplanters with 6,030 acres and 5,333 acres respectively. Laurence Dowdall (4,858 acres) and Sir Thomas Nugent (4,273) were also prominent, while Sir Richard Barnewall and Patrick Netterville obtained decrees for 2,500 and 1,407 acres respectively.[145]

None the less, the Leinster officers were among those Catholics who understandably remained deeply discontented with the implementation of the transplantation scheme. Their main ground for complaint was the apparent shortage of land west of the Shannon. As late as 1659 Sir Robert Talbot was present in London at the head of the tireless Irish Catholic lobby. In that year it was expected that the restored Rump parliament would pass fresh legislation relating to the Irish land settlement. This expectation led Talbot and Colonel Garret Moore jointly to present two petitions to the parliament.[146] Moore, a landowner in Co. Mayo, was among the Connacht officers promised equal treatment with their Leinster comrades under articles of surrender agreed in July 1652. He was assigned almost 3,000 acres as a transplanter.[147] A newsletter written in London at the end of June 1659 noted that Moore had recently arrived in the city and that he was 'joined in [a] commission with Sir R. Talbot from the Irish Catholics'.[148]

Talbot and Moore's first petition was presented at the door of the Commons 'on behalf of themselves and the distressed Irish, Submittees upon Articles of War, and others who are to have a certain proportion of their estates by the Act for Settling of Ireland'. This document recited how, in submitting to the parliament, the Catholics 'did readily subject and put their Consciences, Lives and Fortunes as in a Secure Sanctuary [and had] ever since walked in due conformity to the Government, without the least defection therein'. This was despite the

143 *TSP* iii. 566–7.
144 MS Prendergast 1, fos 245, 248; NLI, MS 11,961, fos 1, 7, 18, 28–9.
145 'Ormond list'.
146 The details of their lobbying in London in 1659 are recited in Boyle, *The answer of a person of quality*, 19–27.
147 *IUC* i. 236–9; 'Ormond list'.
148 *Calendar of the Clarendon state papers*, iv. 254.

fact that 'No Christian nation [could] parallel the sufferings of the petitioners' since the expulsion of the parliament by Cromwell in April 1653. Talbot and Moore informed the parliament that 'rather than ravel into the settlement', they would hereafter 'willingly acquiesce in the Transplantation'. They also requested that some provision be made for Catholics in the new legislation relating to Irish land.[149] These sentiments were echoed in their second petition, in which they also claimed that 'absence, poverty, and the short sitting of the Court for the adjudication of Claims [at Athlone]' had prevented many transplanters from prosecuting their claims.[150]

The content of these petitions suggests that, by the end of the decade, at least some leading transplanters were resigned to their fate and were attempting to ensure for themselves a secure future as landowners in Connacht. The defiance of the Leinster officers in the face of transplantation, so evident in 1653–5, had seemingly been dissipated. Although they requested more land, Talbot and Moore must have known that there was little or none still available in Connacht. At the very least therefore, their petitions must have been designed to ensure that transplanters would not be deprived of the approximately 700,000 acres already granted to them.

In attempting between 1655 and 1659 to implement the transplantation scheme, the central government struggled to achieve its objectives in Dublin and the south-east and elsewhere in the country. Both its drive to remove all Catholics from the south-east and its efforts elsewhere to transplant landowners and soldiers soon encountered significant obstacles. Apart from the inevitable reluctance exhibited by Catholics, the widespread resistance of Protestant landowners, both old and new, and the lack of enthusiasm for the scheme among many local officers and officials combined to limit its effectiveness. The progress reports compiled by some diligent officers served only to confirm this reality. In this context, repeated threats of imprisonment, transportation and even execution for Catholics, and of cashiering for army officers, were not enough to induce general compliance. Some of those Catholics who went to Connacht quickly returned home again while some others flocked to those counties where taxes were either very low or altogether avoidable.

None the less, the substantial legal and administrative workload completed by the commissioners at Athlone and Loughrea demonstrates that despite the range of difficulties which existed, the implementation of the transplantation scheme must be considered as relatively successful. Between 1655 and 1657 up to 2,000 Catholic landowners engaged with the framework that had been put in place to oversee their resettlement in Connacht. Pre-war holdings west of the Shannon were carved up, and around 700,000 acres were redistributed among more than 1,000 local proprietors and a smaller number of newcomers. However, the limited stock of land, as well as a degree of corruption at Loughrea, ensured that not all were ultimately satisfied with estates. Among those who fared best were the Galway townsmen and the Leinster officers. Their cases further demonstrate the

149 Boyle, *The answer of a person of quality*, 19–21.
150 Ibid. 21–2.

nature of the problems with which the government had to contend, as well as revealing the determination of certain well-organised Catholic groups to secure the best possible outcome in what were generally disastrous circumstances. The two Catholic agents active in London in 1659, while dissatisfied with several aspects of the transplantation, evidently saw the scheme as providing a solid base for continued Catholic landownership into the future. As events unfolded in the months that followed, they would switch their focus from preserving the transplantation to arguing instead for the full recovery of their former estates under their restored monarch, Charles II.

5

Transplantation in County Roscommon

The redistribution of land under schemes of plantation and transplantation was to be the main legacy of the Cromwellian period in Ireland. These processes entailed a drastic reduction in Catholic proprietorship, from around 61 per cent of the land of Ireland in 1641 to less than 10 per cent by the end of the 1650s.[1] These figures provide a stark indication of the extent to which Irish landed society was transformed. In order to comprehend the practical consequences of this revolution at the local and familial level, it is necessary to select and zoom in on one section of the map of Cromwellian Ireland.[2] This chapter will explore how the transplantation scheme impacted on landownership patterns in Co. Roscommon. The process of land redistribution in question can be broken down into four parts. First, it is necessary to establish how much land was reserved around towns and garrisons and in the proposed *cordon sanitaire* along the river Shannon intended to insulate Protestant Ireland from Catholic Connacht. The transplanters themselves can be arranged for the purposes of analysis into two groups: the local existing landowners; and the incomers from other counties. Many transplanters quickly sold their assignments of land to another group which would subsequently become known as the Connacht Protestant purchasers. This unplanned aspect of the transplantation played a key role in reconstituting the profile of landholding in Connacht up to 1660. Some context for the changes which occurred in the 1650s can be established by sketching briefly a picture of the landowners of Co. Roscommon prior to the 1641 rebellion.

Before the storm

The boundaries of Co. Roscommon are formed approximately by the river Shannon and its lakes to the east, its tributary the river Suck to the west, and the Curlew mountains to the north. It shape has changed little since the sixteenth

---

[1] John Gerald Simms, 'Land owned by Catholics in Ireland in 1688', *IHS* vii (1957), 180–90 at p. 189; McKenny, 'The restoration land settlement', 39. McKenny's calculations produced a figure of 66% for Catholic landownership in 1641.
[2] Laurence Arnold, 'The Cromwellian settlement of County Dublin, 1652–1660', *Journal of the Royal Society of Antiquaries of Ireland* ci (1971), 146–53; John Cunningham, 'Cromwellian County Mayo', in Gerald Moran and Kieran Rankin (eds), *Mayo: history and society* (forthcoming).

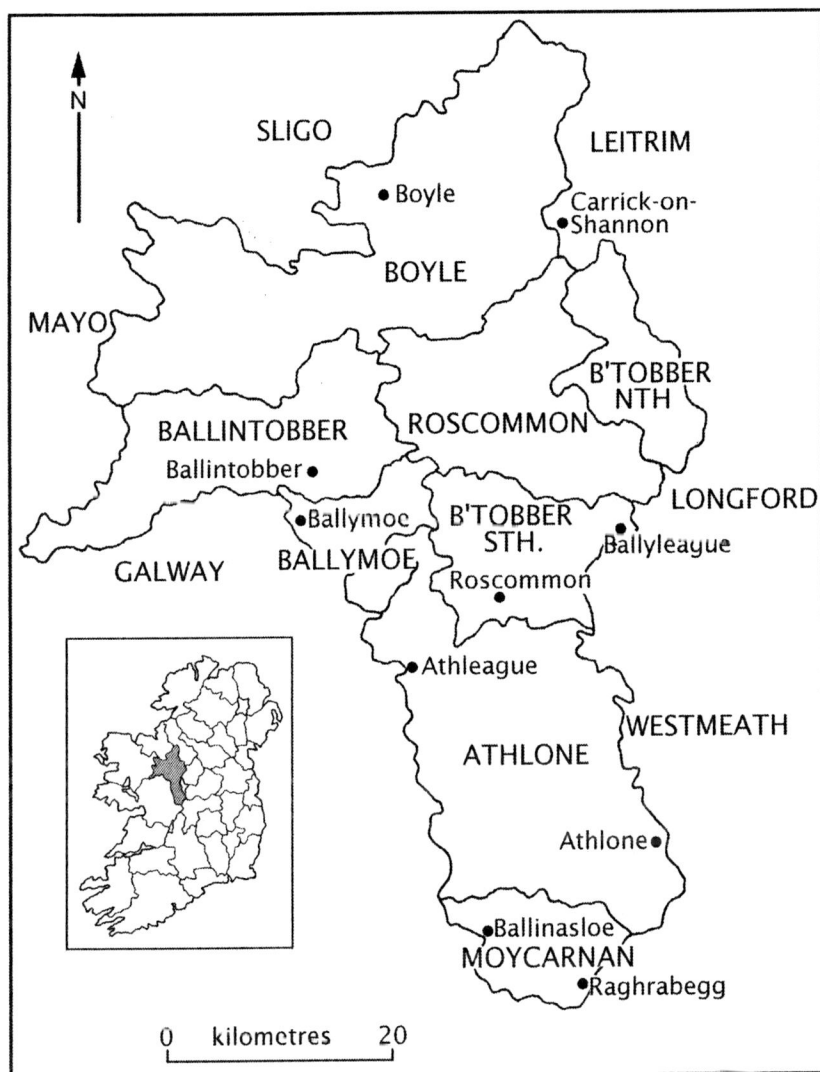

Map 2. County Roscommon in the seventeenth century

century, when the county was shired under the government of Sir Henry Sidney.[3]
At that time most of the county was controlled by Gaelic families; the Kellys in
the south, the McDermot kingdom of Moylurg in the north and the rival families
of O'Connor Don and O'Connor Roe in between. The Old English McDavid
Burke territory of Clanconway also incorporated part of the west of the county.[4]

---

3   Gerard Hayes-McCoy, 'The completion of the Tudor conquest and the advance of the
counter-reformation, 1571–1603', in Moody, Martin and Byrne, A new history of Ireland, iii.
101.
4   See map by Kenneth Nicholls ibid. 2–3.

From south to north, the six baronies which made up the county were Moycarnan, Athlone, Ballymoe, Roscommon, Ballintobber and Boyle. In the mid-1630s Strafford's surveyors found that the county contained approximately 195,000 Irish plantation acres of profitable land.[5]

Of this land the Strafford Survey recorded almost 12 per cent, some 22,644 acres, as belonging to the Anglican Church of Ireland. Almost two-thirds of this was attached to the bishopric of Elphin, with those of Meath, Clonfert and Tuam holding smaller amounts.[6] The lands attached to the lord presidency of Connacht, a provincial governorship established in 1569, represented nearly 5 per cent of the total profitable acreage.[7] Between the 1560s and the 1630s a considerable amount of land in Co. Roscommon had also come into private Protestant possession. A small number of these Protestants were of Gaelic or Old English origin.[8] The majority, however, belonged to New English settler families such as Coote, King, St George and Crofton. All of these families had benefited from grants of former monastic and other lands. The combined holdings of Gaelic, Old English and New English Protestant proprietors equated to approximately 18 per cent of the total profitable acreage.[9] The remaining 65 per cent of the profitable land was in Catholic hands. Members of several Gaelic families, such as McDermot, O'Connor Don and Kelly, continued to hold large estates in the areas where they had once been dominant. Numerous others, including the Naghtens, Fallons and Molloys, owned smaller quantities of land. Old English Catholic families from east of the Shannon, notably Dillons and Nugents whose medieval bases were in neighbouring Co. Westmeath, had also made substantial acquisitions.[10] While landholding patterns in Co. Roscommon were evidently far from static in the decades before 1641, the 1650s would witness changes altogether more far-reaching.

Lines, garrisons and reserved lands

In Co. Roscommon almost all Catholic-owned land was deemed forfeit in the 1650s. The one apparent exception to this rule was an estate of over 1,000 acres owned by Nicholas Barnewall, Viscount Kingsland, in the barony of Ballintobber. Barnewall had played no part in the 1641 rebellion and soon after its outbreak he went to England. Because the Cromwellian authorities could not

---

[5] *The books of survey and distribution*, iii, passim; Isaac Weld, *Statistical survey of the county of Roscommon*, Dublin 1832, 7–11. Simington's total figure of 198,393 acres includes some lands 'discovered' during the implementation of the land settlement. The county also contained a large amount of land categorised as unprofitable. The latter is not included in the figures offered here.

[6] *The books of survey and distribution*, iii, passim.

[7] Ibid.

[8] Ibid. 107–13, 119, 125. Justice James Donnellan was the main Old Irish Protestant landowner. The Old English landowner and convert Thomas Dillon, Viscount Costello-Gallen, would return to Catholicism during the 1640s.

[9] Ibid. passim.

[10] Ibid.

make up their minds what to do with this aged and inoffensive nobleman, he managed to cling on to at least part of his Co. Dublin estates as well as his land in Co. Roscommon throughout the 1650s.[11] The main reduction in the quantity of former Catholic land available for transplanters occurred as a result of the Irish government's decision in 1653 to reserve territory adjacent to the Shannon and around designated towns and garrisons.[12] It also aimed to withhold the substantial amount of property formerly belonging to the outlawed Church of Ireland from redistribution to Catholics. For the most part, this policy relating to church lands was actually adhered to.[13] On the other hand, the results of the efforts made to establish the Shannon line and to create exclusion zones around towns and garrisons would come some way short of the outcome envisaged in 1653.

The main strongpoint in the Shannon line was the town of Athlone. During his visit to Athlone in June 1655, Fleetwood endorsed a proposal to reserve all lands within three miles of the town on the Connacht side.[14] Over the following years some attempt was made to adhere to this plan. In 1656 the Loughrea commissioners set out 1,000 acres 'within three miles of the Shannon' to Colonel Henry Markham and Alderman John Perrin of London.[15] Markham also obtained a lease of a further 743 acres. Captain Lewis Thomas, Ensign Marcus Lenan, Captain Read, Thomas Walpell and the adventurer Erasmus Smith also received land near the town.[16] At the same time, a number of transplanters, both locals and newcomers, were also assigned land in the several parishes adjacent to Athlone, thus ensuring that this area would not become exclusively Protestant-owned and inhabited after all.[17] In the remainder of the county, the proposed Shannon line was even less-well established. North of Athlone, in the baronies of Roscommon, Ballintobber and Boyle, only small quantities of land were reserved.[18] In the extreme south of the county, the main crossing point into King's County in Leinster was at Raghrabegg, modern day Shannonbridge. In 1651 the Catholic garrison there had been commanded by Terence Coghlan, a substantial landowner at Kilcolgan on the east side of the river.[19] Coghlan's estate was subsequently granted to the regicide MP and adventurer Gregory Clement. In May 1656 the latter's agent, Francis Blomer, complained that he was being 'kept out of a house and lands' by Terence Coghlan's widow.[20] Nevertheless, a month later Mary Coghlan was transplanted to lands adjoining the Shannon at Raghrabegg.[21] This outcome would have afforded her relatively easy access to her

---

11 Ibid. 11–50; SP 63/286/22; H. Cromwell and the Irish council to Oliver Cromwell, Dublin, 2 Jan. 1655, MS O'Renehan 2, fo. 568.
12 *IUC* ii. 375–6.
13 Some church land in Moycarnan was set out to transplanters: NAI, MS Headfort 2B 33 18, fos 240v–244r.
14 *IUC* ii. 524.
15 Ibid. 589.
16 MS Headfort 2B 33 18, fos 209r–14r.
17 Ibid.
18 Ibid. fos 335v–336r, 342v–344r.
19 *A contemporary history*, iii. 111, 161; NAI, MS Quit Rent Office, books of survey and distribution 13, fo. 47r.
20 MS Prendergast 2, fo. 360; *IUC* ii. 417.
21 'Ormond list'; MS Headfort 2B 33 18, fo. 244r.

former home, allowing her to continue to harass Blomer if she so wished. Coghlan's case in particular indicates that the plan to create a Catholic-free buffer zone adjacent to the Shannon was not taken very seriously in Co. Roscommon.

The endeavour to exclude transplanters from designated lands around garrisons and strong points outside of those located on the river Shannon also enjoyed mixed results. In 1651 Cromwell's nephew Major John Desborough 'was by providence cast' into possession of the former Brabazon castle at the town of Ballinasloe, a key crossing point on the river Suck.[22] In the mid-1650s Ballinasloe was listed as one of the Connacht garrisons around which one mile of land was to be reserved. These orders reinforced Desborough's hold on Ballinasloe.[23] An official investigation into allegations that he had stolen 100 sheep from the Coghlans in 1652 seems not to have affected his position.[24] Instead, his request for a twenty-one-year lease was approved by his uncle in London, and in 1657 he was resident at Ballinasloe with a garrison of 147 men. None the less, his plan to establish an English plantation 'to set up the trade of cloth making' would soon be derailed.[25]

Desborough was only one of the many individuals who sent petitions to Cromwell. Early in 1657 the lord protector received a plea from William Spenser of Kilcolman, Co. Cork.[26] Spenser, a grandson of the Elizabethan poet and Munster settler Edmund Spenser, was described in the books of survey and distribution as an 'English Papist'.[27] In 1641 he had been a minor resident in Co. Cork with his widowed Catholic mother. In 1657 he claimed to have renounced Catholicism 'since coming to years of discretion'. He also argued that transplantation would place him in peril because his grand-father's writings 'touching the reduction of the Irish to civilitie brought on him the odium of that nation'.[28] Despite a favourable intervention from Cromwell, the authorities in Dublin insisted that Spenser should transplant to Connacht, his Munster estate having been already set out to the army. By that stage in 1657, lands of the magnitude needed to satisfy his entitlements in Connacht were scarce. The Loughrea commissioners solved this problem by granting him over 1,100 acres around Ballinasloe.[29] As a result, Edmund Spenser's grandson displaced Oliver Cromwell's nephew from Brabazon's castle on the banks of the Suck. Desborough may have taken some consolation from the fact that the transplanter for whom he was forced to make way was indeed a Protestant as he had claimed. Spenser married Barbara Edwards, the daughter of one of the Loughrea commissioners, and he was still around to guide to General Ginkel on his march from the siege of Athlone to the battle of Aughrim in 1691.[30]

---

22 SP 63/286/130; *IUC* ii. 628–9.
23 *IUC* ii. 524, 616.
24 NLI, MS 11,961, fo. 109.
25 SP 63/286/130; *IUC* ii. 628–9; BL, MS Add. Petty 72,877, fos 72v, 74r.
26 *IUC* ii. 659.
27 MS Quit Rent Office, books of survey and distribution 6, fos 152v–153r.
28 *IUC* ii. 659.
29 MS Headfort 2B 33 18, fos 241r–242r; 2B 33 16, Clonmacknowen, fos 6–7.
30 Patrick Egan, *The parish of Ballinasloe*, Dublin 1960, 93; William Spenser, *The case of William Spencer of Kilcolman in the county of Cork in the kingdom of Ireland, esq; grandson and heir to Edmond Spencer the poet*, London 1701.

Another key stronghold on the Suck was the town of Athleague, 'a brave seat, and a passage and place of great importance' formerly owned by the marquis of Clanricarde.[31] In October 1640, during a heated argument in the presence of the king, the earl of Strafford had conceded that Clanricarde's estate ought to be excluded from his proposed plantation, but he insisted that he would still need to seize possession of Athleague 'under pretence of the service for the king'.[32] Whatever Strafford's precise motivations, fifteen years later his interest in controlling Athleague would be mirrored by Sir Charles Coote. As lord president of Connacht, and the most senior army officer in the province, Coote was responsible for selecting suitable locations for the posting of garrisons. Rather than proposing to garrison Athleague, he first sought to get possession of the place for himself. Crucially, his position as a Loughrea commissioner would allow him to succeed where Strafford had failed. In November 1655 Coote and his colleagues recommended that Athleague and 2,000 acres adjoining should be granted to Colonel John Fitzpatrick.[33] Although Fitzpatrick had already left the country, the entitlement to land which he had secured in return for his early surrender in March 1652 had still to be satisfied.[34] Having presumably engineered this grant, Coote promptly agreed a thirty-one-year lease of the property with Fitzpatrick's attorney, thus ensuring that this strategic town would rest securely in Protestant hands.[35] By September 1657 Coote had further tightened his grip by posting a foot company from his own regiment at Athleague.[36]

Two other locations which had been included in Coote's list of proposed garrisons were the towns of Ballymoe and Ballintobber.[37] In the former location Captain Daniel Thomas oversaw the building of a new fort named for the lord deputy as Fort Fleetwood.[38] However, most of the land initially reserved around Ballymoe and Ballintobber ultimately found its way into the hands of an English Catholic transplanter, Lady Frances Butler. Butler was the earl of Castlehaven's sister and Ormond's sister-in-law. Her husband Colonel Richard Butler went into exile in the 1650s and his estates in Kilkenny and Tipperary were confiscated.[39] As a result, Lady Butler was forced to turn for relief to the 'piety and pitty' of Oliver Cromwell.[40] Following Cromwell's intervention in the case in 1655, Coote was ordered to 'pitch upon lands' worth £200 per annum in Connacht which could be assigned to Lady Butler.[41] By July 1656 she had been assigned

---

31 *The memoirs and letters of Ulick, marquis of Clanricarde,* ed. John Smyth Bourke, earl of Clanricarde, London 1757, 20.

32 The earl of St Albans and Clanricarde to Secretary Windebank, York, 26 Oct. 1640, SP 16/470/118.

33 NLI, MS 11,959, fo. 296; NAI, MS D19,309.

34 *IUC* i, 149–53.

35 NAI, MS D19,309; MS Headfort 2B 33 18, fos 229v–232r, 233v–238r.

36 MS Add. Petty 72,877, fo. 73.

37 *IUC* ii. 524.

38 Captain Daniel Thomas to H. Cromwell, Fort Fleetwood alias the Bridge of Ballymoe, 11 Oct. 1657, MS Lansdowne 822, fos 212r–v.

39 Bernard Burke, *A genealogical history of the dormant, abeyant, forfeited, and extinct peerages of the British empire,* London 1866, 535.

40 SP 63/287/17.

41 The Irish council to Sir Charles Coote, 24 Feb. 1656, MS Prendergast 1, fo. 548.

almost 3,000 acres at Ballintobber, including O'Connor Don's castle, and 300 acres adjoining the bridge at Ballymoe.[42] In October 1656 her Protestant cousin and occasional correspondent Elizabeth Blennerhassett reported that Butler had 'transplanted into Connacht, and farmes her owne estate'. Blennerhassett may even have been a little envious of her transplanted cousin; she described her own surroundings at Trillick in Co. Tyrone as 'the worst part of Ireland'.[43]

Despite securing a considerable assignment of land in Connacht, Lady Butler remained anxious for the future prospects of her seven children. Moreover, she could expect little assistance from her exiled husband, as he would soon be reduced to reliance on the charity of Abbess Mary Knatchbull of the Benedictine Convent at Ghent.[44] Because the Ballintobber estate was granted for her lifetime only, she was keenly aware that her offspring might face 'misery and ruyne ... in case nothing be left to them to support them' after her death. Early in 1657 Butler sent another petition to the lord protector. She informed Cromwell that her new estate had only yielded £24 in the past year, much less than the £200 to which she was actually entitled. She also sought a ninety-nine year lease of the lands held by her in Connacht.[45] Cromwell obliged by sending the necessary instructions to Dublin in March 1657. Unfortunately for Butler, the Irish government proved less co-operative than before. With land becoming increasing scarce, the council insisted that they could not comply with Cromwell's orders because 'the lands in Connacht and Clare were by Act of Parliament set apart to satisfy the decrees of the Irish'.[46] By January 1658 the determined lady had negotiated a compromise. In return for a once off payment of £600, she offered to forego her entitlement to £200 *per annum*. She proposed to use this £600 to buy unsatisfied Athlone decrees from other transplanters.[47] In this way she could purchase entitlements to an estate not exceeding 3,000 acres without infringing upon any laws. The council consented to this plan but limited the sum of money in question to £500. By July 1658 Butler had purchased the necessary transplanters' decrees. The council accordingly approved the payment of £500 and ordered the surveyor general to settle lands on her not exceeding 3,000 acres.[48] As a result it seems that Butler was confirmed in possession of the lands around Ballintobber. In the process her title was presumably converted from a mere life interest in the estate to one which ensured an inheritance for her children.

These examples show that the plan to create no-Catholic zones around garrisons and towns in Co. Roscommon was not fully implemented, particularly as land became increasingly scarce. Although the ideal of Protestant military outposts supported by bustling Protestant colonies never became a reality, Coote must have been reasonably satisfied with the actual outcome: Ballinasloe was in

---

[42] SP 63/287/17; 'Ormond list'; MS Headfort 2B 33 18, fos 249v–250r, 316v–331r.
[43] Elizabeth Blennerhassett to Lady Mary Hastings, Trillick, 29 Oct. 1656, MS Hastings, Henry E. Huntington Library, San Marino, Box 20.
[44] *Calendar of the Clarendon state papers*, iv. 66.
[45] SP 63/287/17; MS Prendergast 2, fos 682–4.
[46] MS Prendergast 2, fos 682–4.
[47] Ibid.
[48] Ibid.

the hands of a New English Protestant; the proprietor of Ballintobber may have been a Catholic, but she was at least English rather than Irish; and he had secured Athleague for himself. Elsewhere, providing for the security of the garrisons at the towns of Roscommon and Boyle was more straightforward, as most of the land around these strongholds was already Protestant-owned and their commanders were established local proprietors closely allied to Coote. By September 1657 Coote and his comrades were in command of some 726 soldiers stationed in the county.[49] This force was charged with keeping the peace as the numerous local and incoming transplanters all sought to secure the lands assigned to them by the commissioners at Loughrea.

Local transplanters

Between 1655 and 1657 roughly 120,000 acres of profitable lands were assigned to transplanters in Co. Roscommon. This represented 63 per cent of the total profitable acreage.[50] Just 32,116 acres of this land was granted to Catholics originating within the county. The property assigned to the Roscommon transplanters in other counties, around 3,600 acres scattered across Mayo, Galway and Clare, did little to make up their overall losses.[51] At the same time, the number of local Catholic landowners was also drastically reduced, from 523 in 1641 to around 180 by 1657.[52] This remarkable shrinkage of Roscommon's Catholic landed society to one-third of its pre-war size can be attributed to a number of general factors. It may be assumed that some landowners had perished in the war, while others had since gone into exile. The group of individuals who failed to secure decrees at Loughrea due to land shortages must also have included former Roscommon proprietors. Still others probably lacked the financial means to pursue their claims to land before the relevant commissioners.

In line with overall trends across the four counties of the transplantation zone, the sizes of the estates granted to Roscommon transplanters varied greatly. Of the 180 locals 105 secured 100 acres or less. On the other hand, Sir Thomas Nugent and Theobald Dillon were assigned 3,500 and 3,400 acres respectively.[53] Nugent, father-in-law to the earl of Westmeath, had also forfeited extensive estates east of the Shannon. As a former Leinster officer, he was entitled to the equivalent of one-third of his former estate.[54] His grant in the barony of Roscommon was made up for the most part of lands which had belonged to him before the war.[55] In 1641 Theobald Dillon's grandfather Sir Lucas had owned more than 8,000 acres in Roscommon and further lands else-

49 MS Add. Petty 72,877, fos 72–74v.
50 MS Headfort 2B 33 18, passim; *The books of survey and distribution*, iii, passim.
51 Simington, *Transplantation*, 233–78; *The books of survey and distribution*, iii, passim.
52 BL, MS Harleian 2,048, fos 424–429v; 'Ormond list'; McKenny, 'The restoration land settlement', 44.
53 'Ormond list'.
54 MS Egerton 1,762, fo. 181.
55 MS Headfort 2B 33 18, fos 289v–294r, 303v–311r.

where.[56] Sir Lucas had been a leading member of the supreme council of the Catholic confederation before he too secured the benefit of the Leinster articles in 1652.[57] He died in 1655, having been predeceased by his eldest son, Captain Robert Dillon. Their deaths meant that by 1655 the latter's eldest son, Theobald Dillon, could lay claim to a considerable estate.[58]

There were also a number of other interested parties in the Dillon lands. Following their marriage in 1638 and the receipt of a dowry of £2,500, part of the estate had been conveyed to Theobald Dillon's parents.[59] Sir Lucas had also made some provision for his younger sons. Sir Charles Coote too had an interest. In August 1653 Sir Lucas Dillon had borrowed £1,815 from Coote and around £224 from John Boswell of Co. Sligo and entered bonds of £4,448 for the repayment of those sums.[60] Two years later Sir Lucas was dead and the debt was still outstanding.[61] By 1655, therefore, Theobald's widowed mother Rose, his guardian and widowed grandmother Jane, his uncles Theobald, Christopher and Arthur and the indomitable Coote could all lay claim to some stake in the estate. To satisfy Coote, the Dillons agreed that he should be given some of the land due to Theobald Dillon as a transplanter.[62] Coote was duly able to arrange for Dillon's assignment to be set out adjacent to his own estates in the barony of Athlone. In 1656 Theobald and his grandmother secured around 3,400 acres in Athlone, about 1,000 acres of which was promptly transferred to Coote.[63] Meanwhile, the Dillon estate in the barony of Boyle, some 5,200 acres, passed into other hands.

Some further insight into the experiences of local transplanters can be garnered from the evidence relating to other families. In 1641 the lands held by the Kelly family were concentrated in the south of the county. Various members of this family owned 1,200 acres in Moycarnan and they were also the leading Catholic proprietors in six out of fourteen parishes in the barony of Athlone.[64] While they managed to hold onto almost 800 acres in Moycarnan, they were subsequently displaced from many of their holdings in Athlone.[65] The leading transplanter from the family was Colonel John Kelly of Corrabeg in the parish of Athleague. His father Colla had fought under the fourth earl of Clanricarde against the earl of Tyrone at Kinsale in 1601 and he subsequently acquired a large estate in Roscommon and east Galway.[66] This military relationship was renewed

---

[56] *The books of survey and distribution*, iii. 97–119, 155–62; ii. 57–8, 80, 91, 149.

[57] Lodge, *The peerage of Ireland*, iv. 191–3; Athlone decree of Theobald and Lady Jane Dillon, 18 Apr. 1656, MSS De Freyne, NLI, unsorted collection.

[58] Case of Theobald Dillon before the court of claims, 25 May 1663, MSS De Freyne, unsorted collection.

[59] Ibid.

[60] *The Irish statute staple books, 1596–1687*, ed. Jane Ohlmeyer and Éamonn Ó Ciardha, Dublin 1998, 361; *Statute staple database* CD-ROM, ed. Jane Ohlmeyer and Éamonn Ó Ciardha, Dublin 1998, nos 2,983–4.

[61] NLI, MS 11,961, fos 180–1.

[62] Ibid.

[63] MS Headfort 2B 33 18, fos 209r–240r; the claim of Theobald Dillon, 5 Nov. 1662, MSS De Freyne, unsorted collection.

[64] *The books of survey and distribution*, iii. 60–4, 92–128.

[65] MS Headfort 2B 33 18, fos 209r–240r, 241r–244r.

[66] Cronin, 'The foundations of landlordism', 174, 180.

forty years later when John Kelly was appointed as a captain under the fifth earl of Clanricarde.[67] Following his surrender at Jamestown in April 1652, Kelly had retired to his estates, while his son Charles went into exile.[68] In 1655 his petition for land was supported by certificates of approval from Coote and the Old Irish Protestant Justice James Donnellan, and he obtained a decree for 923 acres thereafter.[69] This was more than double the amount granted to any other of the roughly 100 Kelly transplanters originating in Roscommon and Galway.[70]

The estates owned by members of the Fallon family in 1641 were also concentrated in the barony of Athlone, where they held over 3,000 acres.[71] In the 1650s eight individual Fallons were granted a combined total of just 250 acres in the barony, while others were assigned new lands elsewhere.[72] One of those Fallons who received lands in Athlone was Sarah, daughter of Edmond Boy O'Fallon of Finagh in the parish of Dysart. Upon her father's death in 1652, Sarah had inherited his estate of 250 acres of profitable land and 300 acres of bog. In September 1655 she produced two witnesses before the Athlone commissioners who swore that the lands in question were Edmond O'Fallon's 'ancient inheritance time out of mind'.[73] The commissioners were accordingly satisfied that Sarah had good title to the lands and they failed to find any evidence of delinquency against her or her father. As a result, she was decreed the equivalent of two-thirds of her estate 'according to the mercy held forth to recusants not in arms or otherwise aiding in the late rebellion, in and by the said eighth qualification'.[74] According to this decree, Sarah ought to have received at least 165 acres of profitable lands. However, eight months later the Loughrea commissioners assigned her only eighteen acres out of her former estate.[75] In common with the Fallons, the Flanagans, Birnes, McDowells and other local families also saw drastic reductions in their holdings.[76] The Hanlys from Ballintobber barony may have produced the oldest transplanter. In 1656 Murtagh Moyle Hanly presented his claim at Athlone, in which he insisted that he was 'upwards of ninety years old'.[77] If this claim was true, Hanly was older than the county which was being transformed before his very eyes.

In other cases at least one member of a wider family group managed to fare reasonably well. This was true of Feaghra Flinn, a former confederate officer, who retained a sizeable part of his family's former estates in the parish of Kiltullagh.[78] At least some of his relatives sought to survive by other more desperate means; in August 1656 the capture of 'one John Oge fflynn, a ringleader of the Tories in Connacht' was reported by a triumphant Captain Theophilus Sandford. This

---

67 *The memoirs and letters of Clanricarde*, 18–19.
68 *IUC* i. 172–5.
69 NLI, MS 11,961, fos 172–3; MS Headfort 2B 33 18, fos 236v–237r; Simington, *Transplantation*, 132.
70 'Ormond list'.
71 *The books of survey and distribution*, iii. 101–11, 116–17.
72 Simington, *Transplantation*, 124, 237–41, 251, 274, 276.
73 NLI, MS Westport 40,893/5(3).
74 Ibid.
75 'Ormond list'; MS Westport 40,893/5(4).
76 MS Headfort 2B 33 18, passim.
77 NLI, MS 24,597, no. 1.
78 *The memoirs and letters of Clanricarde*, 442; MS Headfort 2B 33 18, fos 347v–351r.

outlaw had been betrayed by one of his associates in return for a pardon.[79] In Ballintobber various members of the O'Connor family secured almost 1,700 acres, roughly one-fifth of their former possessions there. Of this land, nearly 700 acres went to Mary, the widow of Charles O'Connor Don.[80] In the neighbouring barony of Roscommon the O'Connor proprietors suffered a rather more severe decline in their fortunes.[81] Further north, the McDermot lands were reduced from around 13,000 acres to just over 2,000 acres. Of the six members of that family who received assignments, four were widows.[82] As with other local families, the war had evidently taken its toll on the McDermots, and the implementation of the settlement had done little to alleviate their troubles.

Incoming transplanters

Alongside the locals, transplanters originating in twenty-four additional counties also acquired land in Roscommon. Proprietors from the five other counties west of the Shannon secured over 10,000 acres altogether. The 156 transplanters from east of the Shannon were assigned a combined total of 77,000 acres, equal to 40 per cent of the total profitable acreage of the county. Around four-fifths of the land given to these newcomers to the province was redistributed among 117 transplanters who came from Leinster. Ten transplanters from Ulster were granted a combined total of just over 6,000 acres, while twenty-nine individuals from Munster acquired around 7,500 acres. The best-represented county was Meath, with thirty-six transplanters.[83] The average size of the estates assigned to incoming proprietors from the other three provinces was around 490 acres, and many of them also obtained land in other counties as well.[84] Although they fared better than the locals in this respect, they were none the less confronted with a range of difficulties in their new surroundings.

A series of complaints sent up to Dublin in the mid-1650s by newcomers to the barony of Athlone allows some insight into the problems which they faced. At least three petitions of grievance reached the council in the space of just over a year, beginning in March 1655.[85] The chief signatory of these documents was Philip Purcell, formerly of Ballyfoyle, Co. Kilkenny. Purcell's name may have been familiar to the authorities in Dublin. Because he had rendered assistance to Protestant refugees in 1641, he had the dubious honour of being the only Catholic to receive favourable mention in the *Abstract of some few of those barbarous, cruell massacres and murthers* published by Scoutmaster-general Henry Jones in 1652.[86] Purcell appears to have been among the first of the new

---

79 MS Prendergast 2, fo. 405.
80 Simington, *Transplantation*, 249–51.
81 Ibid. 275–6.
82 MS Headfort 2B 33 18, fos 255v–283r; 'Ormond list'; Simington, *Transplantation*, 262–3.
83 Simington, *Transplantation*, 233–78; MS Headfort 2B 33 18, passim.
84 Simington, *Transplantation*, passim.
85 MS Prendergast 1, fos 266–7; 2, fos 369–70.
86 Henry Jones, *An abstract of some few of those barbarous, cruell massacres and murthers, of the Protestants and English in some parts of Ireland*, London 1652, 1.

arrivals in the county, although his grant of 703 acres in the parish of Kilmeane was not actually finalised until June 1657.[87]

Unfortunately, the names of Philip Purcell's fellow petitioners have not survived, but it is evident that he was acting on behalf of the incoming transplanters. In March 1655 they requested permission to send servants 'to bring them provisions from the places from where they are transplanted'. They also complained of being 'turned [out of] their transplantation lands for the disbanded soldiers', presumably in the vicinity of Athlone town.[88] Three weeks later a second petition revealed that the soldiers were not the only ones making life difficult for the newcomers. Some had apparently been 'deprived of their assignments by the former inhabitants of the country and turned into the most unfertill and barren parts'.[89] This problem stemmed in part from the fact that Purcell and his associates had not yet received either decrees at Athlone or final assignments of land from Loughrea. However, their suggestion that this process could be expedited if they were permitted to employ 'Irish native professors of the law to plead for them' won no sympathy in Dublin.[90] A year later, in May 1656, Purcell encountered further trouble when two army officers, Captain Mathias Sandford and Captain Phoenix, levied £700 upon the county in order to meet a debt owed by the state since 1649 to a local Protestant landowner, Captain Edward Ormsby. When Purcell and his tenants refused to pay the £9 demanded of them, Ormsby's men seized three of his cows. Fortunately, Purcell managed to convince the government that as a newcomer to the county he should not be held liable for any share of a debt accrued seven years before.[91] The fate of his cows is unknown.

While Purcell's petitions hint at the tensions that existed between the newcomers and the old proprietors, both groups did sometimes work together to defend their common interests. In February 1657 a joint complaint made by a group of newcomers and locals against Captain James Shaen was considered by the court of exchequer.[92] Shaen was one of the Loughrea commissioners appointed in 1654 to oversee the redistribution of land in Connacht. In February 1656 the council ordered an inquiry into the reported abuses committed by Shaen and another Loughrea commissioner Captain Stephen Squibb as 'persons entrusted to let and set the State's lands in those parts'. They were accused of seizing lands illegally and oppressing transplanters.[93] Allegations of malpractice against Shaen were reinforced a year later when up to eight transplanters in the barony of Athlone saw fit to complain about his behaviour. They protested that they had been 'turned out of doors ... to their grievance, loss and damage' by him.[94] John Naghten, a minor local Protestant proprietor, had also been ejected from his lands.[95] It appears that Shaen had somehow obtained injunctions to

---

87 MS Prendergast 1, fos 266–7; 'Ormond list'; MS Headfort 2B 33 18, fos 234v–235r. In the latter source, Philip Purcell is incorrectly entered as Theobald Purcell.
88 MS Prendergast 1, fos 266–7.
89 Ibid. fo. 267.
90 Ibid.
91 Ibid. MS 2, fos 369–70.
92 NAI, MS Ferguson 10, fos 90–2.
93 IUC ii. 387–9, 569–70.
94 MS Ferguson 10, fos 90–2.
95 Ibid.

allow Protestants to seize possession of lands in Co. Roscommon. While the court of exchequer ordered that John Naghten be restored immediately, it referred the case of the displaced transplanters to two men on the spot: the governor of Athlone, Lieutenant-Colonel Alexander Brayfield, and William Handcock, one of Shaen's accomplices.[96] As in the case of Purcell's cows, the outcome of this dispute is also unclear. However, it serves to demonstrate that transplanters encountered difficulties not only with each other, but also with the questionable practices of unscrupulous officers and officials.

Three of the transplanters affected by Shaen's malpractice had earlier benefitted from a government decision to reserve the barony of Athlone for the satisfaction of 'widows of English extraction'.[97] This proposal was partially implemented, with the result that a total of over 4,500 acres in the barony was granted to ten widows who fitted into this category.[98] Among them was Lady Mary Dongan, widow of Sir John Dongan, late of Castletown, Co. Kildare.[99] Lady Dongan managed to secure somewhat favourable treatment from the authorities in Dublin, perhaps due to the influence of her Protestant uncle-in-law, Judge Thomas Dongan. In 1656 she received a decree for 1,569 acres. She was the only transplanter to receive lands in the parish of St Peter's, immediately adjacent to the town of Athlone.[100] Despite having gone into exile, her eldest son Sir Walter Dongan was granted 1,500 acres as part of his entitlements under the Leinster articles. He had initially fought on the royalist side in the English civil wars before coming home to play a part in the Irish conflict.[101] A further 550 acres were assigned to four of his younger brothers, including William, the future Jacobite earl of Limerick.[102]

Lady Dongan's fortunes can also be linked to that of her own family, the Talbots of Carton, Co. Kildare. At least four of her brothers, including Peter the future archbishop of Dublin, and Richard, later duke of Tyrconnell, went into exile.[103] Her eldest brother, Sir Robert Talbot, acted as chief agent for the Irish Catholics in London for most of the 1650s, while five of her sisters are recorded as transplanters. These were Margaret, the wife of Sir Henry Talbot, and Frances, the widow of James Cusack, who received a joint decree for 740 acres along with her younger sisters Jane, Katherine and Eleanor.[104] This Talbot circle, including the Dongans, managed to secure a remarkable amount of land, much of it in the barony of Athlone. Sir Robert Talbot was given 3,612 acres in the parish of Taughmaconnell, while his brother-in-law Sir Henry secured around 2,500 acres in the county.[105] The latter was on reasonably good terms with the government, and in 1656 the Athlone commissioners reported that he had proved 'a good, but

96   Ibid.
97   IUC ii. 423.
98   Simington, Transplantation, 233–6.
99   Burke, Dormant peerages, 529.
100 'Ormond list'; MS Headfort 2B 33 18, fos 208v–209r, 212v–218r.
101 'Ormond list'; NLI, MS 11,959, fo. 49; IUC i. 32.
102 'Ormond list'; John Dalton, King James's Irish army list, Dublin 1855, 259–63.
103 ODNB, s.v. 'Talbot, Peter (1618/1620–1680)'.
104 'Ormond list'; Burke, Dormant peerages, 529.
105 MS Headfort 2B 33 18, fos 217v–221r; 'Ormond list'.

not constant good affection'.[106] This helps to explain why his wife was able to travel to Dublin in 1657 to secure small sums of money from the state coffers to relieve her husband and children in their 'distressed condition'.[107] The family's ties to their new neighbourhood were strengthened when Sir Henry Talbot's daughter Mary married the prominent local transplanter Theobald Dillon.[108]

Several further Talbots also received land in Co. Roscommon. James Talbot and his wife Helen of Ballyconnell, Co. Cavan, were decreed 2,455 acres, of which 900 acres were set out in Athlone.[109] James Talbot's father Walter had earlier been a servitor in the plantation of Ulster.[110] In common with Sir Robert Talbot, James was married to one of the sisters of the English Catholic nobleman Cecil Calvert, Baron Baltimore.[111] Sir Robert's cousin, John Talbot of Malahide, received nearly 600 acres in Athlone and further lands elsewhere. His son Richard subsequently married Frances Talbot, Sir Robert's only daughter.[112] Lastly, Katherine Archbold alias Talbot, a widow from Co. Dublin, was assigned almost 500 acres in the parish of Taghboy.[113] This brought the various Talbot estates in the barony of Athlone to just over 9,000 acres. In the mid-1650s another marriage, that of the youngest Talbot sister, Eleanor, to Henry O'Neill of Killaleagh, Co. Antrim, further strengthened the family's connections among the transplanted.[114] Like Sir Walter Dongan, O'Neill had also fought for the king in England before eventually ending up as an officer in the Leinster army.[115] Thereafter his efforts to pass himself off as a Protestant enjoyed some success before being scuppered by Sir John Clotworthy, an influential adventurer determined to secure a slice of the O'Neill estate.[116] Henry O'Neill had to settle instead for a Talbot wife and a decree of 5,333 acres in Connacht.[117]

Another group of siblings who featured as transplanters included five Butler ladies, aunts to the marquis of Ormond. The eldest sister, Margaret, the baroness dowager of Upper Ossory, was granted lands in Co. Galway.[118] The second eldest was Lady Katherine Power, the widow of Pierce Power of Curraghmore. At Athlone in 1656 she entered a claim for her jointure lands worth £200 *per annum*, as stipulated by her marriage articles dating from 1601. She ultimately secured

---

106 MS Prendergast 2, fo. 391.

107 Ibid. fo. 669. Sir Robert Talbot's wife also secured some money from the government in 1657.

108 Lodge, *The peerage of Ireland*, iv. 194.

109 'Ormond list'; Simington, *Transplantation*, 234.

110 SP 63/225/225; *CSPI, 1611–1614*, 130–1.

111 George Ely Russell and Donna Valley Russell (eds), *The ark and dove adventurers*, Baltimore 2005, 4.

112 Simington, *Transplantation*, 234; Burke, *Dormant peerages*, 529. For a detailed account of John Talbot of Malahide see Joseph Byrne, *War and peace: the survival of the Talbots of Malahide, 1641–1671*, Dublin 1997.

113 Simington, *Transplantation*, 234.

114 Burke, *Dormant peerages*, 529.

115 SP 63/317/205, 63/314/85; *CSPI, 1660–1662*, 248–9; MS Prendergast 2, fo. 850.

116 MS Egerton 1,762, fos 158–9.

117 'Ormond list'; Simington, *Transplantation*, 82, 100, 135, 163, 207, 259.

118 Simington, *Transplantation*, 86.

280 acres under the terms of the eighth qualification. Her son Pierce also proved legal title to the reversion of these lands. However, as he was found to be within the terms of the seventh qualification, the commissioners decreed that only half of the 280-acre assignment should revert to him at his mother's death.[119] A third sister, Ellena, was married to Pierce Butler, Viscount Ikerrin, whose family obtained a decree for 5,000 acres.[120] Joan and her husband Sir Thomas Esmond were decreed almost 3,500 acres, while Elizabeth and her husband Colonel Richard Burke were decreed almost 1,500 acres.[121] In 1658 the latter succeeded his cousin as sixth earl of Clanricarde.[122] By then most of the former Clanricarde estate in Roscommon and elsewhere in Connacht had been carved up and divided amongst the transplanters. At least some of it had also found its way into the hands of the Protestant Connacht purchasers.

Before looking more closely at the activities of the latter group, it is worth examining a complex case which in some ways spanned the divide between transplanter and Connacht purchaser. The transplanter concerned was the Galway townsman Patrick French FitzStephen, the Connacht purchaser his son Dominick. The Loughrea commissioners were able to satisfy the claims of most Galway townsmen by assigning lands out of their existing estates in Galway, Mayo and Clare. Patrick French's case was more complicated, as much of his estate lay outside of the transplantation zone in Co. Sligo. The French family had become involved in mortgage transactions in Co. Sligo in the early years of the century, most notably with the family of O'Connor Sligo. By the mid-1630s Patrick French held over 5,000 acres in the county under the terms of twenty-seven separate mortgage agreements.[123] At that point Teige O'Connor, the nominal owner of the O'Connor Sligo estate, was on the point of despair. Alongside French's interest, the respective widows of his three predecessors were also entitled to jointures out the property. The three women concerned were Eleanor, the ancient countess dowager of Desmond, her daughter Ellen, and Sarah, the sister of Randall McDonnell, second earl of Antrim.[124] In an effort to rescue his fortunes, Teige O'Connor turned for help to the king and the lord deputy.[125]

Matters came to a head in 1635 when Patrick French attempted to prevent the recently widowed Sarah O'Connor from taking possession of her jointure lands.[126] A subsequent letter from the king ordered that she be protected from the 'unconscionable devices' of Patrick French.[127] With an eye as ever to his own advantage, Strafford swiftly came to the rescue. In return for a payment of £500,

---

[119] MS Pakenham-Mahon 10,125.

[120] 'Ormond list'; MS Prendergast 2, fo. 290.

[121] 'Ormond list'.

[122] ODNB, s.v. 'Ulick Burgh, marquis of Clanricarde (1604–1658)'.

[123] Ó Bríc, 'Galway townsmen', 360–1, 369, 395.

[124] Ibid. 358–61; Anne Chambers, Eleanor countess of Desmond, c. 1545–1638, Dublin 1986, 224–9; Mary O'Dowd, Power, politics and land: Sligo 1568–1688, Belfast 1991, 92–3.

[125] Teige O'Connor to the lord deputy concerning the plantation of Connacht, 16 Oct 1636, MSS De Freyne, unsorted collection.

[126] The answer of Patrick French to a bill of complaint by the earl of Antrim and Dame Sarah O'Connor, 16 Mar. 1635, and Sarah O'Connor's answer to the petition of Strafford and Radcliffe, 14 Nov. 1662, ibid.

[127] CSPI, 1633–1647, 126.

Teige O'Connor agreed to surrender his lands to Sir Philip Percival, who was acting as a trustee for Strafford and his associate Sir George Radcliffe. In return he was to receive a fresh grant of 3,000 acres as part of the planned plantation of Connacht. Strafford and Radcliffe also undertook to pay O'Connor's debts.[128] In 1637 Sarah O'Connor was given a lump sum of £2,000 in lieu of her jointure.[129] While French was also promised £2,000, he remained deeply dissatisfied with the situation.[130]

In November 1640 French travelled to London in the company of his lawyer Geoffrey Browne to petition the English parliament. The unfortunate Teige O'Connor undertook the same journey, only to be drowned en route. None the less, in April 1641 his son and successor, another Teige, seized possession of the O'Connor estate and returned French's lands to him.[131] Following Strafford's execution in May, the English House of Commons sided with French, while the king ordered that the estate be vested in trustees for the families of Strafford and Radcliffe.[132] Thereafter, the O'Connor land dispute was overtaken by the 1641 rebellion.

After the war French had to deal with the new regime rather than with the O'Connors. Despite having been guaranteed his life upon surrendering in July 1652, Teige O'Connor was hanged shortly afterwards in the town of Boyle, the north Roscommon stronghold of the Protestant King family.[133] His widow and children were subsequently decreed 200 acres as transplanters.[134] At Athlone in 1655 Patrick French produced the paperwork and the witnesses necessary to prove his entitlement to the O'Connor Sligo lands. In 1638 Sir Philip Percival had poured scorn on these deeds and papers, suggesting that French should 'goe out of sight and stop bottles with them'.[135] The judges at Athlone proved themselves more accommodating; French obtained a decree for 6,190 acres under the articles of Galway, making him the fifth most substantial transplanter overall. Most of his grant, some 4,912 acres, was carved out of the estate forfeited by Sir Lucas Dillon and the McDermots in the barony of Boyle.[136]

Patrick French settled at Dungar, later Frenchpark, in the parish of Tibohine. In 1656 his Protestant son Dominick took over the estate. Dominick French would later claim that he had actually purchased the lands in question from his father, a distinction which would be of crucial significance post-1660.[137] He was married to Anne, the granddaughter of Edward King, late Protestant bishop of

---

128 Teige O'Connor to the lord deputy concerning the plantation of Connacht, 16 Oct 1636, MSS De Freyne, unsorted collection; O'Dowd, Sligo, 115–16; Terence O'Rorke, The history of Sligo: town and county, Dublin 1890, i. 191–204.
129 Sarah O'Connor's answer to the petition of Strafford and Radcliffe, 14 Nov. 1662, MSS De Freyne, unsorted collection.
130 O'Dowd, Sligo, 116.
131 Ibid. 116, 136; CSPI, 1633–1647, 312.
132 CSPI, 1633–1647, 312; CJ ii. 272–3.
133 O'Rorke, The history of Sligo, i. 144.
134 'Ormond list'.
135 O'Dowd, Sligo, 116.
136 'Ormond list'; MS Headfort 2B 33 18, fos 267v–272r.
137 Petition of Dominick French to the commissioners for the Act of Explanation, c. 1666, MSS De Freyne, unsorted collection.

Elphin and a close ally of French's former adversary the earl of Strafford.[138] The size of Dominick French's estate ensured that he was able to lend assistance to other members of the family. In May 1659 his brother Stephen wrote him a warm letter: 'I have more quetness from my wife than I did expect to have God continue it shee desired me to give unto you thanks she is more proud of the mare then of the monie God keep us all in love and union.'[139] While his wife was content, Stephen French was concerned about current taxation levels, which had apparently risen to 6*d*. per acre. Another brother, Edmond, had recently been arrested in Galway, presumably as part of the effort to rid the town of Catholics.[140] While the French family would remain at Frenchpark until 1952, many other transplanters opted to sell their assignments of land as soon as they could find a willing purchaser.

The Connacht purchasers

In most cases, the individuals who purchased land from the transplanters were Protestant officers and officials active in Connacht. Twenty years earlier, in 1636, Strafford had informed the king that it was possible to 'buy a thousand acres in most parts of Ireland for 600 or 700 pounds'.[141] The land of Connacht was generally less fertile than in many areas east of the Shannon, a circumstance reflected by the terms of the Adventurer's Act of 1642. This legislation valued 1,000 acres in Connacht at just £300, half the rate proposed for the province of Leinster.[142] Breandán Ó Bríc calculated that, in the decades before 1641, 1,000 profitable acres in Connacht usually yielded an annual income of around £200, and that land usually changed hands for six to seven times its annual value.[143] Thus, even allowing for the risk associated with investing in Ireland in the uncertain year of 1642, the rate set down for 1,000 acres in Connacht represented a bargain. However, because the Irish land market was saturated in the 1650s, transplanters who sold their estates could ask even less than the price authorised in the Adventurer's Act. The evidence available for Co. Roscommon in the mid-1650s suggests that land was changing hands for no more than £200 per thousand acres. Furthermore, the vast majority of transplanters had considerably less than 1,000 acres at their disposal. Even substantial transplanters complained bitterly of the meagre income that they derived from their new Connacht estates. Sir Henry Talbot claimed that his grant of around 2,500 acres was worth less than £40 *per annum*, while Lady Frances Butler apparently derived just £24 from her estate of 3,000 acres.[144] In the short term, the securing of a large estate in Connacht provided little security against impoverishment and ruin. It can be no

---

138 ODNB, s.v. 'King, Edward (c.1576–1639)'; Leslie Pine (ed.), *Burke's genealogical and heraldic dictionary of the peerage, baronetage and knightage*, London 1956, 608–9.
139 Stephen French to Dominick French, May 1659, MSS De Freyne, unsorted collection.
140 Ibid.
141 HMC, *Fourth report*, ed. John Romilly and others, London 1874, 291.
142 *A collection of acts and ordinances*, 26.
143 Ó Bríc, 'Galway townsmen', 367, 721–2; O'Dowd, *Sligo*, 92–3.
144 MS Prendergast 2, fo. 381; SP 63/287/17.

surprise, therefore, that many smaller transplanters in particular opted to sell their lots and to join the ranks of the tenantry, either in Connacht or on their old estates elsewhere.

At least five of the Loughrea commissioners were involved in purchasing lands from transplanters.[145] The clerks and other officials appointed to assist them were also well-placed to acquire land at cheap rates. One of these clerks, Christopher Ormsby, came from a family settled in Connacht since the sixteenth century.[146] Along with his cousin Thomas, he was involved in numerous land transactions with transplanters. In 1656 Edmond Butler, formerly of Kiltorcan, Co. Kilkenny, was assigned 100 acres in Ballintobber barony. He subsequently sold this land to Thomas Ormsby for just £20.[147] Also in 1656 Ormsby paid £16 17s. 4d. for an unsatisfied Athlone decree held by Theobald and Patrick Verdon, two brothers transplanted from Co. Louth. Despite relocating to Roscommon, the Verdons had not managed to secure a final settlement of land. Within six days of purchasing their Athlone decree, Thomas Ormsby had secured a grant at Loughrea.[148] In this way the Ormsbys managed to add around 1,500 acres to their existing estates by the end of the 1650s.[149]

The Connacht purchasers active in Co. Roscommon also included two recently arrived Protestant army officers, Captain Theophilus Sandford and Captain Nicholas Mahon. Both men managed to piece together substantial estates which would remain in the hands of their descendants until the twentieth century. In 1657 Sandford purchased the 600 acres recently assigned to Philip Hore, a transplanter from Co. Dublin. This transaction cost him £105.[150] He also acquired land from at least two other Dublin transplanters, John Caddle and John Talbot, formerly of Malahide.[151] Captain Mahon acquired a considerable amount of land from up to eighteen transplanters across several baronies in Co. Roscommon. Among those who sold their lands to him were three members of the Magennis family from Co. Down, Mortagh, Glassny and Edmond McShane.[152] Another transplanter who opted to sell his land to Mahon was Hugh Wyre of Castletown Geoghegan in Co. Westmeath. At Athlone in 1655 Wyre claimed as his inheritance an estate of 360 acres worth £40 per annum, which included 'a great stone house and a park fenced and beautified with a quick sett of thorn'. A year later he was assigned 198 acres scattered across three different baronies in Co. Roscommon.[153] The money that he received from Captain Mahon could not have been more than the equivalent of one year's

145 Blake family records, ii. 214; IRC, Fifteenth report, 102, 189, 203, 233.
146 Edward McLysaght 'Commonwealth state accounts: Ireland, 1650–56', Analecta Hibernica xv (1944), 227–321 at p. 301; 'Ormsby of Ballinamore', <http://www. landedestates.ie> accessed 12 Aug. 2009.
147 Sir Henry Blackall, 'The Butlers of County Clare', North Munster Archaeological Journal vii (1953–7), 153–67 at p. 156; NAI, MS D14,349; MSS Ormsby of Ballinamore, microfilm P. 8,502, no. 29.
148 'Ormond list'; MS Ormsby of Ballinamore, microfilm P. 8,502, nos 9–11.
149 Cunningham, 'Cromwellian County Mayo'.
150 NAI, MS M6,237(3).
151 'Ormond list'; Statute staple database CD–ROM, no. 3,336; NLI, MS 31, fo. 231.
152 MS Pakenham-Mahon 10,125.
153 Ibid.; Simington, Transplantation, passim.

income from his former estate. For many small proprietors like Wyre, transplantation must inevitably have caused an ignominious decline in their social status and living conditions. While the occasional charity of the government provided badly needed relief to a few individuals, most transplanters were undoubtedly left unaided to face a considerable struggle; in the first place to acquire land and then to derive some actual benefit from it, either through husbandry or simply by selling it as quickly as possible.[154]

Roscommon was the smallest of the four counties in the transplantation zone and the vast majority of the roughly 1,815 transplanters received their assignments of land elsewhere. None the less, by examining more closely the implementation of the transplantation in that county, some insight can be gained into how this scheme actually unfolded across Connacht in the second half of the 1650s. Some of the trends evident in Roscommon, such as newcomers being assigned most of the land redistributed, were also in evidence elsewhere.[155] Each of the four counties concerned also had its garrisons, its reserved lands and its Protestant purchasers. The tensions which existed between natives and newcomers in Roscommon must also have been a feature of the transplantation in the other counties. For a great many transplanters the available sources reveal only a sparse amount of information. For others, something more of their experiences can be pieced together. In all cases it is clear that the transplanters faced a sharp adjustment in their circumstances, which can only have compounded the problems bequeathed by a decade of war and conquest; the claim made by Sir Robert Talbot in 1658 that they had 'not a ffift part at most in value of their former estates granted them' may not have been too far off the mark.[156] This outcome placed many in a situation where the best of their limited options was to sell their assignments of land to a low bidder. As a result, even in the four counties set aside for the Catholics, the level of Protestant proprietorship was increased in the 1650s. At the same time, Catholic landholding east of the Shannon had been all but wiped out. Although some of the more drastic elements of the settlement drawn up early in the decade had not been implemented, a revolution in land-ownership had taken place. At the end of the decade, however, as a restoration of the Stuart monarchy beckoned, the Catholics had reason to hope that this revolution would soon be reversed.

---

154 MS Prendergast 2, fo. 669.
155 Simington, *Transplantation*, passim.
156 MS Bellew of Mountbellew 31,946.

6

The Transplanters and the Restoration Land Settlement

In the midst of the political uncertainty which marked the close of the 1650s, many Irish Catholics at home and abroad had reason to hope that they would soon be able to recover their confiscated estates. In December 1659 a gathering of gentlemen and officers in Brussels resolved to petition their exiled king for 'security for their lives, estates, and equal liberty of subjects with England and Scotland; and a liberty of conscience in a modest and humble way'.[1] In May 1660 another group of Irish Catholics sent an address from London to Ormond at Breda. Describing themselves as 'the remnant of our miserable nation', they expressed the hope that their presence in London would enable them to 'reap with the first in this twilight of a coming settlement'.[2] The general outlines of the complex land settlement which unfolded over the following two decades have been reconstructed by a number of historians. Among the more detailed works with a regional focus, Laurence Arnold's study of Co. Dublin is particularly illuminating.[3] The main outcome is undisputed: in contrast to post-1660 developments in England and Scotland, the landownership changes recently wrought in Ireland would for the most part remain intact.[4]

Within the broader context provided by existing scholarship, this chapter will

---

[1] MS Carte 30, fo. 4.

[2] Ibid. fo. 626

[3] Laurence Arnold, The restoration land settlement in County Dublin, 1660–1688, Dublin 1993. See also Carte, The life of Ormond, ii. 200–366; Leland, The history of Ireland, iii. 423–73; Prendergast, Ireland from the restoration to the revolution, 1–56; William Butler, Confiscation in Irish history, Dublin–London 1918, 165–205; Bottigheimer, 'The restoration land settlement', 1–21; John Gerald Simms, 'The restoration, 1660–85', in Moody, Martin and Byrne, A new history of Ireland, iii. 420–53; John Cronin, 'The restoration of the kingdom of Ireland', unpubl. MA diss. NUI Galway 1999; Clarke, Prelude to restoration; Kevin McKenny, The Laggan army in Ireland, 1640–1685, Dublin 2005, 132–56, and 'The restoration land settlement in Ireland: a statistical intepretation'; Michael Perceval-Maxwell, 'The Irish restoration land settlement and its historians', in Dennehy, Restoration Ireland, 19–34.

[4] Hrothgar John Habakkuk, 'Landowners and the civil war', Economic History Review, xviii (1965), 130–51 at pp. 139–42, 147, and 'The land settlement and the restoration of Charles II', Transactions of the Royal Historical Society 5th ser. xxvii (1978), 201–22; Joan Thirsk 'The restoration land settlement', Journal of Modern History xxvi (1954), 315–28 at p. 323.

seek to address the more specific question of how the restoration settlement impacted on the position of the transplanters. For the 1660s three documents in particular were of crucial importance. In the *Gracious declaration* of November 1660, the king acknowledged the competing claims of the Protestants and Catholics and outlined the methods through which the impossible task of satisfying both sides was to be attempted.[5] The legal basis of the approach set down in 1660 was strengthened by the Act of Settlement of 1662, which incorporated the *Gracious declaration* and added a host of clauses in favour of additional groups and individuals.[6] Further legislation, the Act of Explanation of 1665, sought to resolve outstanding difficulties, of which there were a great many.[7] Each of these three documents generally privileged Protestant claims over those of the Catholics. Moreover, the intense competition for Irish land ensured that even where Catholics had in theory secured some form of entitlement to be restored to their former estates, they frequently failed to secure such an outcome in practice. Catholic appeals to the king, to successive Irish governors and to the courts of claims of 1663 and 1666–9 yielded positive results for some, but for the majority the disappointments of the 1650s were merely reinforced. A careful analysis of how the transplantation issue and the transplanters themselves were treated as the *Gracious declaration*, the Act of Settlement and the Act of Explanation were each in turn formulated and implemented in the 1660s should allow a better understanding of the consequences of the Restoration land settlement for that large group of landowners. By 1670 a number of significant issues remained to be addressed. Perhaps the most notable of these was the uncertain position of the many transplanted landowners whose title to land in Connacht under the restored monarchy had not yet been regularised and confirmed. It is necessary, therefore, finally to explore the circumstances under which the transplanters' claims were eventually dealt with in the 1670s as part of a wider effort to bring the implementation of the land settlement to a conclusion.

The *Gracious declaration*

At the Restoration, Irish Catholic hopes of recovering lost ground rested in part on the set of promises made to them over a decade before by the marquis of Ormond. The 1649 articles of peace, the foundation of Ormond's royalist alliance in Ireland, had guaranteed a full pardon for all offences committed since 1641

---

[5] *His majesties gracious declaration for the settlement of his kingdome of Ireland, and satisfaction of the several interests of adventurers, soldiers, and other his majesties subjects there*, Dublin 1660.

[6] *An act for the better execution of his majesties gracious declaration for the settlement of his kingdome of Ireland, and satisfaction of the several interests of adventurers, soldiers, and other his majesties subjects there*, Dublin 1662.

[7] *An act for explaining some doubts arising upon an act intituled, an act for the better execution of his majesties gracious declaration for the settlement of his kingdome of Ireland, and satisfaction of the several interests of adventurers, soldiers, and other his majesties subjects there; and for making some alterations of, and additions unto the said act, for the more speedy and effectual settlement of the said kingdom*, Dublin 1665.

and the restoration of Catholic property.[8] In 1660 Charles II duly referred to his obligations towards his Irish Catholic subjects in the course of an address to the English House of Lords: 'They have shown much affection to me abroad ... and you will have a care for my honour, and of what I have promised to them.'[9] However, the Protestants then in possession of most of the land of Ireland had no intention of making way for the former Catholic proprietors of their estates. The Protestant convention which met in Dublin in February 1660 had as one of its leading priorities the preservation of the land redistribution of the 1650s. It accordingly sought to exclude Catholics both from the anticipated act of indemnity and from membership of the Irish parliament which would be tasked with passing it.[10]

Following his triumphant return to London in May 1660, the king was presented with a raft of conflicting proposals concerning the resolution of the Irish land question. Moreover, Irish Protestant opinion on the matter was far from uniform. Lord Broghill, Sir John Clotworthy and other agents from the Protestant convention sought as far as possible to preserve the *status quo*. They proposed that only Ormond and a few other deserving royalists should be restored to their estates. Sir Charles Coote disagreed, as such an approach would have allowed even those individuals who had opposed the restoration of the monarchy to keep their Irish lands. On the other hand the Old English Protestant Sir Maurice Eustace proposed to overturn many of the recent alterations. Amongst other points he argued that neither the Cromwellian army nor the adventurers enjoyed any legal title to their estates, as they had been granted under the terms of English parliamentary acts which ought to have no force in Ireland. He also pointed out that both groups had secured far more land than they should have done because their assignments had been admeasured in Irish plantation acres, rather than the considerably smaller English statute acres originally stipulated by the Adventurers' Act.[11] Meanwhile, the Catholic agents proposed a full Catholic restoration, after which they would contribute a share of their yearly income to compensate deprived adventurers and soldiers.[12] Ormond's biographer Thomas Carte explained that the king 'was at a loss which to prefer of these interests, which seemed incompatible'. Ormond himself was under no illusions regarding the apparent difficulties which lay ahead; he confessed that 'there must be new discoveries of a new Ireland, for the old will not serve to satisfy these engagements. It remains, then, to determine which party must suffer in the default of means to satisfy all'.[13]

Because the implementation of the transplantation had been essential in enabling the recent plantations, its status now assumed a crucial importance for all parties. Unsurprisingly, there was a sharp divergence between the respective views expressed by the agents representing the Protestant convention and the Catholic interest. Broghill and his colleagues insisted that all transplanters

8   John Milton, *Articles of peace, made and concluded with the Irish rebels and papists by James earle of Ormond ... upon all which are added observations*, London 1649, 6–7.
9   Arnold, *The restoration land settlement*, 38.
10 Clarke, *Prelude to restoration in Ireland*, 298–314.
11 Arnold, *The restoration land settlement*, 40.
12 Ibid.
13 Carte, *Life of Ormond*, ii. 215, 240.

should be barred from restoration because of 'their own voluntary act' in accepting lands in Connacht.[14] The Catholics were led by the lawyer Sir Nicholas Plunkett, a former confederate and one of the transplanted. He countered that the transplanters had been forced 'to accept despicable proportions of land in Connaght or see their wives and children starve before their faces'. Among those who had managed to avoid this 'seven years forced penance' in the west, some had been 'sold as slaves into America', while others were imprisoned 'until they were not able to put bread into their mouths'. Plunkett also pointed to the 1649 articles of peace, arguing that the promises made by Ormond ought now to take precedence over the policies implemented by the Cromwellians.[15] In the face of these Catholic protests, the Protestant convention agents conceded some ground and agreed that Catholics found to be innocent of rebellion and of all other misdemeanours should be restored to their estates.[16] At the same time, they dug in their heels on the wider issue of reversing the transplantation: 'since above 300,000 Protestants were murdered without provocation … who could blame them for putting those Irish … into such a part of the kingdom, as might most probably confine them from the like wickedness in the future'?[17]

As the Protestants and Catholics went about convincing the king of the justice of their contrasting positions, Catholic faith in Ormond, recently created a duke, soon began to waver. In particular, they had expected Ormond to throw his considerable weight behind their central argument concerning the validity of the 1649 articles of peace. With the duke characteristically holding back from anything like decisive action, the Franciscan Peter Walsh observed of his coreligionists that 'a dimnesse and a darkesse [was] seizing their judgements'.[18] In a letter to Ormond in October 1660, Walsh pointed out that many Protestants whom he deemed 'far more heinously criminal' than the Irish Catholics had been almost universally pardoned by the act of indemnity recently passed in the English parliament. Only the regicides and the Irish Catholics had been 'held unworthy to rejoice in the Kings restauration'. Although Walsh conceded that some Catholics had broken the terms agreed with Ormond in 1649, he argued that 'the transplantation [could] not be continued on any such account'. Unless the king could be convinced of this point, he would, according to Walsh, risk 'God's revenge of article-breaking'.[19]

Within days of Walsh's admonition of Ormond, the king was instead won over by a set of proposals presented by Broghill and some other Irish Protestants.[20] By the end of November 1660, Charles had signed *His majesties gracious declaration for the settlement of his kingdom of Ireland*. This document revealed that the adventurers and the soldiers were to keep the property that they had acquired in the

---

[14] MS Gilbert 219, fo. 266.

[15] Ibid. fos 256–79.

[16] Ibid. fos 280–327.

[17] Ibid. fo. 308.

[18] Peter Walsh, *A letter desiring a just and mercifull regard of the Roman Catholicks of Ireland, given about the end of October 1660, to the then marquess, now duke of Ormond and the second time lord lieutenant of that kingdom*, [?]Dublin [?]1662, 1.

[19] Ibid.

[20] Carte, *Life of Ormond*, ii. 215–16.

1650s.[21] Furthermore, effectively all pre-war Protestant landowners were to be restored to their estates and any adventurers or soldiers displaced by them were to receive compensatory reprisals out of other available lands.[22] Another newly-constituted interest group, royalist officers with arrears of pay still outstanding from the 1640s, was to be satisfied with land in Wicklow, Longford, Leitrim and Donegal, as well as grants of property in towns and corporations.[23] These terms alone were enough to make it clear that the Catholics had failed spectacularly in their efforts to overturn the settlement of the 1650s.

The fate of the transplanters was dealt with across several sections of the king's declaration. In keeping with Broghill's earlier claims, the transplantation was described as 'an act of their own, [which] we might without any injustice deny to relieve them in'. None the less, in the interests of 'equitable mercy', any Catholic who could demonstrate unbroken loyalty to the crown since 1641 was to be restored as an innocent. However, property located in corporation towns was deemed off-limits even for innocent Catholics, unless the king should see fit to grant exemptions in individual cases. Transplanters deemed innocent were required to surrender their Connacht assignments.[24] Other Catholics who could not claim or prove innocence were grouped into three main subcategories. First, those who had refused to submit to the agreements negotiated between Ormond and the confederates in the 1640s were deemed to have forfeited all favour. Secondly, those who had observed these agreements and had then later accepted land in Connacht were 'to stand bound ... and not be relieved against their own act'. Lastly, a group of 224 individually-named ensignmen who had fought for the king abroad were to be restored to their estates, provided that they had not obtained decrees for land in Connacht. A number of these men, including Viscount Castleconnell and Sir Ulick Burke of Glinsk, Co. Galway, had in fact received land as transplanters.[25] In any case, the provision made for this large group of Catholics was rendered largely worthless by the stipulation that adventurers and soldiers should not surrender any property to the ensignmen until they had first received other lands in compensation.

The *Gracious declaration* also named thirty-six further individuals who would become known as 'the nominees'. These were for the most part prominent Catholics who 'in an especial manner merited our Grace and favour' but who, due to their prominent roles as confederates in the 1640s, had little hope of being adjudged innocent. Almost half of this group had acquired land as transplanters. They included Lords Westmeath, Ikerrin, Trimleston, Galmoy and Athenry, as well as Sir Richard Barnewall. Despite the king's warm acknowledgement of their past services, the nominees too would have to wait until the adventurers and soldiers were ready to make way for them.[26] The fiction that a vast store of undisposed lands was available to compensate the adventurers and soldiers who stood in the way of the restoration of most of these proprietors enabled the king

21 The *Gracious declaration*, 5–9.
22 Ibid. 12–13.
23 Ibid. 9–12.
24 Ibid. 14–16.
25 Ibid. 18–27.
26 Ibid. 20–1.

to make promises to all sides, when all sides knew that there would not be enough Ireland to go around.

In this context, a decree of innocence, leading to restoration without the requirement for previous reprisals to adventurers and soldiers, assumed great importance for dispossessed Catholic proprietors. However, the team of commissioners appointed in February 1661 to hear their claims inspired little confidence, as most of them had a vested interest in maintaining the existing settlement intact. Furthermore, their instructions set down very strict criteria for innocence, barring even those who had merely lived quietly at home in rebel quarters during the 1640s.[27] The uncertainty surrounding the commissioners' actual powers to grant lands presented a further problem, as their proceedings were authorised merely by an act of state as opposed to an act of parliament. Despite these unpromising circumstances, the transplanter Henry O'Neill attempted to recover his lands. His optimism was grounded upon his war record as a royalist soldier both in England and Ireland in the 1640s. Yet his hopes were dashed by the Cromwellian grantee of his Co. Antrim estate, Sir John Clotworthy. The latter, recently ennobled as Viscount Massarene, was able to block the hearing of O'Neill's claim simply because he had been a transplanter.[28] In any case, it was widely recognised that the commissioners' proceedings were unlikely to resolve the many difficulties which existed, and that an Irish parliament was needed to give the weight of legislative sanction to the proposed land settlement. Parliament was accordingly summoned to meet in May 1661.[29] A disputed election result for the borough of Tuam, Co. Galway, returned the sole Catholic, Geoffrey Browne, but he would never attempt to take up his seat. Instead, he acted once more as agent for the Galway townsmen as the Protestant and Catholic interests renewed their wrangling over Irish land in London.[30]

Debate and division

In the summer of 1661 the Catholic agents at court moved to petition the king before the new bill of settlement then being devised in the Irish parliament had reached London. In one of their many complaints, they objected to the reported imprisonment of some Catholics who had returned from Connacht to other parts of Ireland. They were primarily concerned, however, with the terms of the *Gracious declaration* and with the likely content of the programme being prepared in Dublin. The agents sought leniency for transplanted Catholics 'who only had a few acres given them in meer charity ... [and] those who took decrees and never had any benefit by them'. They also argued that those individuals who received land under the eighth qualification, and were therefore transplanted 'meerly for religion', ought to be restored without any further ado.[31] The eventual Protestant response to this latest Catholic effort was uncompromising, reiterating the point

---

[27] Arnold, *The restoration land settlement*, 42–3.
[28] *Act of settlement*, 55; Major Henry O'Neill to the king, Sept. 1661, SP 63/317/205.
[29] Arnold, *The restoration land settlement*, 43.
[30] ODNB, *s.v.* 'Browne, Geoffrey (c. 1608–1668)'; SP 63/307/98.
[31] MS Gilbert 219, fos 346–53.

that transplantation was apparently 'their own act' and dismissing the validity of the 1649 articles of peace on the grounds that the king had been compelled by necessity to agree to them.[32]

At the end of July 1661 the Irish government dispatched commissioners to London to expedite the royal approval of the draft bills which had been sent over.[33] Their arrival gave the Catholics new grounds for complaint. They objected in particular to the proposed preamble to the bill of settlement, wherein the progress of the 'unnatural rebellion' which had 'manifest[ed] itself by the murther and destruction of many thousands of your said Majesties good and loyal subjects' was rehearsed at length. Sir Nicholas Plunkett viewed this preamble as unnecessary, irrelevant and inaccurate: 'instead of an act of oblivion, here is an bill for passing a brand of infamy'.[34] Plunkett's protests simply created an opportunity for the Protestant agents to rehearse at length before the king their justification for the content of the controversial preamble. They insisted that 'it were preposterous to vest so great a part of that kingdom in your Majesty without declaring the justice of it, which ariseth out of matter of fact'.[35] The 'fact' of the wholesale massacre allegedly executed by the Catholics in 1641 remained one of the strongest weapons in the Protestant arsenal.

Over the following weeks the Catholics continued their protests against other aspects of the impending settlement, with the key issue of reprisals proving particularly controversial. The Catholics insisted that all lands available for reprisals had already been used up in restoring Ormond and a few others. They claimed that because the king had been misinformed on this matter, 'the work of finding reprisals should be put upon those who undertook it', namely the Protestants. The transplantation scheme, 'the acts of the highest force that the cruel hand of the usurper could inflict', was also revisited, but to little avail.[36] The decisive moment in the rancorous debate came eventually in March 1662 when the king was shown a letter dating from 1647 and signed by Sir Nicholas Plunkett which had offered control of Ireland to various continental powers. Although he had recently admitted that 'for my part, rebel for rebel, I had rather trust a Papist rebel than a Presbyterian one', the king took the opportunity to banish Plunkett from the court. All further Catholic petitions were forbidden and within two months the Act of Settlement had been passed in Dublin.[37]

The Orrery-Walsh debate

The struggle between the Protestant and Catholic parties was also inevitably carried beyond the corridors of power. The most notable exchange which occurred in 1662 was the pamphlet debate engaged in by Peter Walsh and Broghill, recently created earl of Orrery. This episode was sparked by Walsh's decision to publish the aforementioned letter which he had sent to Ormond late

---

32 Ibid. fos 354–80.
33 Ibid. fos 344–6.
34 Ibid. fos 405–22.
35 Ibid. fos 422–507.
36 Ibid. fos 568–620.
37 Arnold, *The restoration land settlement*, 46–7.

in 1660.[38] He did so most likely to show his fellow Catholics that he had made every effort to secure official favour for them. The appearance of Walsh's brief vindication of the Catholic cause inspired two robust pamphlets from Orrery, both of which he published anonymously.[39]

Orrery's first work, The Irish colours displayed, seems to have been a hurried response to the publication of Walsh's letter. It emphasised the centuries-old division between the English and the Irish in Ireland and asserted, as Giraldus Cambrensis had done in the twelfth century, that 'the contention between the two parties in Ireland will never have an end'. The Irish could not be trusted because 'bloody animosities were constant and hereditary to them'. Orrery also lamented supposedly savage Irish customs, such as their funeral rites, 'elegantly described by Spencer in his short discourse of Ireland', and still allegedly practised in the north. He insisted that 'the peace and safety of that kingdom can not be provided for by balancing interests between English and Irish, but by boying up one or other of them out of danger of sinking again'. Therefore the Protestant state could not afford to make any significant concessions to Catholics in the new land settlement.[40] Future peace and stability could only be ensured by Protestant predominance within the framework of a Protestant state.

Orrery's second pamphlet added substantially to the arguments which he had made in The Irish colours displayed. Writing anonymously as 'a person of quality', he depicted Walsh's letter as insulting to the king and Ormond, as well as to all Protestants in the three kingdoms, and he sought systematically to undermine the arguments that Walsh had advanced.[41] Orrery sought to demonstrate that the promises made to Catholics in 1649 were now invalid, both because they had been made under duress, and because the Catholics had proceeded to break their side of the bargain by excommunicating Ormond and his followers in 1650. He accepted that many Protestants had transgressed in the recent past and that they were now reaping the benefit of 'his Majesties grace, which is as great as their guilt'. However 'the Irish Papists [could] only claim what is due by Articles, the foundation whereof being dissolv'd on their parts, they can justly claim nothing by them'.[42] Royal grace was apparently inapplicable to Catholics. Orrery also pointed to the lessons of history; 'the conquered never did (some think morally never will) love the Conqueror'. The Irish Catholics, after frequent rebellions against Queen Elizabeth and her successors, were now at last a conquered people. Having endeavoured to strengthen his arguments through reference to the past, Orrery then sought to relate the situation in Ireland to one of the problems which dogged politics and society across early modern Europe. The Catholics' religious principles were, he claimed, inconsistent with loyalty to a Protestant monarch; 'Can his Majesty trust them, if they be not faithful to their Conscience- ingagement? and if they be, can he trust them when their Consciences ingage them to his enemy?'[43]

---

38 Walsh, A letter.
39 For a discussion of these pamphlets see Rankin, Between Spenser and Swift, 177–9.
40 Roger Boyle, earl of Orrery, The Irish colours displayed in a reply of an English Protestant to a late letter of an Irish Roman Catholique: both address'd to his grace the duke of Ormond, London 1662, 1–17.
41 Idem, The answer of a person of quality.
42 Ibid. 7–16.
43 Ibid.

Orrery proceeded to address the more specific issues of transplantation and the readmission of Catholics to the corporations. He claimed that 'many other countreys and ages [had] formerly on less grounds used Transplantation'. He furthered his attack on the transplanters by citing the two petitions presented to parliament by the Leinster officers in mid-1659 in which they had sought, amongst other things, the confirmation of their transplanted estates. Sir Robert Talbot and Colonel Garret Moore, the Catholic agents who presented those petitions, had remained active as lobbyists in London post-1660. They were now censured for adhering to protocol in addressing the restored rump parliament as 'the Supreme Authority'; according to Orrery, 'the very Murtherers of his late Majesty of Glorious Memory [were] the elected sanctuary of the Irish Papists'.[44]

Orrery's skilled and provocative writings inevitably drew a rapid retort from Peter Walsh. He responded to Orrery's first pamphlet, The Irish colours displayed, with a work entitled The Irish colours folded. Walsh evidently did not know the identity of the author who had sought to demolish Catholic claims to favour; he described him only as 'an impudent assertor of strange positions'. He took as his starting point Orrery's seeming adherence to the view 'that this contention between the two parties in Ireland will never have an end'. Walsh dismissed Orrery as a 'man of separation' who aimed only at 'the extirpation of the nation' and he sought instead to depict the restoration of the monarchy as an opportunity to heal old and bitter divisions. History showed that this could be done, as 'the Brittains, the Danes, the Saxons, and the Normans [were] now so incorporated into England, as the memory of all distinction [was] lost amongst them'. By contrast, Orrery was guilty of 'engrafting such numbers of Old English Families upon the Irish stock and interest [and of] imposing on and abusing Spencer's View'. Walsh concluded by again pleading with Ormond to use his position of influence to secure a pardon and equitable treatment for the Irish Catholics. He also expressed the hope that the imminent arrival of Ormond in Ireland as lord lieutenant would mark a new beginning for 'the many other different parties and interests' in Ireland.[45] Although Walsh continued to harbour some optimism, the contents of the Act of Settlement of 1662 clearly represented a defeat for Catholic ambitions and a triumph for those Protestants, such as Orrery, who wished to maintain as far as possible the landholding changes implemented in the 1650s.

Implementing the settlement

The undoubted significance of the Act of Settlement was reflected in James Hardiman's assessment dating from 1825: it was 'an Act in defence and reprobation of which some hundreds of volumes have since been written; but, under which ... the landed property of Ireland had been disposed of and settled, and

---

44 Ibid. 16–32.
45 Peter Walsh, The Irish colours folded, or, The Irish Roman–Catholick's reply to the (pretended) English Protestants answer to the letter desiring a just and mercifall regard of the Roman Catholicks of Ireland (which answer is entitled The Irish colours displayed), addressed (as that answer and letter have been) to his grace the lord duke of Ormond, lord lieutenant general, and general governour of that kingdome, London 1662, 1–32.

continues, in great part, to be enjoyed until this day'.[46] This legislation provided for the establishment of a court of claims, which was to hear all claims to innocence. Along with incorporating the text of the *Gracious declaration*, the act also contained a large number of provisos and additional clauses in favour of various groups and individuals. One clause added eighteen names to the original list of thirty-six nominees to be restored after previous reprisals. Nearly all of those added were transplanters; they included Sir Richard Blake, Sir Robert Talbot, Geoffrey Browne and Edmond Dillon of Drumraney in Co. Westmeath.[47] Another clause confirmed the Protestant Connacht purchasers in possession of the estates which they had acquired in the 1650s.[48] Provision was also made for the prompt restoration of a number of individual transplanters, including Colonel John Fitzpatrick and Sir John Bellew of Co. Louth.[49] The Connacht land vacated by restored persons was to be used to compensate transplanters and others displaced as a consequence of the restoration before previous reprisals of figures such as Lords Clanricarde and Costello-Gallen, both of whom had also secured crucial provisos in the act.[50]

Because innocent landowners were to be restored without the need for previous reprisals to adventurers and soldiers, a decree of innocence offered the best hope of restitution for dispossessed Catholics. The relevant court of claims began its hearings in January 1663. It would close eight months later, with many claimants left unheard. According to Laurence Arnold, the commissioners ruled on 829 cases, with negative or 'nocent' judgements being returned in at least 130 instances.[51] For the transplanters, the problem posed by the short sitting of the court was compounded by the fact that several of its procedural rules also discriminated against them. These rules stipulated that claimants who had not sued for decrees of land in Connacht were to be processed first and that preference would be given to individuals from Co. Dublin and other eastern counties, with Connacht landowners being left until last.[52] As a result, a number of transplanters had the hearing of their claims postponed.[53] In most cases, postponement ensured that the claimant would never be heard. On the other hand, some transplanters benefitted from the fact that the rules which might have prevented them from being heard were not always strictly applied. On its second day in session, the court of claims restored two transplanters, Sir Henry Talbot and Garret Fox. A few days later, the Dongan family also enjoyed success.[54] Overall, close to forty transplanted persons obtained decrees of innocence, while at least three, Donnogh O'Callaghan, John Carroll and Arthur Molloy, were found 'nocent'. A further fifteen heirs or relatives claiming inheritance from

---

46 IRC, *Fifteenth report*, 33.
47 *Act of settlement*, 21, 124.
48 Ibid. 108–9, 121
49 Ibid. 51, 87, 92, 105.
50 Ibid. 109.
51 Arnold, *The restoration land settlement*, 53.
52 John Gerald Simms, 'Introduction', in *Court of claims: submissions and evidence, 1663*, ed. Geraldine Tallon, Dublin 2006, pp. xi–xii.
53 Ibid. 113, 332–3, 377, 385.
54 Deputy keeper of the public records in Ireland, *Nineteenth report*, London 1887, 42–3.

transplanters were also restored.[55] However, the Cromwellian grantees of their former estates were not always willing to give way to innocents, and protracted legal proceedings sometimes ensued.

The proceedings of the court of claims and the implementation of other elements of the Act of Settlement helped further to confuse the picture of landholding in the west. Approximately sixty proprietors restored as innocents laid claim to estates situated within the four-county transplantation zone. However, the terms of the *Gracious declaration* protected transplanters settled on the estates of these innocents from being automatically displaced.[56] This provision caused some confusion and resulted in a large number of complaints being addressed to the court of claims even after August 1663. Sir Henry O'Neill, a recently knighted transplanter, found it necessary to take three separate actions to preserve his entitlements against Connacht innocents, while Connacht purchasers such as Charles Coote, earl of Mountrath, and Sir George Bingham also applied for protection from dispossession.[57] In 1664 the Catholic agents at court reported that 47,000 acres belonging to Connacht innocents remained in the hands of transplanters. On the other hand, the local magnates Clanricarde, Costello-Gallen and Inchiquin had apparently recovered possession of 167,000 acres formerly assigned to transplanters.[58] These circumstances guaranteed intense competition for any Connacht land vacated by restored innocents. Dispossessed transplanters vied, usually without success, with displaced Connacht purchasers, royal favourites and a range of other petitioners.[59] As the implementation of the land settlement quickly met with difficulties in the west and elsewhere, the various parties concerned recognised the urgent need for clarification of several confusing and contradictory aspects of the Act of Settlement. The favoured solution was further legislation.

The Act of Explanation

Throughout the period of its sitting in 1663, the court of claims had given many Protestants cause for alarm. At an early stage one of the commissioners noted that the Irish House of Commons was dismayed because a few Catholics had been restored, 'an act of justice, and therefore and unheard-of crime in this land'.[60] The discovery of Colonel Thomas Blood's armed conspiracy in May 1663 further heightened tensions. By September the Irish privy council had sent over to London a new bill of settlement designed to be more palatable to Protestants. Two months later, the acrimonious debate between the agents representing the Catholic and Protestant parties recommenced, with each side once again seeking

---

55 Ibid. 42–83; *Court of claims*, passim.
56 *Act of settlement*, 26.
57 *Court of claims*, 422, 424, 427. Sir Charles Coote, who played such a key role in implementing the transplantation in the 1650s, was created earl of Mountrath in 1660 and died the following year. He was succeeded by his son, also Charles.
58 MS Gilbert 198, fo. 226.
59 See, for example, the petitions for land in NLI, MS Ormond 2,511, fos 15–17b.
60 Arnold, *The restoration land settlement*, 71.

to limit what the other should have.[61] Unsurprisingly, the voicing of their conflicting claims, which echoed the arguments made earlier in the decade, eventually led to stalemate.[62]

By the summer of 1665 all sides were at last ready to accept a compromise. Crucially, it was agreed that there should be no further trials of innocence. Instead, the adventurers, the soldiers and the Connacht purchasers were to surrender one-third of their estates so as to free up land for reprisals and for the restoration of individuals nominated by the king. This switch towards royal nomination and away from tests of innocence which, given more time, could be undergone by any proprietor ensured that the claims of most Catholics to restoration were now simply jettisoned. From the point of view of those Catholic elites with influence sufficient to secure nomination, this change seemed to increase their chances of recovering more land. This new approach was enshrined in the so-called Act of Explanation passed by the Irish parliament in December 1665. It was made up for the most part of provisos in favour of particular groups and individuals.[63] In one of the more notable clauses, fifty-four Catholic nominees were promised restoration to their former principal seats and 2,000 acres adjoining. These included thirty-three of the nominees named in the Act of Settlement 'for whom no provision hath yet been made'. Of the twenty-one men newly listed, eleven were transplanters or their heirs.[64] Some of these individuals had undoubtedly contributed to the fund of £30,000 which Sir Robert and Colonel Richard Talbot had taken to London 'to get the secluded Irish into their estates'.[65] However, while the use of influence and patronage at court were important factors, the restoration of these leading Catholics continued as before to depend on the discovery of alternative lands to reprise the adventurers and soldiers still in possession of their former estates. As a result, only a handful of the nominees would actually obtain certificates for land from the second court of claims.[66] A number of further clauses of the act were also of consequence to various transplanters, not least the proposed restoration of several more Connacht proprietors without any requirement for previous reprisals.[67]

Among those singled out for restoration in this way was Theobald Burke, Viscount Mayo, whose father had been executed at Galway in 1653.[68] His case was to receive considerable attention from the second court of claims, which sat from January 1666 to January 1669.[69] Although Mayo secured a decree for 33,000 acres, his extensive claims were opposed by numerous transplanters and some Connacht purchasers.[70] While Mayo was willing to concede possession of some land to the well-connected Sir Robert Talbot, other individuals did not have to

---

[61] Ibid. 72.
[62] MS Gilbert 198, fos 208–26.
[63] Act of explanation, passim.
[64] Ibid. 101–2.
[65] HMC, Manuscripts of the earl of Dartmouth, ed. W. O. Hewlett, London 1896, 110.
[66] IRC, Fifteenth report, 123, 219, 222; MS Stowe 213, fo. 202.
[67] Act of explanation, 80–1, 83–4, 137, 145, 148.
[68] Ibid. 137.
[69] Arnold, The restoration land settlement, 97.
[70] NLI, MS 31, fos 175–88, 192v. See also Cunningham, 'Cromwellian County Mayo', forthcoming.

be treated so carefully.[71] In many instances leases were arranged. For example, John Porter, a transplanter from Co. Waterford, agreed to pay Mayo £300 up-front and a further 10s. per year in order to keep possession of his assignment of 488 acres. The terms of such leases often reflected the uncertainty that existed regarding the status of the transplanters. Porter's lease was to terminate if and when 'the said transplantation at Athlone or Loughrea shall be totally and in every respect broken, disproved, annulled ... and taken away by force or meanes of any act of parliament'.[72] Further south in Co. Clare, Daniel O'Brien, son and heir of the former transplanter Viscount Clare, secured a decree for 50,000 acres in December 1666.[73] The second court of claims also confirmed large tracts of land to the Protestant Connacht purchasers.[74] Some deeper sense of how the proceedings of this and the previous court of claims impacted on landholding in Connacht can be acquired by looking once again at developments in Co. Roscommon.

The courts of claims and Co. Roscommon

Under the terms of the Act of Settlement of 1662, twenty-seven proprietors from Co. Roscommon were restored as innocents or in accordance with personal provisos. This group comprised eighteen Catholics and nine Protestants.[75] Among the lands recovered by Clanricarde was his estate in the barony of Athlone, which had been divided between nine transplanters in the 1650s. A report compiled in the 1670s recorded that Clanricarde possessed over 4,500 acres in Roscommon, around the same as his pre-war total, as well as over 105,000 acres in Co. Galway.[76] His fellow nobleman Costello-Gallen claimed almost 6,500 acres in Roscommon, more than five times what he had actually owned in 1641. Along with his own former estate, Costello-Gallen secured the estates forfeited by his uncles William and Thomas Dillon. From the family viewpoint, this made perfect sense. While Costello-Gallen was entitled to be restored without previous reprisals, many of his less influential relatives were barred from recovering their estates because of their failure to secure decrees of innocence.[77] The use of this particular family-orientated strategy appears to have been widespread, with Ormond and Viscount Clare among those accused of being the chief culprits.

Alongside men of influence such as Clanricarde, the two most substantial local transplanters in Co. Roscommon both emerged as Catholic innocents in 1663. Sir Thomas Nugent's son and heir Robert was restored to 4,280 acres in the county.[78] This process was relatively straightforward, as there was no other

---

71 NLI, MS 31, fo. 175; MS Westport, 40,889/12(1).
72 MS Westport, 40,889/6–8.
73 IRC, *Fifteenth report*, 87–8.
74 MS Prendergast 2, fos 1,029–31, 1,037–9.
75 Deputy keeper, *Nineteenth report*, 41–87.
76 *Books of survey and distribution*, i, passim; MS Headfort 2B 33 18, fos 208v–240r; MS Quit Rent, Box 2A. 12. 44, lands held by innocents in Co. Galway, fo. 45.
77 *Act of settlement*, 108–9; *Books of survey and distribution*, i, passim; MS Quit Rent, Box 2A. 12. 44, lands held by innocents in Co. Roscommon, fos 7–8.
78 Deputy keeper, *Nineteenth report*, 47; *Books of survey and distribution*, iii. 75–81.

claimant to the land in question. In contrast, the restoration of Theobald Dillon was a more complicated affair. The schedule of lands presented to the first court of claims by Dillon's attorney John Barber revealed that his inheritance was now in the hands of numerous individuals.[79] Although transplanters had no legal defence against proprietors such as Costello-Gallen who were provided with individual legislative provisos authorising their restoration without previous reprisals, the Act of Settlement did protect them from dispossession by persons equipped solely with decrees of innocence from the court of claims.[80] For this reason, Dillon recovered no more than about half of the 5,200 acres which had formerly belonged to his grandfather in the barony of Boyle.[81] Overall, the number of acres restored to Catholics in Co. Roscommon upon decrees of innocence or upon provisos in the Act of Settlement can be estimated at around 28,000.[82] It is notable that Old English claimants such as Nugent and Dillon fared much better than the more numerous members of Old Irish Catholic families who had between them owned much of the county in 1641. The McDermots were represented solely by the innocent Henry McDermott Roe who recovered around 430 acres, while Owen O'Connor fared slightly better with 633 acres. None of the Kellys or Fallons succeeded in proving their innocence, while one member of the Hanly family may have recovered as little as twenty-two acres.[83]

A few years later, the implementation of the Act of Explanation in Co. Roscommon saw the granting of land to three distinct groups. The least significant group comprised three well-connected Catholics, Viscount Netterville, Colonel Garret Moore and Colonel John Kelly, newly designated for restoration without previous reprisals. Between them, these men recovered around 3,400 acres.[84] More significant were the claims entered before the second court of claims by the Protestant Connacht purchasers. This group included Dominick French, son of the transplanter Patrick French. The requirement for Connacht purchasers to retrench one-third of their estates meant that French had to surrender 1,682 acres, but he nevertheless secured title to a total of 3,144 acres in the county.[85] This grant frustrated the ambitions of Theobald Dillon, the innocent former proprietor of most of French's lands. The remaining Connacht purchasers in the county, around twenty-five individuals, included both members of long-established families and relative newcomers. They were confirmed in possession of roughly 29,000 acres of former Catholic land.[86] This was nearly one quarter of the total which had been granted to transplanters in the county a

---

[79] Decree of innocence of Theobald Dillon, 25 May 1663, MSS De Freyne (unsorted collection).

[80] Act of settlement, 26.

[81] MS Quit Rent, Box 2A. 12. 44, lands held by innocents in Co. Roscommon, fos 3–5.

[82] Ibid. passim; Deputy keeper, Nineteenth report, 42–87; Books of survey and distribution, iii, passim.

[83] Deputy keeper, Nineteenth report, 48, 77–8; MS Quit Rent, Box 2A. 12. 44, lands held by innocents in Co. Roscommon, fo. 6; Books of survey and distribution, iii. 41.

[84] MS Quit Rent, Box 2A. 12. 44, lands held by innocents in Co. Roscommon, fos 9–13; Books of survey and distribution, i. 92–128.

[85] Claim of Dominick French of Dungar, Co. Roscommon, before the commissioners of the second court of claims: MSS De Freyne (unsorted collection).

[86] IRC, Fifteenth report, 45–233.

decade before. Just under half of the land concerned was secured by members of the families of Coote, King, St George, Ormsby and Jones, with the Cootes laying claim to over 6,000 acres.[87] The most notable newcomers were Captain Theophilus Sandford with 2,112 acres and Captain Nicholas Mahon with 1,815 acres.[88]

The third group to secure land in the county under the terms of the Act of Explanation consisted of prominent royalists who for one reason or another had been promised Irish estates. Colonel William Legge and Charles Berkeley, earl of Falmouth, were two Englishmen included in this category. It was they who eventually secured most of the land vacated through the restoration of the innocent Lady Mary Dongan. Falmouth also secured most of the former Kelly lands released by the restoration of Colonel John Fitzpatrick, thus bringing his new estate in the barony of Athlone to over 2,500 acres. Legge obtained 700 acres in the same barony, as well as a large estate in Co. Galway recently released by the innocent transplanter Thomas Luttrell of Co. Dublin.[89] Altogether more substantial was the estate granted to the king's brother and heir James, duke of York. Under the terms of the settlement, York was to be given all estates held by the regicides in Ireland during the 1650s. In practice, however, much of this land was recovered by innocents and York's agents instead sought out alternative properties to satisfy his requirements.[90] His new estate in Co. Roscommon extended to 2,600 acres, most of which had been previously granted to Ormond's sister-in-law Lady Frances Butler in the 1650s.[91] The gains made by York and other favourites ensured that nearly 6,000 acres of former Catholic lands which were supposed to be ring-fenced to reprise dispossessed transplanters or Connacht purchasers were instead diverted to other ends.

In 1641 Catholics had owned around 125,000 profitable acres in Co. Roscommon. Between 1663 and 1669 the courts of claims disposed of just over 70,000 acres of this land. However, less than half of it was restored to Catholics. The substantial acquisition of land by Protestants, begun by the Connacht purchasers in the 1650s and continued through grants to royal favourites in the 1660s, saw the Protestant share increase by more than 38,000 acres.[92] The remarkable decision to grant the lord presidency lands to Viscount Ranelagh upon the abolition of that office in 1672 meant that a further 5 per cent of the county now came into private Protestant hands.[93] This meant that by the mid-1670s Protestants had obtained secure title to approximately 43 per cent of the profitable land in Co. Roscommon, up from 18 per cent in 1641. The share held by the re-established Church of Ireland was unchanged from the pre-war figure of around 12 per cent. On the other hand, the Catholic innocents and the five individual Catholics who benefitted from special legislative provisos had

---

87 Ibid.

88 Ibid. 48, 79, 95, 125.

89 Ibid. 58, 186.

90 Arnold, *The restoration land settlement*, 100.

91 IRC, *Fifteenth report*, 187–9, 348–96.

92 *Books of survey and distribution*, iii, passim.

93 The king to Arthur Capel, earl of Essex, Whitehall, 13 Jan. 1675, MS Stowe 207, fos 51–4.

together secured title to only around 16 per cent of the profitable land.[94] The outstanding 29 per cent, less than 60,000 acres, was held for the most part by transplanters who had not yet enjoyed the opportunity to obtain proper legal title to their estates. Many transplanted proprietors in the neighbouring counties also fell into this same category. At the end of the 1660s, therefore, it was apparent that despite the substantial work carried out in that decade, the process of settling the ownership of estates in Connacht was still far from complete.

The land question in the early 1670s

The beginning of the new decade witnessed an escalation of Catholic efforts to recover more of their former lands. In November 1670 Colonel Richard Talbot was appointed to travel to London on behalf of the fifty-two signatories of a new Catholic petition. At least one-third of this group consisted of transplanters or their heirs, the most prominent being the earl of Westmeath and Baron Trimleston. On 18 January 1671 Talbot presented before the king and council 'the case of his majesties distressed subjects of Ireland who were outed of their estates by the late usurped government and not yet restored'.[95] In the following month the attorney-general Sir Heneage Finch presented a wholly unsympathetic response, in which he sought trenchantly to uphold the existing settlement: 'if this foundation be shaken, noe other can be layd'. On the question of the transplanters, he revealed that 'I have heard it said that they would suffer none to live in Connaght but such who were friends to their republique.'[96] However, despite Finch's opposition, the granting of titles to Irish land was suspended and a commission of inquiry was appointed to review the state of the settlement.[97]

One of the signatories of the Catholic petition was the transplanter Sir Henry Slingsby, a descendant of an English beneficiary of the Munster plantation in the 1580s. While Talbot was busy lobbying in London, Slingsby decided to pursue another route in an effort to improve his position. In a petition which he sent to the lords justice in Dublin in mid-1671, he voiced his discontent regarding the levying of the so-called annual 'quit rents', which had to be paid to the crown by all persons granted land under the Restoration settlement. Slingsby's grievance arose from the fact that he was being 'compelled to pay quit rents out of those lands in Connaught, altho he hath no letters patent'. Having reviewed the situation, the lords justice found that transplanters had 'nothing to shew for their title to those lands they enjoy, but only the allotments made to them thereof in the usurper's time, which are found to be of very little use to them either to defend or recover their rights in any suit'. They accordingly proposed that a commission be appointed to hear the claims of transplanters and to grant letters patent 'for such part of their estates as shall be thought fitt to confirm to them'.

---

[94] *Books of survey and distribution*, i, passim; MS Quit Rent, Box 2A. 12. 44, lands held by innocents in Co. Roscommon; Deputy keeper, *Nineteenth report*, 42–87.

[95] MS Gilbert 198, fos 35–49; *Act of explanation*, 119–20.

[96] MS Gilbert 198, fos 51–74.

[97] Arnold, *The restoration land settlement*, 127.

To this end, the lords justice sent to London a draft letter to be signed by the king.[98] By mid-1671 therefore, it appeared that some progress was at last being made towards settling transplanters in their estates.

However, following the dispatch of the draft to London, this latest Irish government initiative also ground to a halt. The granting of the request made by the lords justice was presumably hindered by the existence of the commission of inquiry established some months earlier in response to Talbot's Catholic petition. That commission too made little or no progress, and in August 1671 a new body with greater powers of investigation was appointed.[99] Although it supposedly enjoyed enhanced competencies, over a year later it was reported that the subcommissioners appointed by this latest commission of inquiry had not yet done any work.[100] Despite this seeming administrative inertia, Protestant fears that the land settlement was about to be overturned were none the less on the increase. By the beginning of 1673 the adventurers and soldiers were again readying themselves to send agents to London to defend their interests.[101]

In this context the newly-arrived lord lieutenant of Ireland, Arthur Capel, earl of Essex, was understandably keen to gauge the prevailing moods in Ireland. In January 1673 he reported that 'the generalitie of the English who enjoy their estates upon these new titles, could not shake off the apprehensions of loosing them again', while 'the Irish doe almost universally discourse, that they will have their lands agen'.[102] However, the course of events in London soon helped to diffuse some of this tension. An upsurge in anti-Catholic sentiment in England saw the House of Commons pass the Test Act, which required office-holders to take the oaths of supremacy and allegiance and to subscribe to a declaration against transubstantiation. The duke of York's refusal to comply with these measures ensured that his earlier conversion to Catholicism would become public knowledge. The fact that the heir to the throne was a Catholic seemed to bode well for the land claims of his coreligionists in Ireland. On the other hand, the English House of Commons demanded that the commission of inquiry on Irish land be suspended and that the Acts of Settlement and Explanation be confirmed. Catholic hopes appeared to be ruined when the king bowed to the will of his parliament. The defeat of their ambitions was symbolised by the Commons' insistence that Colonel Talbot be banished from court.[103] These developments seemed to augur poorly for a more equitable completion of the settlement. None the less, Essex would spend much of the time up to his departure from Ireland in 1677 dealing with vexing issues relating to land. Moreover, his increasing sympathy for Catholic interests opened up the prospect that the transplanters might at last receive a hearing.

---

98 Lords justice to Lord Lieutenant Berkeley, Dublin, 26 June 1671, MS Stowe 214, fo. 97r–v.

99 Arnold, *The restoration land settlement*, 127.

100 Essex to Henry Bennet, earl of Arlington, Dublin, 3 Sept. 1672, MS Stowe 213, fo. 30v.

101 Essex to Arlington, Dublin, 18 Jan. 1673, ibid. fo. 103v.

102 Ibid.; Essex to Arlington, Dublin, 20 Jan. 1673, ibid. fo. 105v; Essex to Arlington, Dublin, 25 Jan. 1673, ibid. fo. 114.

103 Arnold, *The restoration land settlement*, 128.

Essex and the land settlement

Essex's concerns regarding the land settlement were signalled by a letter which he wrote to the secretary of state, Henry Bennet, earl of Arlington, in the opening months of his administration: 'the leaving of men's minds in doubt of their titles to the estates which they enjoy, may produce very ill effects'.[104] He immediately began to seek means further to satisfy the demands of the various parties to the settlement. However, his efforts were constantly under threat from the activities of 'discoverers'. Their method was to seek out lands which had not yet been granted away or which was held under defective titles and then to petition the king for a patent for the property in question. The duke of York in particular employed agents to identify any lands to which he could lay claim.[105] In May 1673 Essex discovered that Sir William Petty and Sir Henry Ingoldsby were attempting to secure a lease of all remaining concealed land, the precise extent of which remained unknown. Essex argued that such an agreement would permit them 'to ravel into the settlement of all men's estates' and he trenchantly denounced Petty's scheming: 'I am confident that in all his majesties three Kingdomes, there lives not a more grating man than Sir Wm Petty.'[106] Petty's own description of discoverers as 'a calamity upon the nation' was evidently self-referential.[107]

In an effort to overcome such problems, Essex sought out a more satisfactory method for identifying and disposing of the store of land which had not yet been granted away by the state. Beginning in the summer of 1673, he oversaw a new and secret inquiry into the land settlement. At its heart was the work carried out by Thomas Taylor, a former subcommissioner in the court of claims. Taylor had apparently kept careful records of all land grants to date, and he accordingly set out with Essex's support to compile 'books of survey and distribution' for each county.[108] In effect, Essex intended that these books would enable the state, rather than individual suitors like Petty, to become the chief discoverer of undisposed lands. He was confident that this method would enable him more equitably to deal with outstanding land entitlements, with a surplus left over for the king to dispose of as he pleased.[109] By May 1675 Taylor had completed his work and Essex began to plan a trip to London, where the key decisions regarding the disposal of the remaining Irish land would be made.[110]

All the while, Essex had sought to persuade the king to suspend all further

---

[104] Essex to Arlington, Dublin, 3 Sept. 1672, MS Stowe 213, fo. 30v.

[105] Essex to the king, Dublin 28 Mar. 1674, MS Stowe 214, fo. 101v; the king to Essex, 27 June 1676, MS Stowe 209, fo. 368r–v; Arnold, *The restoration land settlement*, 115–16, 131.

[106] Essex to Sir Arthur Forbes, Dublin, 19 Apr. 1673, MS Stowe 213, fo. 182r–v; Essex to the lord chancellor, Dublin, 4 May 1673, ibid. fos 189v–190; Essex to William Harbord, Dublin, 28 Mar. 1674, MS Stowe 214, fo. 104.

[107] Arnold, *The restoration land settlement*, 129.

[108] Essex to Harbord, Dublin, 28 Mar. 1674, MS Stowe 214, fos 101v–103.

[109] Essex to the king, Dublin, 4 Jan. 1674, ibid. fos 2–3.

[110] *Letters written by his excellency Arthur Capel, earl of Essex, lord lieutenant of Ireland in the year 1675*, 2nd edn, Dublin 1773, 203.

grants of land until his secret inquiry was complete.[111] While the king apparently agreed in principle with Essex's requests, he found it impossible to refuse petitions from certain individuals. Thus letters in favour of York, Baron Kingston and Sir Theophilus Jones preceded further requests for land from Carlingford, Powerscourt and Orrery. Taylor's labours allowed Essex to deflect at least some of these demands. In response to Orrery's request for a grant of 8,000 acres which he claimed to have discovered, Essex wrote that 'if they are already in Taylor's books, a discoverer can not claim priority'.[112] While Orrery could be rebuffed, the duke of York, with his outstanding claim to 12,000 acres, could not. From London in February 1676 Essex instructed Taylor 'to pick out of the books you have made such a proportion of the best and ancient lands' for York.[113] Lands worth £1,000 *per annum* had also to be found to satisfy the king's mistress, the duchess of Cleveland, after Essex rejected a proposal that she should be gifted the Phoenix Park adjacent to Dublin city.[114] Thus, 'the torture of discoveries' so dreaded by Essex went on apace, albeit in the more orderly fashion enabled by Taylor's data.[115] At the same time, Essex remained anxious to address the demands of those outside the inner circle of royal favouritism, including the many still unsatisfied Irish Catholics.

The case of the nominees

Essex proved particularly sympathetic towards the fifty-four Catholic nominees, the 'little army of men' promised restoration to 2,000 acres of their former estates by the Act of Explanation. He confessed that 'the case of these seems indeed very hard'.[116] Over the previous decade some of the nominees had recovered more than their entitlements, while others had received no land at all. The earl of Westmeath had apparently recovered only around 200 acres of his former estate, although he had managed to cling on to some of his assignment in Connacht. Many of those who had secured some land were still waiting for adventurers and soldiers to be reprised so that they could recover their full entitlements. By May 1673 Essex had calculated that he would need to find 42,132 acres to satisfy the nominees.[117] However, he soon began to worry that this group of men were not alive to the precariousness of their position. Writing to the lord chancellor, he argued 'that the persons who are most clamourous for these nominees and pretend to be their patriotts, are least willing they should ever be satisfied, for it is these mens's desire to keep a clamour on foot, that under the pretext of that, they

---

111 Essex to the king, Dublin, 4 Jan. 1674, MS Stowe 214, fos 2–3; Essex to Harbord, Dublin, 21 Apr. 1674, fos 129–31.

112 Essex to Roger Boyle, 1st earl of Orrery, Dublin, 27 May 1676, MS Stowe 216, fo. 46v; Essex to Secretary Henry Coventry, Dublin, 3 June 1676, fo. 49r–v; Essex to Joseph Williamson, Dublin, 20 June 1676, fo. 70.

113 Essex to Thomas Taylor, London, 24 Feb. 1676, ibid. fo. 11; Essex to the king, Dublin, 17 June 1676, fo. 65v; the king to Essex, 28 Mar. 1676, MS Stowe 209, fo. 167.

114 *Essex papers, 1672–1679*, ed. Osmund Airy (Camden n.s. xlvii, 1890), 122–3.

115 Essex to Coventry, Dublin, 13 June 1676, MS Stowe 216, fo. 60.

116 Essex to Forbes, Dublin, 7 Mar. 1673, MS Stowe 213, fo. 147r–v.

117 Essex to Arlington, Dublin, 17 May 1673, ibid. fos 200v–202.

may as opportunitie shall offer make private advantages for themselves'.[118] He was further dismayed by the reluctance of the nominees to act as one body. In June 1674 a subgroup of eighteen, led by the transplanters Westmeath and Sir Patrick Barnewall, secured a letter of favour from the king.[119] Essex responded by supporting a mission to London undertaken by two other nominees and former transplanters, Sir Thomas Blake of Galway and Edmond Nugent of Co. Westmeath. These two men represented a separate group of twenty-one who, in common with Essex, sought equal treatment for all of the nominees.[120]

Essex's enthusiasm for the Blake-Nugent agency must have been dampened a few weeks later when he learned that Blake had taken ship before Nugent was ready to travel. This behaviour set the tone for their subsequent actions.[121] Having arrived in London by February 1675 both men proceeded to present petitions regarding their own estates.[122] Three months later they finally got around to their official purpose of defending the nominees' collective interest.[123] By the end of July the committee for the affairs of Ireland, with Essex now in attendance, had considered the nominees' position. They ordered that the 'common stock' of undisposed land identified in Taylor's books should be employed to satisfy this group, either by giving them this land directly or by using it to reprise the adventurers and soldiers still in possession of nominees' estates. To enable the execution of this task, Essex was authorised to establish yet another commission of inquiry to determine the outstanding entitlements of various groups to Irish land.[124]

This latter proposal guaranteed further hold-ups and created the prospect that royal favourites and men of influence would now have more time to secure land for themselves.[125] Accordingly, in September 1675, Blake and Nugent presented a fresh petition reciting 'their indigent and necessitous condition, to which delays will prove destructive'.[126] Despite enjoying Essex's support, it is evident that these individuals faced considerable difficulties in securing any practical benefits from the royal favour extended to them in the Act of Explanation. The barriers which hindered their restoration in the 1660s remained in place in the following decade. Moreover, their increasing desperation militated against joint action and served further to undermine their case. In the years after 1675 a handful of nominees did succeed in passing patents for 2,000 acres, but they most likely faced additional problems in securing actual possession of the property in

---

[118] Essex to the lord chancellor, Dublin, 25 Oct. 1673, ibid. fos 318v–319.

[119] CSPD, 1673–1675, 280–1.

[120] Ibid. 412; Essex to Harbord, Dublin, 26 Sept., 14 Oct, 1674, MS Stowe 214, fos 290v–291v, 299v.

[121] Essex to Harbord, Dublin, 8 Nov. 1674, MS Stowe 214, fo. 316v.

[122] MS Stowe 208, fo. 159r–v; the king to Essex, 13 Feb. 1675, MS Stowe 207, fos 147–8; Letters written by Arthur Capel, earl of Essex, 238–9.

[123] H. Thyme to Essex, Whitehall, 25 May 1675, MS Stowe 208, fos 430v–434.

[124] Ibid. fos 185–6, 193.

[125] The king to Essex for Sir Robert Holmes and Colonel Edward Roscarrock, 25 Sept. 1675, ibid. fos 292r–293v; the king and privy council to Essex for Sir Theophilus Jones, 26 Nov., fo. 403; the king to Essex for Lord Kingston, 8 Mar. 1676, MS Stowe 209, fo. 107r–v; the king to Essex for the duke of York, 28 Mar. 1676, fo. 167.

[126] MS Stowe 208, fo. 321r–v; the king to Essex, 1 Oct. 1675, MS Stowe 209, fo. 372.

question.[127] The likelihood that they were never fully satisfied is suggested by the Irish parliament's move as late as 1698 to pass an act barring the right of the nominees to restoration following reprisals to adventurers and soldiers.[128] By that date, some of the nominees had, as a consequence their support for James II, forfeited for a second time what lands they had managed to recover through painstaking effort since 1660.

The pressing need to establish a means for satisfying the nominees was just one of the reasons why Essex had travelled to London in the summer of 1675. By that stage, he had also developed an interest in the fate of another group of Catholic landowners more numerous but less prominent than the largely frustrated nominees; those transplanters who had not yet secured legal title to their land under the terms of the Acts of Settlement and Explanation. Some had lost out to the Connacht magnates restored without previous reprisals after 1660, while others had retained a precarious grip on the lands assigned to them by the Loughrea commissioners in the 1650s. Essex's ambition to bring the land settlement to a satisfactory conclusion meant that the claims of these individuals would also have to be dealt with one way or another. His awareness of this necessity was surely heightened by the worrying content of the various reports which reached him concerning conditions in Connacht.

Connacht in the 1670s

Upon his arrival in Ireland in 1672 Essex's attention was immediately drawn to some of the problems which existed in the west; these would take up more and more of his time over the following five years. Within days of his landing at Dublin, he reported to Arlington that ' I mett with some complaints from divers persons of the Roman persuasion lately admitted to inhabite in the city of Galloway, which in regard is the first business between the English and the Irish that has come before me.'[129] A few weeks later another report from Galway revealed that 'everie Sunday there meets in one house at Mass much greater numbers then the whole garrison consists of'. This gathering was adjudged to be 'no way disorderly either in words or otherwise'.[130] Despite their generally peaceful demeanour, in June 1675 the townsmen gave a warm welcome to a seditious pamphlet published by the exiled Catholic bishop of Ferns, Nicholas French, in which he reportedly justified defensive wars against rulers. A friar who was spying on Essex's behalf described the pamphlet's reception in Galway:

> As for the Bleeding Iphigenia there came three copys to this town sent by Bp French. One for Sr Henry Linch, one for Anthony French and one for Mr Christopher French, they make much of it as it goes from hand to hand. The people are so taken with it that in my opinion if 20000 volumes had come over they would all have bin bought up.[131]

The potential influence which the writings of exiled clerics might have on the

---

127 IRC, *Fifteenth report*, 235, 278.
128 Butler, *Confiscation in Irish history*, 196.
129 Essex to Arlington, Dublin, 17 Aug. 1672, MS Stowe 213, fo. 6v.
130 Essex to Arlington, Dublin, 26 Oct. 1672, ibid. fos 60v–61.
131 Part of a letter from a friar in Connacht to Essex, Galway, 11 June 1675, MS Stowe 216,

usually pliant Catholic population of Galway was not the only cause for concern. Unfounded Catholic expectations that the land settlement was about to be overturned contributed to tensions in Connacht and served to highlight some of the more immediate problems that existed. In February 1673 the Protestant officer Colonel Cary Dillon was forcibly dispossessed of Killymer Castle, Co. Galway, presumably by the Daly family who were its former proprietors.[132] Reports which emanated from Co. Clare towards the end of 1672 revealed problems there also. It was reported locally that a royal act of indemnity had been 'posted up at Ennis, which warranted everyone to enter into his own estate that was not guilty of murder, treason or felony'. This led one Roger McMahon to seize a house and lands that had formerly belonged to his family. McMahon had apparently lodged in the house overnight and had then 'persuaded the children out of doors' while the adult occupants were tending their cattle and fetching water. McMahon was soon arrested by the local constable and brought before a justice of the peace, Viscount Clare, who bound him over to appear at the next assizes.[133] Elsewhere in the same county it was reported that the king 'hath declared that all the Irish papists should be restored to their respective estates at May next'. While at mass on 16 November 1672 two former landowners cited this report when declaring 'that no person concerned in the payment of any rent out of any of their lands should pay the same to any person but themselves, their lands having been given to transplanted persons'. The transplanters in possession, originally from Co. Tipperary, were duly harassed and found it necessary to impound cattle belonging to the trespassing former owners.[134] To make matters worse, an alleged plot by Protestants in Co. Clare to seize Limerick city had been revealed two weeks earlier. One of the prime suspects, an army officer named Captain Walcott, had reportedly 'bewayled the condition of the English in generall, for the Irish were like to have all again, and wished himself out of the kingdome, for the king had given the Irish an act of indemnitie'.[135] The widespread but entirely mistaken belief that Catholics would soon be restored to their estates evidently served to heighten tensions in the west.

Some of the great landowners of the region were also causing difficulties:

> For instance, Lord Clare by the Act of Explanation (p. 80) had the estate of [his brother] Teigh O'Bryen given him, now he finding another Teigh O'Bryen who was a transplanter, he thrust him out of possession, under colour of the Act, and now upon passing a patent has inserted those lands. Many other cases of this and the like nature do occur here.[136]

It was widely believed that some of the most substantial landowners west of the

---

fo. 103; Nicholas French, *The bleeding Iphigenia, or an excellent preface of a work unfinished, published by the authors frind, [sic] with the reasons of publishing it*, London 1675. For an in-depth study of French's career see Jason McHugh, 'Soldier of Christ: the political and ecclesiastical career of Nicholas French, Catholic bishop of Ferns (1603–1678)', unpubl. PhD diss. National University of Ireland Galway 2005.

[132] Essex to Arlington, Dublin, 18 Feb. 1673, MS Stowe 213, fo. 140v.
[133] Ibid. fos 116v–117.
[134] Ibid. fo. 116.
[135] MSS Coventry, Longleat House, Bath, papers relating to Ireland, vol.1, 1601–77, fo. 99.
[136] NAI, MS Wyche 56.

Shannon had secured title to a great deal of land which had not belonged to them before the war. Some did so to assist their relatives, while others simply sought to grab as much land as possible. In some cases it must have suited transplanters to have an influential person secure proper title for their assignment. While this outcome reduced them to the status of tenants, it at least conferred a degree of security. Along with Viscount Clare, Lords Mayo and Costello-Gallen were widely suspected of this malpractice. When Costello-Gallen died without producing a son, Essex reported that 'many people [were] offering at discoveries of several lands which he possessed, and did not of right belong to him'. Referring to the deceased, he also noted that 'the proprietors in his time [that] were glad to shelter themselves under his name' were now 'labouring to get some other great men to patronize their estates'.[137]

The news from the west was not all bad however. William Burke, seventh earl of Clanricarde, was commended by Essex for voluntarily allowing transplanters to take possession of land that had been restored to him.[138] Resident magnates like Clanricarde probably fared better than some absentee landlords when negotiating difficulties with neighbours, transplanters and tenants. One Protestant absentee landlord who held lands in counties Galway and Roscommon, the royal favourite Colonel William Legge, was urged to recruit Protestant tenants, because 'the old inhabitants have so many ways to avoid paying their rent, that one shall never get any satisfactory account, nor punctual payment, unless a man were continually with them'.[139] Matters got much worse for both residents and absentees alike in 1673 and 1674 when 'scarcity of fodder and dearth of cattle' meant that there was 'no hope of rent from Connacht'. In April 1674 a visitor reported that he had been 'eyewitness of the death of many, and [the] continued outcry of the people, by scarcity of corn and horn'.[140] These difficulties in Connacht were inevitably brought to Essex's attention. In April 1674 he reported to London that 'people are in a starving condition, and I doe very much fear for a ffamine this summer, their corne being all spent and their cattle dead'.[141] Allied to the other problems that existed in the west, the threat of famine undoubtedly focused the government's attention on the problems posed by the uncertainties that surrounded the issue of landownership in Connacht. Over the following years, as he sought to ensure that they could obtain proper title to their lands, Essex was to stress repeatedly the poverty of numerous transplanted Catholic landowners in the province.

Essex and the transplanters

The proposal made by the lords justice in 1671 to set up a commission to process transplanters' claims provided a ready-made model which Essex was able quickly to adopt. He duly drafted a new letter and dispatched it for signature by the

---

137 Ibid; MS Stowe 213, fo. 350; *Letters written by Arthur Capel, earl of Essex*, 12–13.
138 MS Wyche 56.
139 HMC, *Dartmouth manuscripts*, 114.
140 Ibid. 117–18.
141 Essex to Arlington, Dublin, 18 Apr. 1674, MS Stowe 214, fo. 124.

king.[142] However, Essex's initiative inevitably aroused immediate opposition in London. The committee for Irish affairs was apparently unaccustomed to dealing with proposals which did not involve some element of private gain, and so its members suspected that Essex's plans for granting land titles in Connacht were part of a secret scheme for personal enrichment.[143] Despite this first round of opposition, Essex persisted. In November 1674 Viscount Ranelagh was dispatched to London to win the king's backing for the appointment of 'persons uninterested in that country' as commissioners to settle land titles in Connacht.[144] No progress was made until after Essex himself arrived in London in the summer of 1675. On 22 September the king signed the necessary letter. This document authorised a new survey of Connacht, to be followed by the confirmation of transplanters' titles and the satisfaction as far as possible of their outstanding claims for land.[145] The importance of these issues was once more impressed on the king during discussions in his bedchamber on 1 December 1675.[146] Following his return to Ireland some months later, Essex was at last in a position to move matters forward.

In June 1676 the lord lieutenant and council issued a proclamation ordering 'all persons concerned in any of the said transplanted lands' to submit their claims before 21 August to a team of commissioners sitting at the King's Inns in Dublin. The five judges charged with overseeing these proceedings were Sir Robert Booth, Sir Charles Meredith, Thomas Radcliffe, Henry Henn and Sir Richard Reynell.[147] Essex had recently described Booth, chief justice of the common pleas, as 'the ablest man we have in his profession here, and ... in all respects as worthy a man as I have ever known'. He ranked Reynell as second only to Booth and endorsed Henry Henn as a man 'uninterested' in Connacht.[148] This team surely inspired more confidence than the Loughrea commissioners had done two decades before. The contrast between the respective teams of commissioners was reinforced by Essex's insistence that they should not 'presume directly or indirectly to purchase any estates or titles subject to your examination or inquiry'.[149] In addition, the legal costs to be borne by transplanters were to be minimised by 'making as few officers, and the fees as narrow as could be', and by allowing the issuing of joint certificates 'for very many of their claims are but for 20 or 30 acres of land'.[150]

While he took care to appoint suitable judges and to keep costs down, Essex was aware that the whole task of settling the transplanters was likely to be complicated by its necessary reliance on the Strafford Survey of Connacht dating from the 1630s. Although these earlier records were widely recognised as inaccu-

---

[142] Essex to Arlington, Dublin, 27 Mar. 1674, ibid. fo. 96v.

[143] Essex to Arlington, Dublin, 2 May 1674, ibid. fos 146–7; Essex to Harbord, Dublin, 6 May 1674, fo. 155v.

[144] Ibid. fo. 329v.

[145] The king to Essex, Whitehall, 22 Sept. 1675, MS Stowe 208, fos 285–286v.

[146] MS Wyche, envelope 2/99.

[147] Lord lieutenant and council, *Whereas his majestie by his gracious letters, bearing date the two and twentieth day of September last ... 26 June 1676*, Dublin 1676.

[148] *Essex papers*, 104–5; MS Stowe 214, fo. 329v.

[149] MS Wyche 66.

[150] Essex to Coventry, Dublin, 23 Sept. 1676, MS Stowe 216, fo. 211.

rate and defective, the farmers who controlled the Irish revenue at this time refused to provide the estimated £1,000 needed to cover the costs of a new survey. As a result, the commissioners had no choice but to employ the existing survey as best they could.[151]

The court of claims for transplanters

Towards the end of 1676 Sir George Rawdon reported that 'The Court of Claims for settling the Transplanters in Connaught fills the town with Irish. They sit morning and evening.'[152] Over the previous months many Catholics had flocked to Dublin to process their claims. One of those who made the journey from the west was Ignatius French. In September 1676 he declared that 'the Court proceeds very well in favour of the transplanters, specially those that are in possession'.[153] However, there is evidence to suggest that at least some of the problems which existed at Loughrea two decades before were now replicated on a smaller scale. In June 1677, for example, the Galway lawyer Sir Henry Lynch intimated that he secured his certificate for land only by paying off an official who had 'eng[ine]ered judgment' against him.[154] Whether or not he was aware of such issues, Essex also expressed his general satisfaction with proceedings: 'those poor people who have indeed suffered much misery and want are much pleased, but some greater ones who have wrongfully thrust them out of their estates ... I hear are not so well satisfied'.[155] Wary of the ambitions of these 'greater ones', Essex pursued various strategies in an effort to foil them. Early in 1677 he sent his new secretary Cyril Wyche to London to shore up royal support for his policy towards the transplanters.[156] Wyche soon reported back that he had 'discoursed a little about the settlement of Connacht' with the king, who appeared satisfied with the work.[157] Essex also sought, through Sir Nicholas Plunkett, to enlist the support of the Irish Catholics at court.[158] However, the letters of reassurance, the chocolates and the Spanish tobacco sent back by Wyche could do little to ease Essex's growing worry that his plans for Connacht were about to be derailed.[159]

It was perhaps inevitable that the ongoing clamour from all sides for grants of Irish land would impact on the proceedings relating to Connacht. By February 1677 Essex had received letters sent from London on behalf of two Catholics, Colonel Milo Power and the nominee Arthur Magennis, Viscount Iveagh.[160] The latter, upon his return from military service in exile, had failed to recover any of

---

151 Essex to Coventry, 8 July 1676, ibid. fos 80v–81.
152 *CSPD, 1676–1677*, 450.
153 *Blake family records*, ii. 117.
154 Kenneth Nicholls, 'The Lynch Blosse papers', *Analecta Hibernica* xxix (1980), 115–218 at p. 128.
155 Essex to Coventry, Dublin, 23 Sept. 1676, MS Stowe 216, fo. 211.
156 Essex to the king, Dublin, 13 Jan. 1677, MS Stowe 217, fo. 10.
157 Cyril Wyche to Essex, St James's Square, 23 Jan. 1677, MS Stowe 211, fo. 55.
158 Essex to Wyche, Dublin, 12 Feb. 1677, MS Stowe 217, fo. 49v.
159 Wyche to Essex, St James's Square, 24 Feb. 1677, MS Stowe 211, fo. 141.
160 Essex to Wyche, 12 Feb. 1677, MS Stowe 217, fo. 49v; Essex to Wyche, Dublin, 19 May 1677, fo. 178; Essex to Williamson, Dublin, 19 May 1677, fo. 179.

his former estate of around 45,000 acres in Co. Down. In the 1670s Iveagh was still actively seeking to discover land which could be used to satisfy his entitlement to 2,000 acres. In 1672 the king had authorised a grant to Iveagh of 2,500 acres of land allegedly vacated by innocent transplanters, but for some reason no letters patent were issued.[161] This property included 600 acres of former O'Flaherty land at Bunowen in west Co. Galway which had been granted to Arthur Geoghegan of Castletown, Co. Westmeath, in 1657.[162] In 1663 Geoghegan's grandson and heir Edward was restored as an innocent, but Geoghegan himself kept possession of his Connacht estate and subsequently conveyed it to his second son Arthur.[163] In 1676 Arthur and his widowed mother Giles submitted a claim for the land. Iveagh, who remained determined to secure the property, responded by sending a protest to the king. Although the court of claims for transplanters had already ruled in favour of the Geoghegans, the king ordered Essex to have the proceedings halted so that the case could be reviewed.[164]

The lord lieutenant was dismayed by this 'extraordinary direction.[165] In a letter to Wyche he warned that any move to satisfy petitioners such as Iveagh 'would break the whole business of Connacht'.[166] He also insisted that because 'these commissioners of Connacht are a court of Judicature', it would be highly irregular for him to try to put a stop to any of their work. Instead, he expressed the hope that the commission, whose purpose 'was only to relieve some few poor Irish who have bin most unjustly and injuriously dealt with', would be allowed to continue without interference.[167] The king eventually made up his mind on the Iveagh-Geoghegan case in October 1677, when he instructed the commissioners to proceed 'according to justice'.[168] As they had already twice ruled in favour of Geoghegan, only one outcome was now likely.[169] Thereafter the effort made by Iveagh's relative and man on the spot Teige O'Flaherty to keep the Geoghegans out of the estate at Bunowen would prove futile. In 1678 he was imprisoned and fined £500 at the Galway assizes. The sentencing judge, Sir Robert Booth, was well-informed on the matter, as he had recently passed judgement upon it in his role as a commissioner for Connacht.[170]

It was widely expected that the work carried out by Booth and his fellow commissioners would enable the discovery of a stock of as yet undisposed land in Connacht. Essex intended that this surplus should be redistributed among the many transplanters who possessed less than the quantity of land decreed to them

161 ODNB, s.v. 'Magennis, Arthur, third Viscount Magennis of Iveagh (1623/1626–1683)'; IRC, Fifteenth report, 652; CSPD, 1672, 287–8.
162 CSPD, 1672, 287–8; CSPD, 1677–1678, 410–11.
163 Deputy keeper, Nineteenth report, 82; IRC, Fifteenth report, 250.
164 CSPD, 1676–77, 509–10, 518; Essex to Wyche, Dublin, 19 May 1677, MS Stowe 217, fo. 178.
165 Essex to Wyche, Dublin, 19 May 1677, MS Stowe 217, fo. 178.
166 Essex to Wyche, Dublin, 12 Feb. 1677, ibid. fo. 49v.
167 Essex to Wyche, Dublin, 19 May 1677, ibid. fo. 178.
168 CSPD, 1677–1678, 410–11.
169 IRC, Fifteenth report, 250.
170 CSPD: Charles II, addenda, 1660–1685, ed. F. H. Blackburne Daniell and Francis Bickley, London 1939, 471–5.

by the Athlone commissioners in the 1650s. However, the likelihood that land would be discovered inevitably aroused interest on both sides of the Irish sea and Essex quickly found himself at odds with figures more formidable than Iveagh. By April 1677 the courtier and writer John Wilmot, earl of Rochester, had succeeded in identifying around 3,500 available acres in Connacht. In a petition to the king, he requested that this and other land in Connacht up to a total of 10,000 acres be conferred on him.[171] Essex again flatly rejected this proposal, insisting that 'a great many poor families would be ruined' if Rochester had his way.[172] It would set a precedent for the earls of Burlington and Arran, Baron Colooney, Colonel Cary Dillon, Sir Oliver St George and others who were also actively seeking grants. In a letter sent to Secretary Coventry in July 1677, Essex reiterated his support for the transplanters, pointing out that 'when upon an equal right a rich man and a poor man pretend to a small parcel of land ... the poor man ought to have the preference'.[173] Despite Essex's stance, a few weeks earlier Sir Henry Lynch had reported that the estate claimed by one of his associates, 'poor Nicholas', had been 'put into the stock' and granted away to the Protestant peer Viscount Powerscourt. Lynch accordingly urged his wife to 'advise those friends of mine to regarde their owne interest more than they doe and not to suffer themselves to be destroyed'.[174]

While the proceedings of the commissioners were not always strictly in keeping with Essex's mission to support 'poor creatures against those that are potent', in the summer of 1677 he remained satisfied with their work. In July he reported that the claims of almost 1,000 families who possessed some land in Connacht had been settled.[175] A further progress report sent to London a month later revealed that the outstanding claims of transplanters 'who have yet received nothing' stood at 237,000 acres, while the stock available to satisfy them was less than 50,000 acres. The commissioners proposed to distribute this land to transplanters holding no land, in the hope that they would end up with at least one-third of the amount originally decreed to them by the Athlone commissioners. If any land remained after this process had been completed, it was to be given to transplanters in possession of property belonging to Connacht innocents.[176] Yet even these limited measures soon met with opposition, this time from members of the Irish privy council who also happened to be Protestant Connacht purchasers. These men too had lost some land as a result of the restoration of magnates such as Clanricarde, and they were determined to secure the available store of land for themselves. Thus, in the last days of his regime, Essex was forced to continue his efforts to defend his policies and to convince others of 'the justice, equality, and charity of the thing'.[177] There is no evidence that Ormond displayed any great interest in the matter after his return to the helm in Dublin in August 1677. On the other hand, it is likely that the task of

---

171 CSPD, 1677–1678, 89–90.
172 Essex to Coventry, Dublin, 23 June 1677, MS Stowe 217, fo. 197v.
173 Essex to Coventry, Dublin, 14 July 1677, ibid. fo. 224.
174 Nicholls, 'Lynch Blosse papers', 127.
175 Essex to Coventry, Dublin, 14 July 1677, MS Stowe 217, fo. 224.
176 Essex to Coventry, Dublin, 4 Aug. 1677, ibid. fo. 247v.
177 Ibid. fo. 248.

settling the transplanters had already progressed to the point where the commissioners could proceed to a conclusion without very much governmental supervision.

Settling the transplanters

According to a report compiled almost two centuries ago, the commissioners issued a total of 580 'Connacht certificates' which authorised their holders to pass letters patent for the lands listed therein.[178] The first certificate to be enrolled was that of George Browne, son of the deceased transplanter and nominee John Browne of the Neale, Co. Mayo. The latter had been assigned 1,263 acres in 1656. In March 1677 his son obtained a certificate for an estate of 1,092 acres, out of which he was required to pay an annual quit rent of just over £11.[179] Some of these certificates, which were destroyed in 1922, were issued jointly to two or more transplanters. The surviving *index nominum* contains around 1,850 entries. Moreover, the frequency with which the names of the restored Connacht lords featured in these certificates reflects the extent to which their entitlements, real and alleged, conflicted with transplanters' claims. Clanricarde received eighty-one mentions; Costello-Gallen forty-seven.[180] The fragmentary evidence available also suggests that the commissioners were authorised to investigate the frequently-made claims of impropriety against some larger landowners.[181] In many instances the *Books of survey and distribution* return two or more grantees to the same portion of land. In cases where noblemen or others had passed flawed patents for land which they had never owned in the first place, the transplanters' freshly acquired title was presumably superior.[182] Nevertheless, the task of successfully prising lands from the hands of a local magnate was quite another matter.[183]

As the commissioners went about their work of granting acres, various individuals moved quickly to trade in Connacht land, thus replicating somewhat the pattern of twenty years before. This time, however, the going rates were much higher, as the land market was no longer saturated and the new land titles on offer provided greater reassurance to purchasers. In the 1650s Alderman John Blake of Galway had been transplanted to east Co. Galway.[184] By 1668 three of his sons, rather than wandering around the fields of Mullaghmore, had established themselves as merchants in the West Indies. Two of them returned home in the mid-1670s, by which time their eldest brother Thomas had already re-established the family's position as Galway merchants. Their transatlantic commercial activities meant that in the late 1670s the Blake brothers were in a strong position to buy up land in Connacht. In 1677 they were able to focus their

---

[178] IRC, *Fifteenth report*, 576.
[179] Ibid. 577–9; 'Ormond list'.
[180] IRC, *Fifteenth report*, 580–7.
[181] MS Wyche 56.
[182] IRC, *Fifteenth report*, 317–28; *Books of survey and distribution*, ii, passim.
[183] MS Ormsby of Ballinamore, microfilm P. 8,502, no. 59.
[184] Simington, *Transplantation*, 178.

sights on other transplanters who, having at last secured title to their lands, were willing to sell their estates. Thomas Blake duly purchased 600 acres in Co. Mayo from the Co. Waterford transplanter John Porter. The transaction cost him £580, as well as the price of a petticoat for Porter's wife. It is not clear how this deal affected the lease which Porter had agreed with Viscount Mayo for the same land a decade before. Blake, who was trying to piece together an estate for his younger brother Henry, also agreed to buy 597 acres in Co. Galway from another Co. Waterford transplanter, Edward Gough, this time for £625. Thomas Blake explained that although these transactions represented 'a dear bargain ... lands nowadays are so hard to be bought that it is almost impossible to light on any bargain'.[185] At the same time, Blake was anxious to secure the family in possession of the land assigned in the 1650s to his now-aged father. In November 1676 he wrote to his attorney, Ignatius French, in Dublin as follows: 'I beseech you lose no time in procuring the certificate, for my father longs to see it.'[186]

The Blakes were also active in the trading of deficiencies, or outstanding entitlements to land under unsatisfied Athlone decrees. Thomas Blake's father-in-law assigned part of his deficiency of 824 acres to him in lieu of the £150 still due to Blake from his wife's marriage portion.[187] It is not clear if he actually managed to secure satisfaction of this entitlement. The Protestant Ormsbys of Ballinamore, who had been active Connacht purchasers in the 1650s, also speculated in deficiencies. In April 1677, amongst other transactions, Christopher Ormsby purchased an entitlement to 336 acres from Con O'Neill for £33 12s.[188] This low price reflected the risk that the purchasers of deficiencies might never succeed in actually acquiring the land due upon them. However, this strategy did sometimes pay off. Having purchased deficiencies equal to 306 acres from transplanters, William Moore and John Barber managed to secure a certificate for this quantity of land in the barony of Athlone in 1678.[189]

The complexity of such transactions, the many multiple grants of individual parcels of land and some inconsistencies in the records together complicate any effort to ascertain comprehensive figures for the final outcome of the Restoration land settlement in Connacht. None the less, some approximate calculations can be offered. According to tables compiled by the Irish record commissioners in the 1820s, around 520 grants of letters patent were made in the late 1670s and early 1680s for lands within the four counties of Galway, Mayo, Roscommon and Clare. The vast majority of those granted patents were transplanters, but some Connacht purchasers and other Protestants also featured.[190] Overall therefore, it appears that less than one-third of the original transplanters eventually secured some land in Connacht under the terms of the Restoration settlement. In Co. Roscommon the court of claims for transplanters confirmed around 5,800 acres to

---

185 *Irish immigrants in the land of Canaan: letters and memoirs from colonial and revolutionary America, 1675–1815*, ed. Kerby Miller and others, Oxford 2003, 121–4; *Blake family records*, ii. 119–20.

186 *Blake family records*, ii. 118.

187 Ibid. 113.

188 MS Ormsby, microfilm P. 8,502, nos 35, 46.

189 MS Hussey-Walsh 6, Library of the Irish Genealogical Research Society, London, fo. 1,448.

190 IRC, *Fifteenth report*, 234–80.

Conclusion

The fate of many transplanted families and their estates can be traced up to the end of the seventeenth century and beyond. The persistence and local influence of some is reflected in placenames such as Frenchpark, Brabazon Park, Mount Dillon, Mount Talbot, Mount Bellew and O'Callaghan's Mills.[1] A number of transplanters or their heirs were prominent in the war in Ireland between 1689 and 1691. For example, Theobald Dillon, by then seventh Viscount Costello-Gallen, raised two regiments for James II and was among the more than 7,000 men killed at Aughrim on 12 August 1691. His wife Mary, daughter of Sir Henry Talbot, fell victim a few weeks later to 'the second bomb thrown into Limerick by K. William's army'.[2] Thereafter, the Dillon regiment entered French service, where it remained active until its last colonel, another Theobald, was slaughtered by his own troops at the opening of the Franco-Austrian war in 1792.[3] The Dillons were among the numerous Catholic adherents of James II who salvaged their estates either under the articles of Galway and Limerick or by having their outlawries reversed. Subsequently, the implementation of the 'penal laws' against Catholics ensured that many of these landed families would conform to Protestantism in the course of the eighteenth century. The seventeenth Viscount Costello-Gallen eventually sold the family's estate of 93,652 acres to the Congested Districts' Board in 1899. The house at Lough Glynn was then purchased by the Catholic bishop of Elphin and became home to a Franciscan convent, before being purchased in 2003 for close to €2,000,000 by a property developer who intended to construct a luxury hotel. More recently it has featured in media reports concerning the National Asset Management Agency, a body established by the Irish government in 2009 in response to the collapse of the country's property market.[4]

Of the transplanted families who persisted until the late nineteenth century, many were then swept away by the momentous campaign against 'Cromwellian' landlords. The Talbot mansion at Mount Talbot in Co. Roscommon was among the 'big houses' burnt in civil war in 1922.[5] At Killyan in Co. Galway, the Cheevers family survived as Catholic landlords until 1935 on the estate that had been confirmed to their transplanted ancestor John Cheevers in the late 1670s. At that point, the last of their property was compulsorily purchased by the Land Commission and their house demolished. The latter structure apparently incorporated the crude dwelling occupied by the family following their relocation from

---

[1] A particularly useful online scholarly resource for the subsequent period is the Connacht Landed Estates Database, <http://www.Landedestates.ie>.
[2] Lodge, *The peerage of Ireland*, iv. 194.
[3] *DIB*, s.v. 'Dillon, Comte Theobald (1745–92)'.
[4] 'Dillon (Viscount)', <http://www.landedestates.ie> accessed 1 Aug. 2009; <http://namawinelake.wordpress.com/the–developers> accessed 28 Feb. 2011.
[5] 'Talbot (Mount Talbot)', <http://www.landedestates.ie> accessed 1 Aug. 2009.

Co. Meath in the 1650s: 'it was found that the walls of the original house were formed of huge boulders of uncut stone, the spaces in between them being filled with sods of turf'.[6] By the 1930s the Cheevers's knowledge of that dark chapter of their history owed more to the pages of Prendergast's *Cromwellian settlement* than to any authentic family tradition. They had adopted as their ancestor the wrong Cheevers, Walter of Monkstown, Co. Dublin, whose transplantation along with his wife and five young children had been reconstructed in detail by Prendergast.[7] The popular understanding of the transplantation which developed following the publication of Prendergast's work in 1865 had also been embraced by the Cheevers family: they were 'offered by Cromwell "Hell or Connaught" (hell, if they renounced the Catholic religion and kept their possessions, Connaught or banishment, if they refused)'.[8] Given no choice at all under de Valera's government in 1935, they packed their silver, burned their papers and left for England, from whence an earlier forebear had come with Strongbow in the twelfth century.[9]

The transplantation, which evidently shaped so many individual family histories, also played a fundamental role in the wider history of the country. Undoubtedly it was essential to the formation of the relatively stable Protestant state which emerged eventually from the turmoil of seventeenth-century Ireland. Elsewhere in early modern Europe, other rulers also confiscated land and expulsed population groups in an effort to render their kingdoms more centralised, loyal and secure.[10] Ireland represented a radical instance of this phenomenon, but it was certainly not unique. The developments which occurred in mid seventeenth-century Ireland can also be viewed in a British Atlantic colonial context. In the 1650s thousands of men, women and children were shipped from the country to the West Indies, an episode labelled by a recent historian as 'the ethnic cleansing of Ireland'.[11] Some of the men who conquered Ireland also went on to capture Hispaniola in 1655. Moreover, a number of contemporary observers viewed the settlement of Ireland and Cromwell's western design as two components of a single endeavour, although Colonel Richard Lawrence favoured 'the inlargement of the English nation so near itself' over any prospect of adventures in the West Indies.[12] Alison Games has also drawn attention to this empire-building aspect, pinpointing the English involvement in Ireland in the 1650s as part of the transition towards more direct state participation in a process which did much to shape the modern world.[13]

---

6 Cheevers (Killian), <http://www.landedestates.ie> accessed 1 Aug. 2009; Frederica Cheevers, *Cheevers of Killyan*, Dublin 1936, 11, 24.

7 Prendergast, *The Cromwellian settlement*, 176–8; Cheevers, *Cheevers of Killyan*, 3–4.

8 Cheevers, *Cheevers of Killyan*, 4.

9 Ibid. 24. In a petition sent to the king after 1660 John Cheevers sought the recovery of the lands granted to his family by Henry II: Prendergast, *The Cromwellian settlement*, 176.

10 Tomáš Knoz, 'Die Konfiscationen nach 1620 in (erb)länderübergreifender Perspektive: Thesen zu westentlichen Wirkungen, Aspekten und Prinzipien des Konfiscationsprozesses', in Petr Mat'a and Thomas Winkelbauer (eds), *Die Habsburgermonarchie: 1620 bis 1740*, Stuttgart 2006, 99–100.

11 Seán O'Callaghan, *To hell or Barbados: the ethnic cleansing of Ireland*, Dingle 2000.

12 Lawrence, *England's great interest*, 3, 8–9, 22, 30.

13 Games, *The web of empire*, ch. viii.

In twenty-first-century Ireland, popular awareness of the land settlement of the 1650s remains remarkably high, the 'Cromwellian' label remains potent, and Cromwell's image continues to feature in the famous gable wall murals of Belfast. Yet a search for more meaningful parallels between past and present, if they must be pursued, inevitably now leads beyond the island. Ethno-religious conflicts and competitions for land are very far from becoming solely historical phenomena. One instance which generates some apparent echoes from seventeenth-century Ireland is the ongoing move by many governments and investment companies to buy up large tracts of African land for food security purposes. In November 2010 a village elder in Mali protested that 'all we want before they break our houses and take our fields is for them to show us the new houses where we will live, and the new fields where we will work'.[14] In 1654 the inhabitants of Limerick had like-wise sought 'some certain place of habitation ... lest, if they were straggling about, they might perish by exposure to insults and various perils of life and fortune'.[15]

The evident historical significance of the transplantation to Connacht, combined with its apparent connectivity to multiple contexts and possible parallels, means that it is incumbent on historians to address the question of what the transplantation actually entailed. However, several factors, not least the enthusiasm with which nineteenth-century scholars embraced the subject, and the subsequent destruction of so much of the source material that they employed, have helped to delay the execution of a comprehensive reappraisal. The present work, by exploring the background, the implementation and the outcomes of the transplantation, has endeavoured to fulfil this key task. It should enable the importance of the transplantation more fully to be understood and facilitate its integration as a more meaningful scholarly subject into Irish, three-kingdoms, European and other historical contexts. The latter step may in turn enable new perspectives and alternative methods for researching and understanding this complex and consequential episode.[16]

It ought to be worthwhile to conclude then by drawing attention once again to some of the revisions and additions which have been offered here to the received history of the transplantation. In the first place, a simple widening of the chronological scope, taking into account both the years of conquest and the period of the Restoration, has facilitated the creation of a much clearer picture of the immediate prelude to the transplantation, as well as its complicated aftermath. This has the effect of bringing out of the shadows two individuals in particular, the first of whom is Henry Ireton. Ireton's contribution to the design of the settlement has usually been swallowed up in the historiographical chasm between conquest and settlement. However, the linking of the various settlement proposals which emerged during the conquest to what followed afterwards makes it clear that Ireton was the chief architect of the 'Cromwellian' settlement.[17] While plantation and transplantation were very far from being new ideas, close

---

[14] *International Herald Tribune*, 23 Dec. 2010, 1, 17.
[15] Maurice Lenihan, *History of Limerick*, Dublin 1866, 189.
[16] For example, understanding of the Restoration land settlement could undoubtedly be improved through the application of the techniques now widely used in network analysis.
[17] Cunningham, 'Cromwell and the "Cromwellian" settlement of Ireland', 922.

scrutiny of Ireton's words and deeds helps to answer the question of why post-war policy towards the Catholics in particular took the form that it did. Numerous other factors were also important, not least the various articles of surrender agreed in 1652 which ultimately helped to temper the severity of Ireton's approach. Against this somewhat confused background, the Catholics ultimately emerged from the conquest with entitlements to land more extensive than Ireton or anyone else on the side of the victors seems to have intended.

As early as 1651 Ireton had linked his concession of continued Catholic proprietorship to the prospect of some form of transplantation. The subsequent transplantation to Connacht was finally approved in London in July 1653, but the policy was certainly known about in official circles in Dublin some months before. Thus, Gardiner's assumption that Oliver Cromwell personally played a key role in developing the policy during that summer cannot be sustained.[18] When the relevant instructions arrived in Dublin, it was clear that the Irish government had been empowered to transplant effectively the entire Catholic population across the Shannon. It had, however, no desire to do so, and official policy was quickly moderated to focus attention on landowners and soldiers. Gardiner's argument that this shift towards moderation did not occur until two years later has again been influential, but equally misguided.[19] In 1654 Charles Fleetwood, rather than endeavouring to uproot the majority of the population, was busy defending his limited transplantation policy against the threat posed by the presence of Catholic lobbyists in London. In common with their Protestant counterparts, these Catholics sought and sometimes obtained a sympathetic hearing from Cromwell, something which could not be expected in Dublin.[20]

Once this threat had been overcome early in 1655, Fleetwood and his council were able to press ahead with the implementation of the scheme. However, as was the case elsewhere in early modern Europe, the effective execution of government policy in Ireland in the mid-1650s relied on the co-operation of locally based proprietors, officers and officials.[21] The obstruction offered by Protestant landowners both old and new meant that this co-operation was not always forthcoming. Assiduous officials could draw up lists of those to be transplanted, but that was not enough to make it so. Catholic reluctance, voiced in the many petitions sent up to Dublin, was also an inevitable factor. None the less, many landowners did relocate and the respective teams of transplantation commissioners at Athlone and Loughrea carried out monumental administrative tasks in deciding claims and allocating land to over 1,800 transplanters. At the same time, the fragmentary evidence which survives sustains the contemporary Catholic allegations of corruption and fraud at Loughrea. The implementation of the rulings made by these teams of commissioners utterly transformed patterns of landholding in Connacht. Chapter 5 provides a deeper insight than any hitherto available into the working out of this process on the ground. It reconstructs the

---

18 Ibid. 921–2.
19 Idem, 'The Gookin-Lawrence pamphlet debate', 63–80.
20 Idem, 'Cromwell and the "Cromwellian" settlement of Ireland', 919–37.
21 Jörg Deventer, 'Adelskonfessionalisierung? Überlegungen zum *Rollenspiel* katholischer Adelseliten im Milieu der Bikonfessionalität', in Gerhard Ammerer and others, (eds), *Bündnispartner und Konkurrenten der Landesfürsten? Die Stände in der Habsburgermonarchie*, Vienna–Munich 2007, 442–60.

complex processes of truncation, redistribution, transfer and consolidation which occurred, putting some flesh on the skeleton provided by Robert Simington's statistics.[22] Among the more notable trends which emerge are the granting of most of the land to newcomers and the buying up of thousands of acres by the Connacht Protestant purchasers.

Post-1660 the overall level of Catholic landholding in Ireland recovered somewhat from the historic low reached in the 1650s.[23] Yet this benefitted only a minority: those who had had time to prove their innocence; and those for whom various combinations of influence, merit and social status were sufficient to secure favourable treatment. At the upper levels of the aristocracy, Jane Ohlmeyer has found that the most influential members of the Catholic nobility were able to recover and even expand their holdings after the Restoration.[24] The mass of sources surviving from the period means that it is also possible to trace the experiences of the less fortunate, including the nominees and the transplanters. The study of these groups here complements the research conducted by Ohlmeyer on the aristocracy and by Kevin McKenny on the so-called 1649 offi- cers, thus filling more of the gaps in understanding of the labyrinthine Restora- tion land settlement.[25] It also throws light on that second figure lurking with Ireton in the shadows: the earl of Essex. The period of his government constitutes something of a historiographical vacuum, partially because Ormond's great biog- rapher, Thomas Carte, did not leave a trail for others to follow.[26] Yet Essex's volu- minous correspondence provides many fresh insights into the circumstances in which the remaining transplanters were eventually confirmed in their estates. It thus becomes evident that the working out of the transplantation did not end with the death of Cromwell or at the return of the king, but only when the Cath- olics concerned secured letters patent for their estates in the late 1670s.

At many points throughout the period examined, co-operation between Cath- olics and Protestants can be observed; ties of patronage and friendship often transgressed the religious divide. Ultimately, however, the overall outcome of the land settlement represented the triumph of Orrery's vision, as expressed in 1662, that the Protestant minority ought to enjoy precedence in Irish landed society.[27] A few decades later William Petty was to observe that 'upon the playing of the game or match the English won, and have ... a Gamester's right at least to their estates'.[28] However, as it turned out, the result of the 'game' had not yet been finally decided. In Co. Roscommon in the 1680s the Protestant clergyman John Keogh, himself the son of a mixed marriage, encountered old soldiers ready to

---

[22] Simington, *Transplantation*.

[23] Simms, 'The restoration, 1660–85', 420–53; Kevin McKenny, 'The restoration land settlement in Ireland: a statistical interpretation', in Dennehy, *Restoration Ireland*, 35–52.

[24] Jane Ohlmeyer's forthcoming monograph on the peerage in early modern Ireland prom- ises to transform knowledge of this crucial subject. I am grateful to her for permitting me to read some relevant chapters prior to publication.

[25] Kevin McKenny, 'Charles II's Irish cavaliers: the 1649 officers and the restoration land settlement', *IHS* xxviii (1993), 409–25.

[26] Carte, *The life of Ormond*.

[27] Boyle, *Irish colours displayed*, 8–9.

[28] Petty, *The political anatomy of Ireland*, 24.

identify 'the plains remarkable for the battles fought in the year 1641 and after' and willing to recall in detail the six bloody 'breaches' which had occurred between local Catholic and Protestant forces.[29] As these old wounds remained in evidence, Keogh tellingly refused to reveal whether the county was 'inhabited thickly or thinly'. Such matters, he explained, were not 'a thing permanent, but according to diversity of times of war or peace, famine, plague or plenty ... and so not fit to be put in a lasting record'.[30] Alongside war, plague and famine, the transplantation had played a key role in shaping the society of which Keogh was a part. It had greatly weakened Catholic Ireland but, contrary to Orrery's hopes, the Protestants were not yet 'out of danger of sinking again'.[31] That would require another war.

29 NLI, MS 3,649; ODNB, s.v. 'Keogh, John (c. 1650–1725)'.
30 NLI, MS 3,649.
31 Boyle, Irish colours displayed, 9.

Bibliography

Unpublished primary sources

Aberystwyth, National Library of Wales
11,440D

Bath, Longleat House
MS Coventry, papers relating to Ireland, vol. 1, 1601–77

Dublin, Gilbert Library
MSS Gilbert 198, 208, 219

Dublin, King's Inns
MSS Prendergast 1, 2, 3, 4, 5

Dublin, Marsh's Library
Z2.1.7
Z3.1.1
Z3.2.17(2)

Dublin, National Archives of Ireland
1A.52.42
MSS Blake of Ballyglunin M 6,931, 6,932, 6,935
D 14,349, 19,309, 20,681
MS Ferguson 9, 10, 13
MSS Headfort 2B.33.16, 2A.33.17, 2A.33.18
M 6,237(3)
MS Quit Rent Box 2A.12.44; MS Quit Rent Office, books of survey and distribution 13
MSS Wyche 2/99, 56, 66, 146, 147

Dublin, National Library of Ireland
MSS 31, 758, 839, 3,649, 11,959, 11,960, 11,961, 24,597(1), 24,597(2)
MSS Bellew of Mountbellew 31,900, 31,901, 31,917, 31,945, 31,946, 31,947, 31,966
MSS De Freyne (unsorted collection)
MS Gilbert 857
MSS Ormond 2,511, 2,515
MSS Ormsby of Ballinamore (NLI Microfilm P. 8502)
MS Pakenham-Mahon 10,125
MSS Westport 40,889/6, 40,889/7, 40,889/8, 40,889/8(4), 40,893/2(11), 40,893/5(3), 40,893/5(4), 40,889/12(1)

Dublin, Royal Irish Academy
MSS Purcell 4.A. 42

Dublin, Trinity College
MSS 817, 830, 844, 866

Galway, James Hardiman Library
MSS Hearne of Hearnebrook LE 26

Kew, The National Archives
State papers SP 16, 25, 63

London, British Library
MSS Add 4,771, 19,845, 28,854, 72,858, (Petty) 72,877
MSS Egerton 212, 1,048, 1,761, 1,762, 1,779
MS Egmont 46,937
MS Harleian 2,048
MSS Lansdowne 821, 822, 823
MSS Stowe 200–17, 1,038

London, House of Lords Record Office
HL/PO/JO/10/1/282

London, Irish Genealogical Research Society Library
MS Hussey-Walsh 6

Maynooth, Russell Library, St Patrick's College
MS O'Renehan 2

Oxford, Bodleian Library
MSS Carte 29, 30, 41, 63, 67, 74, 159, 213
MS Firth C5

San Marino, Henry E. Huntington Library
MSS Hastings Box 20

Wexford, St Peter's College
MS Hore 60

Published primary sources

An act for the better execution of his majesties gracious declaration for the settlement of his kingdome of Ireland, and satisfaction of the several interests of adventurers, soldiers, and other his majesties subjects there, Dublin 1662
An act for explaining some doubts arising upon an act intituled, an act for the better execution of his majesties gracious declaration for the settlement of his kingdome of Ireland, and satisfaction of the several interests of adventurers, soldiers, and other his majesties subjects there; and for making some alterations of, and additions unto the said act, for the more speedy and effectual settlement of the said kingdom, Dublin 1665
Acts and ordinances of the English interregnum, 1642–1660, ed. Charles Firth and Robert Rait, London 1911
Adair, Patrick, *A true narrative of the rise and progress of the Presbyterian Church in Ireland, 1623–1670*, ed. William Dool Killen, Belfast 1866

Ainsworth, John and Edward Mac Lysaght, 'Nugent papers', *Analecta Hibernica* xx (1958), 126–215

Articles of agreement, made, concluded, and agreed on, at Dublin, the eighteenth day of June, 1647, Dublin 1647

Blake family records, 1600 to 1700, ed. Martin Blake, London 1902–5

Boate, Gerard, *Irelands naturall history*, London 1652

Books of survey and distribution, ed. Robert Simington, Dublin 1949–67

Borlase, Edmund, *The history of the execrable Irish rebellion*, 2nd edn, Dublin 1743

Boyle, Roger, earl of Orrery, *The answer of a person of quality to a scandalous letter lately printed and subscribed by P.W. intituled, A letter desiring a just and merciful regard of the Roman Catholicks of Ireland*, Dublin 1662

—— *The Irish colours displayed in a reply of an English Protestant to a late letter of an Irish Roman Catholique: both address'd to his grace the duke of Ormond*, London 1662

Butler Yeats, William, *The collected poems of W.B. Yeats*, Toronto 1956

Calendar of the Clarendon state papers, ed. Octavius Ogle and others, Oxford 1869–1970

Calendar of the Orrery papers, ed. Edward MacLysaght, Dublin 1941

Calendar of state papers domestic: Charles II, addenda, 1660–1685, ed. F. H. Blackburne Daniell and Francis Bickley, London 1939

Calendar of state papers preserved in the Public Records Office, domestic series, 1547–1695, London 1856–1972

Calendar of state papers relating to Ireland, 1509–1670, London 1860–1912

Capel, Arthur, earl of Essex, *Letters written by his excellency Arthur Capel, earl of Essex, lord lieutenant of Ireland in the year 1675*, 2nd edn, Dublin 1773

The Carte manuscripts in the Bodleian Library, Oxford, ed. John Prendergast and Charles Russell, London 1871

A census of Ireland, circa 1659, ed. Seámus Pender, Dublin 1939

Certain acts and declarations made by the ecclesiasticall congregation of the arch-bishops, bishops, and other prelates: met at Clonmacnoise the fourth day of December 1649, London 1650

The civil survey, ed. Robert Simington, Dublin 1931–61

The Clarke papers, ed. Charles Firth (Camden n. s. xlix, lix, lxi, lxii, 1891–1901)

A collection of acts and ordinances, ed. Henry Scobell, London 1658

A collection of the state papers of John Thurloe, ed. Thomas Birch, London 1742

A collection of the state letters of the right honourable Roger Boyle, ed. Thomas Morrice, London 1743

The compossicion booke of Conought, ed. Alexander Martin Freeman, Dublin 1936

The constitutional documents of the puritan revolution, 1625–1660, ed. Samuel Gardiner, 3rd edn, Oxford 1906

A contemporary history of Irish affairs, from 1641 to 1652, ed. John Gilbert, Dublin 1879–80

Court of claims: submissions and evidence, 1663, ed. Geraldine Tallon, Dublin 2006

Cox, Richard, *Hibernia anglicana, or the history of Ireland, from the conquest thereof by the English, to this present time*, London 1689–90

Cromwell, Oliver, *A declaration by the lord lieutenant of Ireland: concerning his resolutions for the peace and safety of Ireland, and the free injoyment of the rights of the people*, London 1649

Cunningham, Bernadette, 'Clanricard letters: letters and papers, 1605–1673, preserved in the National Library of Ireland Manuscript 3,111', *Journal of the Galway Archaeological and Historical Society* xlviii (1996), 162–208

Deputy keeper of the public records in Ireland, Tenth report, Dublin 1878

—— *Fourteenth report*, Dublin 1882

—— *Nineteenth report*, Dublin 1887

The diary of Thomas Burton, ed. John Towill Rutt, London 1828

An duanaire, 1600–1900: poems of the Dispossessed, ed. Thomas Kinsella and Seán O Tuama, Mountrath 1981

Duanaire Dáibid Uí Bruadair, ed. John Mac Erlean (Irish Texts Society, 1910–17)

Duanaire Gaedhilge, ed. Róisin Ó h-Ógáin, Dublin 1921

Essex papers, 1672–1679, ed. Osmund Airy (Camden n.s. xlvii, 1890)

Five seventeenth-century political poems, ed. Cecile O'Rahilly, Dublin 1952

French, Nicholas, The bleeding Iphigenia, or an excellent preface of a work unfinished, published by the authors frind [sic], with the reasons of publishing it, London 1675

Further instructions unto Charles Fleetwood esq., lieutenant general of the army in Ireland, Edmund Ludlow esq., lieutenant general of the horse, Miles Corbet esq., and John Jones esq., London 1653

The Gladstone diaries, ed. Henry Colin Gray Matthew, Oxford 1982

Gookin, Vincent, The author and case of transplanting the Irish into Connaught vindicated, from the unjust aspersions of Colonel Richard Laurence, London 1655

—— The great case of transplantation in Ireland discussed, London 1655

The great expedition for Ireland by way of underwriting proposed, London 1642

Grey, Zachary, An impartial examination of the fourth volume of Mr. Daniel Neal's history of the puritans, London 1739

Hartlib, Samuel, 'The epistle dedicatory', in Boate, Irelands naturall history

His majesties gracious declaration for the settlement of his kingdome of Ireland, and satisfaction of the several interests of adventurers, soldiers, and other his majesties subjects there, Dublin 1660

Historical collections, ed. John Rushworth, London 1680–1701

HMC, Fourth report, ed. John Romilly and others, London 1874

—— Seventh report, ed. George Jessel and others, London 1879

—— Manuscripts of his grace the duke of Portland, ed. F. H. Blackburne Daniell, London 1891

—— Manuscripts of the marquess of Ormonde, ed. John Gilbert and Sidney Ratcliff, o.s. London 1895–1909

—— Manuscripts of the earl of Dartmouth, ed. W. O. Hewlett, London 1896

—— Calendar of the manuscripts of the marquess of Ormonde, ed. Francis Elrington Ball and Caesar Litton Falkiner, n.s. London 1902–20

—— Manuscripts of the earl of Egmont, ed. Sophia Lomas, London 1905–9

History of the confederation and war in Ireland, 1641–49, ed. John Gilbert, Dublin 1882–91

The history of the survey of Ireland, commonly called the Down Survey, ed. Thomas Larcom, Dublin 1851

Hutchinson, Lucy, Memoirs of Colonel Hutchinson, London 1908

Hyde, Edward, earl of Clarendon, The life of Edward, earl of Clarendon, Oxford 1759

Inedited letters of Cromwell, Col. Jones, Bradshaw and other regicides, ed. Joseph Meyer, Liverpool 1861

IRC, Reports of the commissioners appointed by his majesty to execute the measures recommended in an address of the House of Commons respecting the public records of Ireland; with supplements and appendixes, Dublin 1811–25

Ireland in the seventeenth century, or the Irish massacres of 1641, ed. Mary Hickson, London 1884

Ireland under the Commonwealth: being a selection of documents relating to the government of Ireland from 1651 to 1659, ed. Robert Dunlop, Manchester 1913

Ireton, Henry, A declaration and proclamation of the lord deputy-general of Ireland, concerning the present hand of God in the visitation of the plague, London 1650

—— A letter from the lord deputy-general of Ireland unto the honorable William Lenthal, London 1651

The Irish and Anglo-Irish landed gentry, ed. John O'Hart, Dublin 1884

Irish immigrants in the land of Canaan: letters and memoirs from colonial and revolutionary America, 1675–1815, ed. Kerby Miller and others, Oxford 2003

The Irish statute staple books, 1596–1687, ed. Jane Ohlmeyer and Éamonn Ó Ciardha, Dublin 1998

Jones, Henry, A remonstrance of divers remarkeable passages concerning the Church and kingdome of Ireland, London 1642

—— An abstract of some few of those barbarous, cruel massacres and murthers, of the Protestants and English in some parts of Ireland, London 1652

Journals of the House of Commons, 1547–1714, London 1742

Journals of the House of Lords, 1578–1714, London 1767

Lawrence, Richard, The interest of England in the Irish transplantation, stated, London 1655

—— England's great interest in the well planting of Ireland with English people, discussed, Dublin 1656

The letters and speeches of Oliver Cromwell with elucidations by Thomas Carlyle, ed. Sophia Lomas, London 1904

Ludlow, Edmund, Memoirs of Edmund Ludlow, Vivay 1698

[MacCaffrey, James], 'Commonwealth records', Archivium Hibernicum vi (1917), 175–202; vii (1918–21), 20–66

MacLysaght, Edward, 'Commonwealth state accounts: Ireland, 1650–56', Analecta Hibernica xv (1944), 227–321

McNeill, Charles, 'Report on the Rawlinson collection of manuscripts', Analecta Hibernica i (1930), 12–178

The memoirs and letters of Ulick, marquis of Clanricarde, ed. John Smyth Bourke, earl of Clanricarde, London 1757

Memorials of the great civil wars in England from 1646 to 1652, ed. Henry Cary, London 1842

Milton, John, Articles of peace, made and concluded with the Irish rebels, and papists, by James earle of Ormond ... upon all which are added observations, London 1649

The Montgomery manuscripts, 1603–1706, ed. George Hill, Belfast 1867

Nicholls, Kenneth, 'The Lynch Blosse papers', Analecta Hibernica xxix (1980), 115–218

O'Flaherty, Roderic, A chorographical description of West or H-Iar Connaught, ed. James Hardiman, Dublin 1846

O'Mahony, S. C., 'Cromwellian transplantation from county Limerick, 1653', North Munster Archaeological Journal xlii (2000), 29–51

Original letters and papers of state addressed to Oliver Cromwell, ed. John Nickolls, London 1743

Owen, John, The labouring saints dismission to rest: a sermon preached at the funeral of the right honourable Henry Ireton lord deputy of Ireland, London 1652

Petty, William, The political anatomy of Ireland, London 1691

The present posture and condition of Ireland, London 1652

Propositions approved of and granted by the deputy-general of Ireland to Colonel Richard Laurence, for the raising in England and transporting into Ireland, a regiment of twelve hundred footmen, London 1650

Sad newes from Ireland: how the Lord has been pleased to chastize the parliaments forces by a loss from the rebels, London 1651

Scotland and the Commonwealth: letters and papers relating to the military government of Scotland, from August 1651 to December 1653, ed. Charles Firth (Scottish History Society 1st ser. xviii, 1885)

Severall letters from Ireland, London 1649

Simington, Robert, The transplantation to Connaught, 1654–1658, Dublin 1970

The speeches of the right honourable Henry Grattan, in the Irish, and in the imperial parliament, ed. Henry Grattan, Dublin 1822

Spenser, William, The case of William Spencer of Kilcolman in the county of Cork in the kingdom of Ireland, esq; grandson and heir to Edmond Spencer the poet, London 1701

The state of the Irish affairs, for the honourable members of the houses of parliament, as they lye represented before them, from the committee of adventurers, London 1645

Talbot, Peter, The polititians cathechisme for his instruction in divine faith and moral honesty, Antwerp 1658

The Tanner letters, ed. Charles McNeill, Dublin 1943

Temple, John, The Irish rebellion, London 1646

True account of the late bloody and inhumane conspiracy against his highness the lord protector and this Commonwealth, London 1654

Tudor and Stuart proclamations, 1485–1714, ed. Robert Steele, Oxford 1910

Walsh, Peter, *The Irish colours folded, or, The Irish Roman-Catholick's reply to the (pretended) English Protestants answer to the letter desiring a just and mercifall regard of the Roman Catholicks of Ireland (which answer is entitled The Irish colours displayed), addressed (as that answer and letter have been) to his grace the lord duke of Ormond, lord lieutenant general, and general governour of that kingdome*, London 1662

—— *A letter desiring a just and mercifull regard of the Roman Catholicks of Ireland, given about the end of October 1660, to the then marquess, now duke of Ormond and the second time lord lieutenant of that kingdom*, [?]Dublin [?]1662

Waring, Thomas, *A brief narration of the plotting, beginning, and carrying on of that execrable rebellion and butcherie in Ireland*, London 1650

—— *An answer to certain seditious and Jesuitical queres heretofore purposely and maliciously cast out to retard and hinder the English forces in their going over into Ireland*, London 1651

Whitelocke, Bulstrode, *Memorials of the English affairs*, London 1682

The writings and speeches of Oliver Cromwell, ed. Wilbur Cortez Abbott, Cambridge, MA 1937–47

Newsbooks (London)

The Faithful Scout
Mercurius Politicus
A Perfect Diurnall of Some Passages and Proceedings of, and in Relation to the Armies of England, Ireland, and Scotland
Several Proceedings in Parliament

Proclamations

A declaration and commission for three months' assessment of £10,000 ... 6 September 1655, Dublin 1655 (BL, 806.i.14(4))

A declaration for making sale of the corn ... 7 March 1654[5], Dublin 1655 (BL, 806.i.14(13))

A declaration that all Irish papists remaining within Dublin ... 18 May 1655, Dublin 1655 (BL, 806.i.14(19))

A declaration, that all persons holding custodiams, or leases from the state ... 21 May 1655, Dublin 1655 (BL, 806.i.14(20))

His highness council having taken ... 7 April 1656, Dublin 1656 (BL, 806.i.14(29))

Upon consideration had ... 12 February 1654[5], Dublin 1655 (BL, 806.i.14(11))

Whereas by a commission ... 23 May 1655, Dublin 1655 (NAI, M 3,159)

Whereas by a declaration ... [1656], Dublin 1656 (BL, 806.i.14(31))

Whereas the late commissioners ... 21 May 1655, Dublin 1655 (BL, 806.i.14(21))

Whereas his majestie by his gracious letters, bearing date the two and twentieth day of September last ... 26 June 1676, Dublin 1676

Whereas by an order ... 27 February 1654[5], Dublin 1655 (BL, 806.i.14(12))

Whereas by our proclamation, bearing date the twenty sixth day of June last ... 19 February 1676[7], Dublin 1677

Whereas in pursuance of ... 14 July 1655, Dublin 1655 (BL, 806.i.14 (25))

Whereas the right honourable the commissioners ... Carrickfergus, 23 May 1653, Dublin 1653 (BL, 816.m.17(74))

Newspapers

International Herald Tribune, Paris 1887–
The Irish Independent, Dublin, 1905–
The Irish Times, Dublin 1859–

Secondary sources

Adamson, John, *The noble revolt: the overthrow of Charles I*, London 2007

Ammerer, Gerhard and others (eds), *Bündnispartner und Konkurrenten der Landesfürsten? Die Stände in der Habsburgermonarchie*, Vienna–Munich 2007

Armitage, David (ed.), *British political thought in history, literature and theory, 1500–1800*, Cambridge 2006

Armstrong, Robert, *Protestant war: the 'British' of Ireland and wars of the three kingdoms*, Manchester 2005

Arnold, Laurence, 'The Cromwellian settlement of County Dublin, 1652–1660', *Journal of the Royal Society of Antiquaries of Ireland* ci (1971), 146–53

—— 'The Irish court of claims of 1663', *IHS* xxiv (1985), 417–30

—— *The restoration land settlement in County Dublin, 1660–1688*, Dublin 1993

Bagwell, Richard, *Ireland under the Stuarts and during the interregnum*, London 1909–16

Barber, Sarah, 'Scotland and Ireland under the Commonwealth: a question of loyalty', in Barber and Ellis, *Conquest and union*, 195–221

—— 'Settlement, transplantation and expulsion: a comparative study of the placement of peoples', in Ciaran Brady and Jane Ohlmeyer (eds), *British interventions in early modern Ireland*, Cambridge 2005, 280–98

—— and Steven Ellis (eds), *Conquest and union: fashioning a British state, 1485–1725*, London–New York 1995

Barnard, Toby, 'Planters and policies in Cromwellian Ireland', *P&P* lxi (1973), 31–69

—— 'Crises of identity among Irish Protestants, 1641–1685', *P&P* cxxvii (May 1990), 58–78

—— '1641: a bibliographical essay', in Brian Mac Cuarta (ed.), *Ulster 1641: aspects of the rising*, rev. edn, Belfast 1993, 173–86

—— 'Land and the limits of loyalty: the second earl of Cork and first earl of Burlington', in Toby Barnard and Jane Clark (eds), *Lord Burlington: architecture, art and life*, London 1994, 167–99

—— 'The Protestant interest', in Ohlmeyer, *Ireland from independence to occupation*, 218–40

—— *Cromwellian Ireland: English government and reform in Ireland, 1649–1660*, Oxford 2000

—— *A new anatomy of Ireland: the Irish Protestants, 1649–1770*, New Haven–London 2003

Barry, James, 'The Cromwellian settlement of the county of Limerick', *Journal of the Limerick Field Club* i, ii, iii (1897–1904), i/4, 16–33; ii. 43–9, 211–16, 257–68; iii/9, 18–24; iii/10, 58–63; iii/11, 160–5; iii/12, 230–7

Beaumont, Gustave de, *L'Irlande: sociale, politique et religeuse*, Paris 1839

Beresford Ellis, Peter, *Hell or Connaught: the Cromwellian colonisation of Ireland, 1652–1660*, Belfast 1988

Blackall, Sir Henry, 'The Butlers of County Clare', *North Munster Archaeological Journal* vii (1953–7), 153–67

Bottigheimer, Karl, *English money and Irish land: the 'adventurers' in the Cromwellian settlement of Ireland*, Oxford 1971

—— 'The restoration land settlement in Ireland: a structural view', *IHS* xviii (1972), 1–21

Bradshaw, Brendan, Andrew Hadfield and Willy Maley (eds), *Representing Ireland: literature and the origins of conflict, 1534–1660*, Cambridge 1993

—— and John Morrill (eds), *The British problem, c. 1534–1707: state formation in the Atlantic archipelago*, London 1996

Brady, Ciaran and Jane Ohlmeyer (eds), *British interventions in early modern Ireland*, Cambridge 2005

Burgess, Glenn (ed.), *The new British history*, London–New York 1999

Burke, Bernard, *A genealogical history of the dormant, abeyant, forfeited and extinct peerages*, London 1883

Burke's Irish family records, London 1976

Butler, William, *Confiscation in Irish history*, 2nd edn, Dublin–London 1918

Byrne, Joseph, *War and peace: the survival of the Talbots of Malahide, 1641–1671*, Dublin 1997

Canny, Nicholas, 'Identity formation in Ireland: the emergence of the Anglo-Irish', in Canny and Padgen, *Colonial identity*, 159–212

—— *Making Ireland British, 1580–1650*, Oxford 2001

—— 'The intersections between Irish and British political thought in the early-modern centuries', in David Armitage (ed.), *British political thought in history, literature and theory, 1500–1800*, Cambridge 2006, 67–88

—— (ed.), *The Oxford history of the British empire*, I: *The origins of empire to 1689*, Oxford 1998

—— and Anthony Padgen (eds), *Colonial identity in the Atlantic world*, Princeton 1987

Carey, Mathew, *Vindiciae hibernicae, or, Ireland vindicated*, Philadelphia 1819

Carey, Vincent and Ute Lotz–Heumann (eds), *Taking sides? Colonial and confessional mentalities in early modern Ireland*, Dublin 2003

Carlin, Norah, 'Extreme or mainstream? The English independents and the Cromwellian reconquest of Ireland, 1649–1651', in Bradshaw, Hadfield and Maley, *Representing Ireland*, 209–26

Carrigan, William, *The history and antiquities of the diocese of Ossory*, Dublin 1905

Carte, Thomas, *The life of James, duke of Ormond*, London 1735–6

Chambers, Anne, *Eleanor countess of Desmond, c. 1545–1638*, Dublin 1986

Cheevers, Frederica, *Cheevers of Killyan*, Dublin 1936

Clarke, Aidan, *The Old English in Ireland, 1625–1642*, London 1966

—— *Prelude to restoration in Ireland: the end of the Commonwealth, 1659–1660*, Cambridge 1999

Cokayne, George Edward and others, *The complete peerage*, rev. edn, Gloucester 1987

Connolly, James, *The re-conquest of Ireland*, rev. edn, Dublin 1983

Connolly, Sean, *Divided kingdom: Ireland, 1630–1800*, Oxford 2008

Corish, Patrick, 'The Cromwellian conquest, 1649–53', in Moody, Martin and Byrne, *New history of Ireland*, iii. 336–52

—— 'The Cromwellian regime', in Moody, Martin, and Byrne, *New history of Ireland*, iii. 353–85

Coughlan, Patricia, 'Counter-currents in colonial discourse: the political thought of Vincent and Daniel Gookin', in Ohlmeyer, *Political thought*, 56–82

Coward, Barry, *The Cromwellian protectorate*, Manchester–New York 2002

Cunningham, John, 'Oliver Cromwell and the "Cromwellian" settlement of Ireland', *HJ* liii (2010), 919–37

—— 'The Gookin–Lawrence pamphlet debate and transplantation in Cromwellian Ireland', in Ciara Breathnach, Liam Chambers and Anthony McElligott (eds), *Power in history: from the medieval to the post-modern world* (Historical Studies xxvii, 2011), 63–80

—— 'The transplanters' certificates and the historiography of Cromwellian Ireland', *IHS* xxxix (2011), 376–95

—— 'Cromwellian County Mayo', in Gerald Moran and Kieran Rankin (eds), *Mayo: history and society* (forthcoming)

Curry, John, *An historical and critical review of the civil wars in Ireland*, Dublin 1775

Dalton, John, *King James's Irish army list*, Dublin 1855

Dennehy, Coleman (ed.), *Restoration Ireland*, Aldershot 2008

Deventer, Jörg, 'Adelskonfessionalisierung? Überlegungen zum *Rollenspiel* katholischer Adelseliten im Milieu der Bikonfessionalität', in Ammerer, *Bündnispartner und Konkurrenten der Landesfürsten?*, 442–60

Dooley, Terence, *The land for the people: the land question in independent Ireland*, Dublin 2004

Edwards, David, Padraig Lenihan and Clodagh Tait (eds), *Age of atrocity: violence and political conflict in early modern Ireland*, Dublin 2007

Egan, Patrick, *The parish of Ballinasloe*, Dublin 1960

Farr, David, *Henry Ireton and the English revolution*, Woodbridge 2006

Firth, Charles, *The last years of the protectorate*, London 1909

—— 'Robert Dunlop', *History* xv (1931), 320–4

Foster, Roy, *Modern Ireland, 1600–1972*, London 1989

Froude, James Anthony, *The English in Ireland in the eighteenth century*, London 1872–4

Games, Alison, *The web of empire: English cosmopolitans in an age of expansion, 1560–1660*, Oxford 2008

Gardiner, Samuel, 'The transplantation to Connaught', *EHR* xiv (1899), 700–34

—— *History of the Commonwealth and protectorate*, London 1903

Gentles, Ian, *The new model army in England, Scotland and Ireland, 1645–1653*, Oxford 1992

—— 'Review of Sean Kelsey, *Inventing a republic: the political culture of the English Commonwealth, 1649–53*', *American Historical Review* civ (1999), 634–5

Gillespie, Raymond, 'Landed society and the interregnum in Scotland and Ireland', in Mitchison and Roebuck, *Economy and society in Scotland and Ireland*, 38–47

Gleeson, Dermot, *The last lords of Ormond*, London 1938

Grace, Sheffield, *Memoirs of the family of Grace*, London 1827

Grey, Zachary, *An impartial examination of the fourth volume of Mr. Daniel Neal's history of the puritans*, London 1739

Gribben, Crawford, *God's Irishmen: theological debates in Cromwellian Ireland*, Oxford 2007

Habakkuk, Hrothgar John, 'Landowners and the civil war', *Economic History Review* n.s. xviii (1965), 130–51

—— 'The land settlement and the restoration of Charles II', *Transactions of the Royal Historical Society* 5th ser. xxviii (1978), 201–22

Hardiman, James, *The history of the town and county of the town of Galway*, Dublin 1820

Hardinge, William, 'On circumstances attending the outbreak of civil war in Ireland on 23rd October, 1641', *Transactions of the Royal Irish Academy, Antiquities* xxiv (1873), 379–420

Harris, Tim, 'Restoration Ireland – themes and problems', in Dennehy, *Restoration Ireland*, 1–18

Hayes-McCoy, Gerald, 'The completion of the Tudor conquest and the advance of the Counter-reformation, 1571–1603', in Moody, Martin and Byrne, *New history of Ireland*, iii. 94–141

Hill, Christopher, *God's Englishman: Oliver Cromwell and the English revolution*, London 1970

Hore, Philip, *History of the town and county of Wexford*, London 1900–11

Kearney, Hugh, *Strafford in Ireland, 1633–41: a study in absolutism*, Manchester 1959

Kenyon, John and Jane Ohlmeyer (eds), *The civil wars: a military history of England, Scotland and Ireland, 1639–1660*, Oxford 1998

Knoz, Tomáš, 'Die Konfiscationen nach 1620 in (erb)länderübergreifender Perspektive: Thesen zu westentlichen Wirkungen, Aspekten und Prinzipien des Konfiscationsprozesses', in Mat'a and Winkelbauer, *Die Habsburgermonarchie*, 99–131

Krugler, John, *English and Catholic: the Lords Baltimore in the seventeenth century*, Baltimore–London 2004

Lawless, Emily and Mrs Arthur Bronson, *The story of Ireland*, New York 1896

Lecky, William Edward Hartpole, *History of Ireland in the eighteenth century*, London 1892

Leland, Thomas, *The history of Ireland from the invasion of Henry II*, Dublin 1773

Lenihan, Maurice, *History of Limerick*, Dublin 1866

Lenihan, Pádraig, 'War and population, 1649–52', *Irish Economic and Social History* xxiv (1997), 1–21

Lingard, John, *The history of England from the first invasion by the Romans, to the accession of William and Mary*, 6th edn, Dublin 1878

Little, Patrick, 'The first unionists? Irish Protestant attitudes to union with England, 1653–9', *IHS* xxxii (2000), 44–58

—— *Lord Broghill and the Cromwellian union with Ireland and Scotland*, Oxford 2004

—— (ed.), *The Cromwellian protectorate*, Woodbridge 2007

Lodge, John, *The peerage of Ireland*, Dublin 1789

Love, Walter, 'Civil war in Ireland: appearances in three centuries of historical writing', *Emory University Quarterly* xxii (1966), 57–62

Lyons, Mary Ann and Thomas O'Connor (eds), *Irish communities in early modern Europe*, Dublin 2006

McCarthy, Justin, *Ireland and her story*, New York 1903

McCarthy-Murrogh, Michael, *The Munster plantation*, Oxford 1986

Mac Cuarta, Brian (ed.), *Ulster 1641: aspects of the rising*, rev. edn, Belfast 1993

Mac Curtain, Margaret and Mary O'Dowd (eds), *Women in early modern Ireland*, Edinburgh 1991

McElligott, Jason, *Cromwell our chief of enemies*, Dundalk 1994

Mac Giolla Coille, Breandán, 'Robert Christopher Simington 1885–1976', *Analecta Hibernica* xxviii (1978), pp. xviii–xix

McKenny, Kevin, 'Charles II's Irish cavaliers: the 1649 officers and the restoration land settlement', *IHS* xxviii (1993), 409–25

—— *The Laggan army in Ireland, 1640–1685*, Dublin 2005

—— 'The restoration land settlement in Ireland: a statistical interpretation', in Dennehy, *Restoration Ireland*, 35–52

Mat'a, Petr and Thomas Winkelbauer (eds), *Die Habsburgermonarchie: 1620 bis 1740*, Stuttgart 2006

Mathew, Henry and Brian Harrison (eds), *Oxford dictionary of national biography*, Oxford 2004

Mendle, Michael (ed.), *The Putney debates of 1647*, Cambridge 2001

Miller, John, *Popery and politics in England, 1660–1688*, Cambridge 1973

Mitchison, Rosalind and Peter Roebuck (eds), *Economy and society in Scotland and Ireland, 1500–1939*, Edinburgh 1988

Moody, Theodore, Francis Martin and Francis Byrne (eds), *A new history of Ireland, III: Early modern Ireland, 1534–1691*, Oxford 1976

Moran, Patrick, *Historical sketch of the persecutions suffered by the Catholics of Ireland under the rule of Cromwell and the puritans*, Dublin 1862

Morrill, John, 'Introduction', in Kenyon and Ohlmeyer, *The civil wars*, pp. xxix–xxiv.

—— 'The Drogheda massacre in Cromwellian context', in Edwards, Lenihan and Tait, *Age of atrocity*, 242–65

—— *Oliver Cromwell*, Oxford 2007

—— 'Cromwell, Parliament, Ireland and a Commonwealth in crisis: 1652 revisited', *Parliamentary History* xxx (2011), 193–214

—— (ed.), *Oliver Cromwell and the English revolution*, London 1990

Mullett, Michael, *Catholics in Britain and Ireland, 1558–1829*, Basingstoke–London 1998

Murphy, Denis, *Cromwell in Ireland: a history of Cromwell's Irish campaign*, Dublin 1883

O'Callaghan, Seán, *To hell or Barbados: the ethnic cleansing of Ireland*, Dingle 2000

O'Dowd, Mary, *Power, politics and land: Sligo 1568–1688*, Belfast 1991

O'Mahony, S. C., 'Cromwellian transplantation from county Limerick, 1653', *North Munster Archaeological Journal* xlii (2000), 29–51

O'Rorke, Terence, *The history of Sligo: town and county*, Dublin 1890

O'Siochrú, Micheál, *Confederate Ireland, 1642–1649: a constitutional and political analysis*, Dublin 1998

—— 'The duke of Lorraine and the international struggle for Ireland, 1649–1653', *HJ* xlviii (2005), 905–32

—— 'Atrocity, codes of conduct and the Irish in the British civil wars, 1641–1653', *P&P* cxcv (2007), 55–86

—— *God's executioner: Oliver Cromwell and the conquest of Ireland*, London 2008

—— (ed.), *Kingdoms in crisis: Ireland in the 1640s*, Dublin 2001

O'Sullivan, Harold, *John Bellew: a seventeenth century man of many parts, 1605–1679*, Dublin 2000

O'Sullivan, Mary Donovan, *Old Galway*, Cambridge 1942

Ohlmeyer, Jane, *Civil war and restoration in the three Stuart kingdoms: the political career of Randall McDonnell, marquis of Antrim, 1609–1683*, Cambridge 1993

—— (ed.), *Ireland from independence to occupation, 1641–1660*, Cambridge 1995

—— (ed.), *Political thought in seventeenth-century Ireland*, Cambridge 2000

Oranmore and Browne, Lord, 'The Brownes of Castlemacgarrett', *Journal of the Galway Archaeological and Historical Society* v (1907–8), 48–59, 165–77, 227–38

Perceval-Maxwell, Michael, *The outbreak of the Irish rebellion of 1641*, Dublin 1994

—— 'The Irish restoration land settlement and its historians', in Dennehy, *Restoration Ireland*, 19–34

Pine, Leslie, (ed.), *Burke's genealogical and heraldic history of the peerage, baronetage and knightage*, London 1956

Prendergast, John, *The Cromwellian settlement of Ireland*, 2nd edn, London 1870

—— *Ireland from the restoration to the revolution*, London 1887

Ramsey, Robert, *Henry Cromwell*, London 1933

—— *Henry Ireton*, London 1949

Rankin, Deana, *Between Spenser and Swift: English writing in Ireland in the seventeenth century*, Cambridge 2005

Reid, James, *The history of the Presbyterian Church in Ireland*, Edinburgh 1834

Reilly, Tom, *Cromwell: an honourable enemy*, London 2000

Richardson, R. C. (ed.), *Images of Oliver Cromwell: essays for and by Roger Howell*, Manchester 1993

Roots, Ivan (ed.), *The great rebellion, 1642–1660*, London 1966

Russell, Conrad, 'The British background to the Irish rebellion of 1641', *Historical Research* lxi (1988), 166–82

Russell, George Ely and Donna Valley Russell (eds), *The ark and dove adventurers*, Baltimore 2005

Scott, Jonathan, *England's troubles: seventeenth-century English political instability in European context*, Cambridge 2000

Seymour, St John, *The Puritans in Ireland, 1649–1661*, Oxford 1921

Sharpe, Hercules, *Genealogical history of the family of Brabazon*, Paris 1825

Shaw Mason, William, *A statistical account, or parochial survey of Ireland*, Dublin 1814–19

Simms, John Gerald, 'Land owned by Catholics in Ireland in 1688', *IHS* vii (1951), 180–90

—— 'Mayo landowners in the seventeenth century', *Journal of the Royal Society of Antiquaries of Ireland*, xcv (1965), 237–47

—— 'The restoration, 1660–85', in Moody, Martin and Byrne, *New history of Ireland*, iii. 420–53

—— 'Introduction', in *Court of claims: submissions and evidence, 1663*, ed. Geraldine Tallon, Dublin 2006

Smith, David (ed.), *Cromwell and the interregnum*, Oxford 2003

Smyth, William, *Map-making, landscapes and memory: a geography of colonial and early modern Ireland, c. 1530–1750*, Cork 2006

Stevenson, David, 'Cromwell, Scotland and Ireland', in Morrill, *Cromwell and the English revolution*, 149–80

—— *Scottish covenanters and Irish confederates*, Belfast 1991

Taylor, William Cooke, *History of Ireland*, New York 1833

Thirsk, Joan, 'The restoration land settlement', *Journal of Modern History* xxvi (1954), 315–28

Underdown, David, *Pride's purge: politics in the puritan revolution*, Oxford 1971

Warner, Ferdinando, *The history of the rebellion and civil war in Ireland*, London 1767

Weld, Isaac, *Statistical survey of the county of Roscommon*, Dublin 1832

Wheeler, James Scott, *Cromwell in Ireland*, New York–Dublin 1999

—— *The Irish and British wars, 1637–1654: triumph, tragedy and failure*, London–New York 2002

Woodhouse, Arthur, *Puritanism and liberty*, 2nd edn, London 1974

Wood-Martin, William, *History of Sligo*, Dublin 1882

Woolrych, Austin, *From Commonwealth to protectorate*, Oxford 1982

Worden, Blair, *The rump parliament*, Cambridge 1974

—— 'Providence and politics in Cromwellian England', *P&P* cix (1985), 55–99

Young, John, (ed.), *Celtic dimensions of the British civil wars*, Edinburgh 1997

Unpublished theses

Cronin, John, 'The restoration of the kingdom of Ireland, 1659–1662', MA, NUI Galway 1999

Cronin, Timothy, 'The foundations of landlordism in the barony of Athlone', MA, NUI Galway 1977

Forkan, Kevin, 'Scottish-Protestant Ulster and the crisis of the three kingdoms, 1637–1652', PhD, NUI Galway 2003

McHugh, Jason, 'Soldier of Christ: the political and ecclesiastical career of Nicholas French, Catholic bishop of Ferns (1603–1678)', PhD, NUI Galway 2005

Menarry, David, 'The Irish and Scottish landed elites from regicide to restoration', PhD, Aberdeen 2001

Ó Bríc, Breandán, 'Galway townsmen as owners of land in Connaught, 1585–1641', MA, NUI Galway 1974

Ó Murchadha, Ciarán, 'Land and society in seventeenth-century Clare', PhD, NUI Galway 1982

Yuan, Cheng, 'The politics of the English army in Ireland during the interregnum', PhD, Brown University 1981

Databases

Connacht landed estates database <http://www.landedestates.ie>

EUobserver <http://euobserver.com/9/31302>

NAMA wine lake <http://namawinelake.wordpress.com>

Index

tion (1660), 123–4; and housing, 150; instructions for, 37–9, 153; intended scope of, 38–44, 153; and land claims, 83–5, 142; legacy of, 100, 150–1; and legal fees, 85, 107; and legal title, 134, 146; and local officials, 74, 75, 78, 80, 98, 153; in the localities, 79–82, 152; moderation of, 7, 39, 45–6, 64–5, 70, 153; oppression under, 88, 111–12, 143; origins of, 15–16, 22, 26–8, 33, 153; perceptions of, 1–2, 5, 134, 151, 152; persons refusing to undergo, 81, 98; persons returning after, 80–1, 98, 124; petitions concerning, 46, 68, 81, 95–6, 97–8, 153; and poverty, 141, 143, 144, 145; pre-1641, 8; progress of, 46, 71, 80–1, 85–6; Protestant opposition to, 76–81, 98; and provisional land grants, 44–5, 97; punishments relating to, 39, 41, 71, 74–5, 98; queries concerning, 80; resistance to, 7, 35, 51–3, 57–68, 73; rules for, 38–9, 41–2, 70; shortage of land for, 86–7, 90, 93, 97, 98, 107, 148; size of grants under, 89, 93, 97, 110, 118; sufferings under, 87, 98,111, 113, 122; tensions generated by, 111, 118; threats to, 61, 68; transplanters' certificates for, 44–5, 47; and Viscount Mayo, 130–1. *See also* commissioners for transplantation (Athlone); commissioners for transplantation (Loughrea); Connacht purchasers; court of claims (1670s); nominees; Restoration land settlement; Roscommon; women.
transportation: to the colonies, 2, 74–5, 77, 98, 122, 151; to Europe, 15, 21, 23, 25, 26, 31
Trillick, Co. Tyrone, 106
Trim, precinct of, 46
Trimleston, eighth Baron, *see* Barnewall, Matthias
Trimleston, ninth Baron, *see* Barnewall, Robert
Tuam, bishopric of, 102
Tuam, borough of, Co. Galway, 124
Tudors, 4, 8, 39, 101, 102, 108, 126
Tyrconnell, first duke of, *see* Talbot, Richard
Tyrone, County, 106
Tyrone, second earl of, *see* O'Neill, Hugh

Ulster, 1, 33, 81; plantation in, 33, 93, 113; transplanters from, 89, 110

Ulster, commissioners for, *see* commissioners for Ulster
Ulster, precinct of, 36
Ulster Scots, 9, 76; and the committee for articles, 51–3; and Cromwell, 50–1, 53; exempted from transplantation, 52–3; suspicions concerning, 36, 48; transplantation of, 27, 34, 36–7, 40, 48
United States of America, 2
Upper Ossory, baroness of, *see* Fitzpatrick, Margaret

vacant land, theory of, 8, 39
Venables, Col. Robert, 36–7
Verdon, Patrick, 117
Verdon, Theobald, 117
Virginia, 27

Walcott, Capt. Thomas, 140
Wales, Gerald of, *see* Giraldus Cambrensis
Waller, Maj.-Gen. Sir Hardress, 24, 33 n. 8
Wallis, Thomas, 84
Walpell, Thomas, 103
Walsh, Fr Peter, 122, 125–7
Walsh, Thomas, archbishop of Cashel, 19
Waring, Thomas, 21
Warner, Ferdinando, 5, 6
Waterford, city, Co. Waterford, 14, 15–16
Waterford, County, 33, 37, 40, 113–14, 131, 147
Weaver, John, 11 n. 2. *See also* commissioners of parliament (1650–4).
Wentworth, Thomas, first earl of Strafford, 105, 114–16; proposed plantations of, 57, 59, 89, 102, 115
West Indies, 77, 146, 151
Westmeath, countess of, *see* Nugent, Jane
Westmeath, County, 34, 84, 102, 117–18, 128, 138
Westmeath, first earl of, *see* Nugent, Richard
Westmeath, second earl of, *see* Nugent, Richard
Wexford, County, 75, 76, 78, 114
Wexford, town, Co. Wexford, 11, 12, 14, 40
Whalley, Henry, 54–5
Wicklow, County, 16, 27, 76, 78–9, 82, 123
Wicklow mountains, 16, 36
William I, 'the Conqueror', king of England, 8
William III and II, king of England, Scotland and Ireland, 150